JUNGIAN PSYCHOTHERAPY AND CONTEMPORARY INFANT RESEARCH

Infant research observations and hypotheses have raised serious questions about previous, mainstream psychoanalytic theories of earliest child development.

In *Jungian Psychotherapy and Contemporary Infant Research* Mario Jacoby looks at how these observations are relevant to psychotherapeutic and Jungian analytical practice. Using recent findings in infant research, along with practical examples from therapeutic practice, he shows how early emotional exchange processes, though becoming superimposed in adult life by rational control and various defences, remain operative and become reactivated in situations of intimacy.

Jungian Psychotherapy and Contemporary Infant Research will be of interest to both professionals and students involved in analytical psychology and psychotherapy.

Mario Jacoby is a training and supervising analyst at the C.G. Jung Institute in Zurich. He is the author of *Individuation and Narcissism* (1991) and *Shame and the Origins of Self Esteem* (1993).

JUNGIAN PSYCHOTHERAPY AND CONTEMPORARY INFANT RESEARCH

Basic patterns of emotional exchange

Mario Jacoby

Translated from German, in collaboration with the author, by Robert Weathers

London and New York

First published 1999
by Routledge
11 New Fetter Lane, London EC4P 4EE

Simultaneously published in the USA and Canada
by Routledge
29 West 35th Street, New York, NY 10001

Routledge is an imprint of the Taylor & Francis Group

© 1999 Mario Jacoby

Originally published in 1998 as *Grundformen seelischer
Astauschprozesse: Jungsche Therapie und neuere Kleinkindforschung*

Typeset in Times by Keystroke, Jacaranda Lodge, Wolverhampton
Printed and bound in Great Britain by Biddles Ltd, Guildford and King's Lynn

British Library Cataloguing in Publication Data
A catalogue record for this book is available from the British Library

Library of Congress Cataloging in Publication Data
Jacoby, Mario.
[Grundformen seelischer Astauschprozesse. English]
Jungian therapy and modern infant research : early patterns of
emotional exchange / Mario Jacoby.
        p.   cm.
Includes bibliographical references and index.
1. Jungian psychology. 2. Infant psychology—Research. 3. Child
psychotherapy—Research. I. Title.
RC506.J3413 1999
618.92′8914—dc21   99–29347
                                                                                            CIP

ISBN 0–415–20142–X (hbk)

CONTENTS

CONTENTS

CONTENTS

CONTENTS

ACKNOWLEDGMENTS

I would like here to express my appreciation; first, to the many analysands who agreed to enter into an emotional exchange process with me which, among other things, was the initial impetus to reflect on the very process so central to this book. Some of these analysands gave me permission to introduce brief vignettes comprising our clinical interactions of their dream material, for which I am extraordinarily grateful. Personal specifics were altered to make them unidentifiable, thus allowing the pertinent issue to be, as it were, lifted out. I also received much welcome encouragement through my discussions with many training candidates in supervision, many of whom have now become esteemed colleagues. Most worthy of my appreciation are my colleagues of many years from two supervision groups which meet on a regular basis, and in which our congenial interactions often bring surprising results to light, pointing to new directions in our work. I also want to thank the participants of the Assisi Conferences and Seminars in Vermont (directed by Michael Conforti) for their most helpful and lively response on the occasion of a clinical workshop which I gave on the subject of the book. Likewise I am grateful for the stimulating week I was allowed to spend at the Jung Institute of Los Angeles, discussing this subject in a series of seminars with colleagues and analysts in training. I was also invited to share my ideas in London (Association of Jungian Analysts and Independent Group of Analytical Psychologists), Dublin (Irish Analytical Psychology Association), New York (Center for Depth Psychology and Jungian Studies, at the time directed by Donald Kalsched) and at the San Francisco Jung Institute. I am grateful for all these opportunities and learned much from the participants' shared interests and critical questions.

Joseph Lichtenberg, from Washington, DC, with whom I have a personal connection, deserves my special thanks. In our several conversations, he illustrated to me how newborn research can serve as the foundation of refining psychotherapeutic advances in clinical work with adults. I also had the opportunity to visit several of his supervision seminars, which are full of enormously rich ideas and insight. Along with Lichtenberg, *Daniel Stern* clearly plays a leading role in this book. I certainly hope I do their contributions justice, even as I attempt to convey these ideas from the vantage point of my Jungian background and my corresponding professional experience and personal equation. I would like to thank *Dr Lotte Köhler* (from Munich), once more, in that she originally brought newborn research and Daniel Stern's work, in particular, to my attention. For many illuminating remarks in reference to Kohut's self-psychology, I thank my friend, *Ernest Wolf* (in Chicago), himself formerly a collaborator of Kohut. Special thanks are due to *Marianne Schiess*, lecturer at Walter Publishers. Besides her exemplary editorial work for the German edition, she at times also provided me with crucial encouragement for this project, which was highly welcome, and probably quite necessary for the completion of this labor-intensive manuscript.

It was specially felicitous for me to meet *Dr Robert Weathers*, Professor at the Pepperdine University in Los Angeles, who volunteered to embark on the arduous task of translating this text from the German. It meant an intense collaboration between us by e-mail, and I was very touched by his empathic sensitivity and his willingness to transmit into English idiom all the nuances that I want to express. I am immensely grateful to him. Many thanks are also due to *Violet Mesrkhani*, the most helpful graduate assistant to Robert Weathers. She gave much steadfast translation and clerical assistance throughout the entire project, including compiling the index. Thanks are due also to *Edwina Welham* and to *Kate Hawes*, both at Routledge, for their gracious encouragement of this publication. Last, but not least, I want to express my most heartfelt appreciation to my wife, Doris Jacoby-Guyot, for her sympathetic understanding and loving support.

Mario Jacoby

Note from author

Purely for the sake of readability and style I decided not to repeat at *every* opportunity that I am thinking of and wish to address members of both sexes. For me, this is such a basic assumption that I may refrain at certain places from the constant repetition of using "he and she" in the text, hoping that the contents of this book show that I am anything but a supporter of fixed, patriarchal structures.

INTRODUCTION

Infant research, especially the work being done in America, has increasingly gained in influence in the last decades, growing in its impact upon psychoanalytic practice. Infant research observations and hypotheses have raised serious questions about previous, mainstream psychoanalytic theories of earliest child development. Within the scope of this study, it is certainly not possible to comprehensively delineate the numerous, intricate findings of research in infant development. (For an introductory, summary description of this research, see Martin Dornes' two outstanding volumes: *The Competent Newborn* [*Der kompetente Säugling*] [1993] and *Early Childhood* [*Die frühe Kindheit*] [1997]. Unfortunately, these works are not yet translated into English.) It is much more my intent to provide an overview of those findings, which to me seem highly relevant to psychotherapeutic, particularly Jungian analytical, practice, and to compare and examine such findings with regard to their psychotherapeutic utility. (It should be mentioned in advance that modern infant research is to be distinguished from "Infant Observation", as introduced by E. Bick in London [Harris and Bick, 1987; Zinkin, 1991].)

First of all, quite naturally there arises the question as to what interest Jungian psychotherapy might have in infant research; or, put differently, why to me, as an analyst who is chiefly interested in Jungian analytical psychology, the results of infant research (especially the work of J. Lichtenberg and D. Stern) appear extremely significant. At first glance, it appears as if the Jungian orientation towards the symbolic exploration of the unconscious psyche is worlds apart from the highly detailed research on the subjective, interpersonal world of the newborn conducted by means of scientific experiments and the most modern research technologies. The answer to this question lies, in my opinion, in the infant researchers' implicit intent to touch upon fundamental questions about the very character of human nature. From the Jungian standpoint one could say that infant research seeks to understand, with the utmost specificity and accuracy, the concrete manifestation of a uniquely human process of psychic unfolding. This process could be described from a Jungian point of view as the gradual incarnation of the self within the individual.

In the sense of Platonic philosophy, I like to imagine that there is a foundational human "idea," the form of essential humanness, underlying each individual human existence. Even though this form, or idea, has taken millions of years to evolve, it is embodied afresh as a universal blueprint in every infant at birth, and is the basis for the organization of that baby's maturation and development (see also Slavin and Kriegman, 1992). It is as if nature, or a "creator of the universe", carried within itself the pre-existing idea of every species, and therefore also the species *Homo sapiens*, which in Judeo-Christian tradition is expressed through the mythical representation that God created humans in His own image. It seems that, within each individual human being, there is hidden knowledge steering that individual's proper psychological and bodily maturation. Because we are naturally social beings, this maturation process will also be influenced by society right from the start, first, through the absolutely necessary interactional exchange processes between the infant and its primary caregivers.

Through the previous mythical representation, of God creating humans in His own image, we are already faced with a central concern of Jungian psychology. It should at this point be briefly mentioned that the messages of myths and fairytales were in general interpreted by Jung to be an expression of the unconscious psyche. Myths and fairytales are related to dreams, as all three may, in a symbolic fashion, provide helpful information about psychological events. It was Jung's lifelong goal to learn to better understand this symbolic language inherent in unconscious processes, and to attempt to search for some key to its interpretation. At the same time, he felt compelled to accept that there are highly ordered and potent forces which manifest themselves, on the one hand, in our instinctive behavior patterns, and, on the other hand, in our collective images or visualized sequences in our individual imaginations. Jung designated these potent forces as "archetypes." The archetypes are, in and of themselves, invisible, and can only be indirectly experienced through their effects; that is, through their instinctual energy and their symbolic counterparts. They compose, based on Jung's ideas, the unconscious and essential ground of our being, which in itself can never be recognized consciously, even though its countless *manifestations* may become more strikingly evident in our experiences over the course of a lifetime.

At the same time, within the essence of each individual lies the desire to solve the riddles of human existence. There is an archetypally determined, deeply felt need to transform the unknown into the known, to give the "nameless" a name. This need is the basis of myth-formation, which throughout history has served to aid humans as they adapt to the vicissitudes of life. It is these life circumstances upon which myth bestows its sense of meaning. Myth also serves humans as they struggle to cope with existential fears. Myth transforms the threatening experience of "cosmic emptiness" into a new perspective which provides the subjective experience of containment. It is a psychological fact that ultimately humans cannot exist in a chaotic world. They require, for their safety and orientation, organizing structures (e.g., in the form of collective myths) that correspond closely with an overall personal philosophy of life and, particularly, with central images of what it is to be human.

Aristotle talked about the human as a "Zoon politikon," a living being that can only exist in social relationships, and we will see that in infant research the human need for social belonging is attributed to an inborn motivational system (Lichtenberg, 1989a). Hence the question of what is truly human nature continuously intersects with socially mediated assumptions and value hierarchies, which may deem necessary, or at least greatly influence, any given view of human nature.

Thus understood, it is simply impossible to address the question of human nature apart from cultural and social influences. And precisely because the answers to the question regarding the essence of what it is to be human can never satisfy completely, the question continues to be posed anew. This is certainly the case in infant research. The formulation of the key question that is implicitly asked throughout these research projects can be stated as follows: What happens precisely at that moment, that place, where the human "idea" incarnates itself within the individual human? How does individual anthropogenesis, the psychological birth of the essentially human, appear in its earliest maturational stages? And most importantly: By what means are the infant's life-giving processes of exchange and interaction with its caregiving environment actively promoted, disturbed, or outright hindered? In any case, it is now possible to see how the question of what it is to be human, including all normative aspects of physical and psychosocial development, is not one of only philosophical interest. Especially in the field of psychotherapy, which most often deals with the detailed analysis of the many routes of faulty development, this question has imminent, practical meaning.

With that, I arrive at the subject of this book in a more focused sense, that of *emotional exchanges as therapy*. In this context, one should keep in mind that Jung, already as early as the 1920s, wrote:

> For, twist and turn the matter as we may, the relation between doctor and patient remains a personal one within the impersonal framework of professional treatment. By no device can the treatment be anything but the product of *mutual influence* (my emphasis), in which the whole being of the doctor as well as that of his patient plays its part.
>
> (Jung, 1929a, par. 163)

In other words, one could say that psychotherapy deals with a more or less rich palette of emotional exchange processes between the analysand and the analyst. This means that so-called "individual therapy" (even though this usually involves *two* persons) deals with both therapy partners, who together are referencing the experiential world, the conflicts, and the emotional exchange processes occurring within the client. Within this context (i.e., Jung's "impersonal framework" of medical treatment; see quote above), emotional exchanges are desirable: the most truly frank openness of the analysand, and the highest corresponding "resonance" or "optimal responsiveness" of the analyst (Wolf, 1988).

In Jungian psychotherapy, the free and creative forming of relationships is very desirable, and the emotional exchange process can take on the most diverse forms, ranging from mutually inspiring and impressive dreams and a beneficial attunement between the therapy partners, to "non-exchange" (which is often its own kind of "exchange," as when it is a result of misunderstandings, feelings of hurt, talking over one another, or other obstacles to communication and connection).

Emotional exchange is also the most essential aspect in the findings of infant research, whereby the deciding influence on a child's maturation process is attributed to the different qualities of interplay between caretaker and child. There is always the question: By what kind of early forms of emotional exchange processes is anthropogenesis promoted, disturbed, or outright hindered? The elements of these original relational connections remain operative in the mature adult, though they become superimposed by the adult's navigating life and its vicissitudes by means of such tools as reason, defenses, and other forms of psychological compensation.

The study of some aspects of primary relational connections, and the promoting or hindering effects they have on maturation, has moved me, as an analyst, to formulate the following questions: How do the findings of infant research relate to the psychological ideas of Jungian analytical psychology? And to which extent could psychoanalytic psychotherapy in general, and Jungian psychotherapy and analysis in particular, be enriched by incorporating certain aspects of these findings? My clinically related experience in examining these questions has convinced me that the incorporation of this research paradigm needs to be, to a far wider extent, considered as serving quite beneficially Jungian approaches to psychotherapy. It may hopefully contribute to a more sensitive grasp of what is taking place on an emotional level and what is therapeutically necessary within the interactive field. Finally, it may also begin to provide some hypotheses concerning the most fundamental features of our emotional life, and the factors that contribute to, or inhibit, its maturation and differentiation. I have to leave it up to the readers if they arrive at similar conclusions. I hope so.

Part 1

ABOUT THE PSYCHOLOGY OF THE INFANT

1

THE CHILD IN THE IMAGINATION OF THE ADULT

The child archetype

Children play a central role in countless myths and fairytales. Much has been written about child deities, such as the Greek Hermes-child, the Zeus-child, the Egyptian Horus-child, and the Christ-child. Further, heroic children, such as Herakles, or the Moses-child, are also well known. In fairytales, children are said to be born with a "lucky skin" (for example, in "The Devil with the Three Golden Hairs"). In any case, their birth happens under magical circumstances of all kinds. Conception or birth is often based in the supernatural (for example, the virgin birth of the Christ-child, or the conception of the Egyptian Horus-child by a ritual phallus). It is characteristic for such children to have a special fate or destiny, whose course follows a fixed and definite story-line. They are abandoned, left to fend for themselves, and saved in wondrous ways, often under dangerous circumstances. Later, as adults, they take on a dominant, divine, heroic, perhaps even royal status (see also Rank, 1909).

Such widespread and common representations point to an archetype that motivates corresponding fantasies and emotions. One must imagine the child archetype, as every archetype, in terms of an invisible, governing structure that manifests itself in the actual symbol of a child and which may constellate an opening to the most diverse dimensions of human experience. In a psychological sense, one will therefore ask what possible meanings are inherent in such archetypal occurrences which revolve around the image of the child.

The following considerations, which are based on Jung's work "The psychology of the child archetype" (Jung, 1940), are to serve the aforementioned purpose. But first, a warning from Jung:

> No archetype can be reduced to a simple formula. It is a vessel which we can never empty, and never fill. It has a potential

existence only, and when it takes shape in matter it is no longer what it was. It persists throughout the ages and requires inter- preting ever anew. The archetypes are the imperishable elements of the unconscious, but they change their shape continually.

(Jung, 1940, par. 301)

In any case, getting back to the child archetype, it is necessary to imagine inner psychic contents which revolve around the image of the child. They are called forth from this image and arranged thematically around this motif. There are such emotions, thoughts, fantasies, and impulses, all referring to the image of the child, which occur in the adult, and at times already in the adolescent, although not yet in the infant itself. Infants living their "being-as-infant" are identical with this experience, and do not yet have the capacity to reflect on how actually being an infant affects them, and what their infantile feelings of life imply about human existence on any greater scale.

Jung expressly emphasized that the actual child is not the cause or prerequisite for the existence of the archetypal child motif (Jung, 1940, par. 273, fn.). Rather, the empirical representation of the actual child is, in psychological reality, only one means of expressing an inner, psychic fact which cannot be conceptualized or articulated more precisely. That is why the mythical representation of the child is most certainly not a mere copy of the empirical child, but rather operates as a clearly recog- nizable symbol of its own: "It is a wonder-child, a divine child, begotten, born, and brought up in quite extraordinary circumstances" (Jung, 1940, par. 273, fn.). However, it seems to me that this statement by Jung contradicts his otherwise very clear and convincing assertion that the archetype, in itself imperceptible, only takes on a metaphorical or symbolic appearance when it encounters the "empirical facts" (Jung, 1928a, par. 300). Therefore, one surely concludes that this "psychic fact that cannot be formulated more exactly" could not take on its outer Gestalt without the experience of the existence of actual children. The child motif, in its symbolism, must therefore be associated with the image of the concrete child; and above all, with the meaning and signifi- cance which the child's existence may have in the psyche of the adult. Only in this way is the corresponding experience capable of being expressed or understood as a symbolic image of the child.

Hence the child motif can take on the most diverse symbolic mean- ings. When it appears in dreams, for example, it can present as an image of certain things from one's own childhood which one has forgotten (Jung, 1940, par. 274). It is not an unusual phenomenon for the dreamer, in his dream, to see himself as a child. This may be due to his having cut himself off too radically from his childhood roots over the course of his life. "He has thus become unchildlike and artificial, and has lost his roots" (Jung, 1940, par. 274). In this way the dreamer is in a sense called upon to get in touch with his childhood roots, which at the same time contain the truth of his original character or nature.

Based on Jung's interpretation, it is important – and here exists a crucial parallel to infant research findings – to consider the child motif not merely as something that was, and has long since passed. It is also intended to serve the purpose of compensating for, or correcting, the often one-sided nature of adult consciousness. Even in the adult, the vital relationship with one's childlike side has very significant meaning, especially insofar as it is still mostly naive, spontaneous, and playful, and close to the adult's instinctive/emotional roots.

A further, essential aspect of the child motif is its future character. It can often be interpreted as a direct symbol of future possibilities. So believed Jung: "The occurrence of the child motif in the psychology of the individual signifies as a rule an anticipation of future developments, even though at first sight it may seem like a retrospective configuration" (Jung, 1940, par. 278). It often becomes apparent that the "child," when appearing in dreams, points to something new, perhaps preparing for a future personality change or transformation. Jung said that, in the individuation process, the "child" anticipates the figure, or Gestalt, which comes from the synthesis of conscious and unconscious personal elements. That is why it is a symbol of uniting the opposites; that is, a symbol of emotional wholeness. In any case, the child motif is, for Jung, primarily a symbol of the self, especially when it appears as a divine or heroic child.

As mentioned before, the child, in many myths and fairytales, is first abandoned, persecuted, and placed in great danger, before it takes on its particular role prescribed by fate or destiny. It then often becomes the new ruler, receiving a powerful or dominant title. The psychological interpretation, that this could symbolize a perspective of renewal, as organized by the self, would correspond to some empirical, experienced facts. That is, at first obstacles appear in the face of new content, ideas, and adjustments which conservative, preserving aspects of the personality want to resist. For some innovations of attitude, as everybody knows, it is endlessly difficult to push through to success. And admittedly, it is also often questionable as to whether the new truly deserves support; or if holding on to the time-tested is not the better solution. Whether certain personality changes turn out for the better or worse depends on the viewpoint of the judgment. For example, when an aggression-inhibited person slowly develops assertiveness, or when the woman emerging from her previous role definition as a wife or mother suddenly announces her own life needs, interfering factors arise immediately from within the dynamics of the family unit. The new is at the very least doubted, and perhaps actively militated against, by those in the surrounding environment. Intrapsychically, as well, there are forces that often set up resistance, which want to uphold the old, even when it is the result of a neurotic equilibrium. In psychoanalysis, the preserving forces often embody the inner resistance to the changes introduced and intended by the therapist.

Without a doubt, the archetypal/symbolic image of the "child" is equipped with a wealth of possible meanings, which are of no minor significance for our own vitality and development, as well as our capacity for renewal. These inner experiences are all symbolized in the image of the child.

At this point, one must certainly be made aware of a further complication. The archetypal image of the child is often unconsciously projected on to concrete children. Is there not, behind some wishes to have children, the barely concealed drive for one's own self-realization or self-renewal? Or perhaps a fantasy that if one had children, one's marriage or partnership could be saved and made indissoluble, and that everything would be better? Surely a motivating force resides in the child archetype, and is overtly, or in an encoded fashion, often thematically integrated into some nightly dreams. In any case, there is often the resulting question: On which level should such dreams be interpreted. . . . Is it about granting a genuine wish, which had previously been rejected, to have a literal child? Or is it about a renewal of the inner attitude, about new creative ideas, about granting the "child" its rightful dues?

The symbolic and concrete child in the imagination of the adult

At this point it should be emphasized that the archetypal or symbolic child needs to be differentiated from the concrete reality of literal children whenever possible. This differentiation is of immensely practical importance for parents, teachers, therapists; in short, for all who deal with children. To acquire insight into the child's world, it is imperative to get in touch with one's own childlikeness, and to become aware of one's own needs for self-renewal, stimulation, fulfillment, and self-realization. Parents should take the freely given opportunity to thoroughly enjoy their heightened sense of self by means of the great blessing given by children.

Taking pleasure in children, one's own enjoyment of children, one's pride in them, the feeling of deep bonding, newly acquired meaning in life gained through children – all of these are direct effects of the child archetype, and provide great meaning for parents, as well as for the child.

Yet one should also bear in mind that the unconscious projection of the child archetype can eventually have very burdensome effects on one's own, literal child. Such a child then becomes the bearer of parental hopes and needs which relate to that parent's own sense of personal fulfillment in life. The child's "special beauty," "extraordinary talent," "sunny disposition," in the mind of the parent, will perhaps bring that child the attention and respect in life that was not given to his parents. "You are my one and only. I exist only for you. You are my life!" Such a pronouncement, whether or not spoken out loud by the parent, may have certain justification in relation to the young infant; but it takes away, even rapes, the maturing child's increasing striving for autonomy. Guilt complexes are thereby already pre-programmed, as it were, manifesting themselves at each moment when the child later wants to go his own way. How can the child disappoint these particular expectations of such "tenderly loving" parents, for whom the child is their "one and only"? The child's individual and unique existence will be undermined by so much "love," and by the burden of unreasonable, even unrealizable, expectations. Such a child suffers the consequences of being invested with the narcissistic needs of the parents.

The unconscious projection of the symbolic child on to the actual, concrete child is often due to the parents, either the father or the mother, or both together, not having access to fulfillment in life from within their own inner resources. Therefore, it is not of much use when outsiders, such as the therapist, preach that the symbolic child must be distinguished from the real one. In order for such a distinction to not remain only in the intellect, but rather to reach its full effect, the parents must, with the help of the therapist, excavate or reconstruct the buried doorway to the inner child and to their own personal resources and vitality.

The complication described here, which exists due to unconscious projections of the symbolic on to the real child, presents a problem for wholesome personality development for a number of reasons. We will return to this clinically relevant subject again; namely, in the context of the subtle observations of emotional exchanges provided by infant research. However, I would like to reiterate that the parents' capability of finding joy in the autonomous development of their descendants, and achieving a truly supportive influence on this development, depends on their connection to the child archetype as it applies to their own personal development and capacity for self-renewal.

Many people, even some expectant parents, are for some reason psychologically cut off from the child archetype. It is hard for them to acquire a sympathetic understanding of the world of the infant. Rather, they experience the demands of the child as overwhelming. Perhaps they are unsure, out of fear, whether they are dealing with the child in the right manner. Perhaps they immerse themselves in one of the countless books that forever blame mothers for all the child's difficulties or problems; with the result that they become even more insecure, and tense up even more when dealing with their child.

The child in dreams

As mentioned earlier, children in dreams appear in endless variations. Dreams may relate to one's own, or otherwise familiar, children; but they may also be about child characters who do not correspond to literal, biological reality, and are more or less pure fantasy products. The more unrealistic such dream children are, the further they are removed from biologic reality, the more they take on a symbolic, archetypal meaning. In reference to this, some examples from my clinical practice are relevant. A male dreamer becomes pregnant; or the dreamer's aged mother gives birth to a child again; or a child has foreign, Oriental or Negroid features, is unnaturally small, animal-like, or already wise, exists only as a head, etc. Such motifs hardly point to a concrete pregnancy or a real child, but to a psychological content which is expressed in a corresponding symbolic form. Something still foreign, somehow abstruse, but perhaps capable of development, draws attention to itself and likes to be noticed by the dreamer. In clinical practice, however, it is useful, as soon as childlike figures appear, to first of all attend to the memories and feelings of the dreamer which are connected with his own childhood, before one tries to arrive at any possible symbolic meaning by way of amplification. What is always most important, of course, are the spontaneous associations and ideas of the dreamer.

Parents often dream of their own children; the interpretation of this follows best the so-called "objective level" of understanding (see Jung, 1921, par. 779). It is possible, for example, that a mother experiences in a dream certain qualities of her child which have escaped her conscious awareness. Thus the dream refers to a subliminal, "objective" reality of her child. At the same time, however, it is her own dream; as such, it belongs simultaneously to her own fantasy, her own emotional world. Therefore, it is in all cases also necessary and beneficial to take the "subjective level" of understanding into consideration (Jung, 1921, par. 812). This raises the question of what could, though the dreamer is unconscious of it, be going on in the literal relationship between the mother and her child. This question supplies a bridge to the "subjective-level" approach, with an attitude by which the dreamer directs his entire attention to his own experience, to his own feelings and thoughts, in connection to the respective child. Based on this, a further question may be posed: What meaning does the child assume in the "psychic household" of the dreamer? Does it also have a symbolic quality for the dreamer's own experience? Behind the actual little person, the child, appear the workings of an archetypal aspect. The parent–child relationship is, on the one hand, intimately personal, and on the other hand, also collectively archetypal, since it is universal in its impact. The conscious differentiation of these two components serves to counteract problematic and burdensome confusion and projections.

Furthermore, I would again like to return to the earlier point that, for Jung, the child motif in dreams could also be "a picture of certain forgotten things in our childhood" (Jung, 1940, par. 273). This very important statement by Jung is unfortunately often overlooked by enthusiastic Jungians in favor of a more "purely Jungian" symbolic interpretation. When, for example, a 3-year-old child appears in a dream, what is asked too early on is to what symbolic content this picture relates. It is understood that the child must symbolize a content that manifested itself, for the first time, three years before (that is, the symbolic child was born three years ago). What is important, however, is to first consider such a dream as a stimulus for memories of one's childhood, in this instance, at 3 years of age. Establishing a connection with buried memories is an essential function of dreams.

Dream example from clinical practice

In the following, I would like to provide an example of a dream which obviously must be viewed as a manifestation of the child archetype and which impressed the dreamer accordingly. A 38-year-old man, who was at the end of his training as a Jungian analyst, dreamt the following:

> He is invited to the house of C. G. Jung for tea. Jung comes to him as a very alert, intelligent child with many toys. He is accompanied by his governess and wants to play with the dreamer. The dreamer accepts the offer, and both are highly excited and absorbed in their play. After a while the governess expresses that the young Jung now needs to withdraw. Both the child, Jung, as well as the dreamer, are very sad about stopping their game.

The following relates to the dreamer's life situation. As mentioned above, he was at the end of his long training as a Jungian analyst, and, in light of that, this dream appeared highly significant to him. During his training-related analysis, Jung's figure had appeared repeatedly in his dreams. For a long time now there had been the constellation of a powerful and all-knowing old, wise man manifesting itself in his dreams. This also corresponded to the conscious fascination and idealization that Jung and Jungian psychology had exerted on him. He had understood the way of individuation described by Jung as a pathway to salvation, and was at that time utterly convinced that he had found in Jungian psychology that very philosophy concerning the world and self. It was, for him, exactly the view for which he had always been searching.

Subsequent to this realization, however, he repeatedly experienced depressively colored phases in which all of that "Jungian-ism" suddenly could have been "bullshit" and appeared as some grandiose illusion to him. Soon enough, though, the previous idealization would then set in once again.

Towards the end of his training, he experienced a period of time in which the character of Jung in his dreams grew increasingly older, behaved strangely, and apparently uttered senseless statements. My analysand attempted to construe this nonsense as deeply meaningful paradoxes, with the accompanying idea that all this could be a form of the Zen Buddhist "koan," or riddle. Zen masters employ such koans to reduce rational thinking to absurdity in order to dissuade their students from rational considerations, because rationality is viewed to be in the way of a more essential, inner experience.

Eventually the dreamer could no longer refuse the realization that his "inner Jung" (meaning his view of Jung as a symbolic inner figure, which operates from the unconscious) must have been afflicted with senile dementia and was in urgent need of renewal.

In this context, the earlier dream, in which Jung appears as a playful child, makes profound sense, and is worthy of our explicit commentary on some of its components. The dreamer is invited to a renewed meeting with "Jung," meaning that which Jung and Jungian psychology means to him. To his surprise, Jung is not the respectful, old, wise man, but a playful child who is under the protective care of a governess. The governess also determines the measured amount of time during which play can take place. The dreamer associated something with the governess which he shared with me during a session, half-laughing, half-embarrassed. He was led to think of some enthusiastic female followers of Jung who still strictly protected Jung's statements from being mistaken or misunderstood. They saw themselves quite evidently as the guardians of the Jungian heritage and set strict rules at the Jung Institute to determine exactly which approach to the psyche is genuine, "as defined by Jung," and which position threatens to "water-down" or "dilute" the "Jungian Spirit." This was also the criterion by which the personality of each of the candidates was judged and their potential contribution to Jungian psychology assessed. The dreamer apparently feels that a direct meeting and discussion with Jung is not allowable unless it be with just such a protective guardian.

In any case, the real surprise in this dream is occasioned by Jung's mode of appearing as a playful child. It seems to me to be of great importance that the dreamer is not paralyzed by respect, rather that he is spontaneously involved in playing, so that an experience of togetherness, a playful exchange, takes place. Thus he does not come to Jung in order to devoutly absorb that which the old and brilliant wise man has to tell him.

For the dreamer, Jung has taken on the figure, or Gestalt, of the child; or rather the reverse: the child symbol appears in the figure of Jung. Whatever meaning the child symbol holds for the dreamer – whether it refers back to his own childlike nature, his spontaneous naivete, his "true self" as defined by Winnicott, his need for renewal, his playful creativity, his vitality, or his youthful religious faith – it is somehow connected to Jung and Jungian psychology. However, this is not an idealizing fusion with all of "what Jung said" with uncritical identification; but rather, this represents for the dreamer a playful and creative personal relationship with the profound stimulation which Jungian psychology still brings him.

In this way he acquires an approach or attitude that is deemed optimal for the beginning Jungian analyst, as it is essential to create an atmosphere which enables the freeing of spontaneity in the emotional exchange. Jung once formulated his therapeutic goal as follows:

> My aim is to bring about a psychic state in which my patient begins to experiment with his own nature – a state of fluidity, change, and growth where nothing is eternally fixed and hopelessly petrified.
>
> (Jung, 1929a, par. 99)

The dream of the analysand is quite fitting at this point of the book before the following theoretical section, consisting of a short overview of some Jungian and psychoanalytic explanations of infant development. In reference to that, I would first like to quote from Heinz Kohut, who accepted inconsistencies within psychoanalytic theorizing insofar as, in his opinion:

All worthwhile theorizing is tentative, probing, provisional – contains an element of playfulness. I am using the word playfulness advisedly to contrast the basic attitude of creative science from that of dogmatic religion.

(Kohut, 1977, pp. 206–207)

2

THE "CLINICAL" AND THE "OBSERVED" INFANT

Introductory remarks

The expressions, the "clinical" or "clinically reconstructed" child, came from D. Stern (1985). With these expressions, he wanted to emphasize how they differ from the "observed" infant that is assessed with empirical methods in new research approaches.

As is well known, the developmental history of the presenting clinical problem is, with regard to the therapeutic method of Freudian psychoanalysis, always the centermost concern. It is assumed that the origin of disorders lies in early childhood, meaning that it rests upon early childhood conflicts or, in more contemporary theoretical developments (such as Kohut), also upon early childhood deficits. In therapy, it is therefore essential to obtain access to these early childhood wounds. The questions at hand then are: What kind of early childhood conflicts and/or injuries are at the basis of the present distress; and at what age, or rather at which developmental stage, was the child subject to such decisive pathological influences? It is believed that one can arrive at a more or less satisfactory answer by carefully noting childhood memories, dreams, and, last but not least, transference. In transference to the analyst, central childhood patterns will be repeated, and can therefore be "reconstructed" to a certain degree by the therapist. The different psychoanalytic theories of child development and early socialization rest extensively on such reconstructions. In this way, the "clinically reconstructed child" is created.

In contrast, the "observed" infant that Stern discusses (Stern, 1985) is accessible only in terms of direct research, at least in part experimental, and is therefore the "product" of modern infant studies. There are many points about which there is no agreement between the psychoanalytically reconstructed and the experimentally observed child. Researchers, such as J. Lichtenberg and D. Stern, are psychoanalysts as well as infant researchers; both have the intention to promote dialogue between analysts and infant researchers. Both concern themselves with the question of how the "clinical" and "observed" infant could be brought closer together, a reconciliation that would contribute to progress in psychoanalytic practice, and further differentiate and modify clinical technique.

For the practice of Jungian psychology, this gap between the "clinical" and the "observed" child has, at least so far, not seemed to have much urgency or even relevance. Jung himself, and the so-called "classical" orientation of analytical psychology, dealt hardly at all with reconstructions of the early childhood situation. Those Jungians who are concerned are much more heavily represented in the branches of analytic psychology which integrate psychoanalytic viewpoints of early child development into their therapeutic approach. This is especially true for those Jungian analysts of the so-called "London School" (Samuels, 1985). For the latter approach, the ideas of Melanie Klein, which already point to a very active inner emotional world in the infant, have met with widespread approval (Fordham, 1989, pp. 213–224; Zinkin, 1991, pp. 37–62).

Jung's views on early childhood development

In 1910, Jung himself, at a time when he was still close to Freud, wrote the essay "Psychic conflicts in a child" (Jung, 1910, pars. 1–79). This was supposed to be a supportive addition to Freud's writings about "Little Hans" (Freud, 1909). With warmth and interest, Jung described a father's observations of his daughter who, at between 4 and 5 years old, was deeply interested in where children (her little brother) came from. These observations by Jung, of the little girl Anna, appeared in three editions in three different periods of his work (1910, 1915, 1938); it is very interesting to follow the development of his psychological approach as reflected in his different forewords to the same text. In the work's first edition, one strongly senses the influence of Freudian drive-theory. For the second edition, in 1915, Jung wrote a foreword in which he strongly relativized his Freudian influenced theses from 1910. Indeed, he still assigned to "sexual interest . . . a not inconsiderable role in the nascent process of the infantile thinking," but believed that the child's sexual interest does not really just strive towards an immediate sexual goal, "but far more towards the development of thinking. Were this not so, the solution of the conflict could be reached solely through the attainment of a sexual goal, and not through the mediation of an intellectual concept. But precisely the latter is the case" (Jung, 1915, p. 4). In a similar manner, Jung emphasized that he did not interpret "the thinking function as just a makeshift function of sexuality," which is then "compelled to pass over into the thinking function" (ibid., 1915, p. 5). In other words, in "infantile sexuality," he saw "the beginnings of a future sexual function," as well as "the seeds of higher spiritual functions" (ibid.). Here, he challenged Freud's theory of the "polymorphous-perverse" tendency of the child, replacing it with his notion of the child's "polyvalent disposition." In this way Jung contributed a piece of his own theory to the "clinically reconstructed child."

In 1938, in the third edition of the same "modest and factual report," Jung placed even the idea of a "polyvalent germinal disposition" of the child into question. This had caused him some doubt. This foreword contains the following, often cited sentences:

> Theories in psychology are the very devil. It is true that we need certain points of view for their orienting and heuristic value; but they should always be regarded as mere auxiliary concepts that can be laid aside at any time. . . . No doubt theory is the best cloak for lack of experience and ignorance, but the consequences are depressing: bigotedness, superficiality, and scientific sectarianism.
>
> (Jung, 1938, p. 7)

Thus the idea of the "clinically reconstructed child," for many Jungian therapists, may be attributed to such a "devilish theory" which can easily be cast aside and devalued.

In the meantime, Jung himself came to the conclusion that, psychologically, infants are part of the parental psyche. In a lecture given in 1923, he stated:

> The prime psychological condition is one of fusion with the psychology of the parents, an individual psychology being only potentially present. Hence it is that the nervous and psychic disorders of children right up to school age depend very largely on disturbances in the psychic world of the parents.
>
> (Jung, 1926, par. 106)

This thesis of the often quite decisive meaning of the parents was at that time necessary, and is in part also confirmed in modern infant research. In its exclusiveness however, as Jung at that time represented it, the "clinically reconstructed child" completely disappears from the picture, and so to speak gets lost in the psyche of the parents. Hence, for too long it has been considered irrelevant in Jungian practice.

Theories of the Jungian analysts: M. Fordham and E. Neumann

Michael Fordham was, besides Frances G. Wickes (1923), one of the first analysts of the Jungian school who dedicated himself to the therapeutic analysis of children. Based on his experiences, he became convinced that, from the very beginning, the child is also psychologically its own individual, and not simply an appendage of the maternal or parental psyche. In this manner, he elaborated fascinating and articulate theories of early child development which, in many respects, do not deviate significantly from the "observed" infant of modern infant research (Fordham, 1969). According to his view, even in the analysis of adult patients, reconstructions of corresponding childhood experiences are of central meaning. He expresses himself thus: "The analysis of the childhood of adults first and of small children later was facilitated by the use of reconstructions or postulates about the childhood and infancy of a patient" (Fordham, 1969, p. 107). A reconstruction is made possible by the analyst who, based on the many specifics provided in dreams, and through careful observation of the subtleties of transference and countertransference reactions, formulates hypotheses, from his theoretical knowledge, that can either be confirmed, disputed, or modified by the patient. A reconstruction can lead to a memory appearing in the patient through which certain hunches may then be confirmed. In addition, facts centering around a specific situation, which the patient does not remember, may then be brought together:

> By using reconstructions alongside memories it is possible to build up a picture of a period in infancy or childhood which fits the psychology of the patient so well that it carries conviction.
>
> (Fordham, 1969, p. 107)

It appears very significant to me that Fordham follows this with a warning. That is, he points out that it is difficult to figure out, or even prove, if a reconstruction completely agrees with the earlier reality. In the end, the determining factor is the meaning which the reconstruction has for the patient.

Another important restriction must be noted here: a consensual agreement coming from the patient does not always warrant the correctness of a reconstruction. As is well known, the meaning assigned to the analyst's interpretation can itself become distorted by the patient's transference-based emotions. In order to properly assess the impact of the patient's particular reactions at least somewhat accurately, the analyst needs a lot of therapeutic finesse. It is therefore a challenging undertaking to attain agreement between the past and the present through reconstruction. Opinions regarding the extent to which such an agreement is therapeutically necessary certainly differ.

In any case, Fordham postulated here the vital importance of direct infant observation. Already in 1969, he indicated that, in order to be more certain, there need to be reciprocal relationships between explanations based on reconstructions of infancy and direct observations during the first weeks and months of life. "There are now good working hypotheses explaining much infant behavior" (Fordham, 1969, p. 108).

Thus Fordham postulated the value of investigating the observed infant with as much exactness as possible in order to make more credible, hence more effective, specific reconstructions in analysis.

Another Jungian analyst, Erich Neumann in Tel Aviv, devised a picture of the child, and its development, at the end of the 1950s (Neumann, 1973). Various child therapists in Israel provided him with the empirical material for his work. In particular, they brought him children's drawings, photographs of child's play with sandtray figures, sketches of roleplays with children, etc. Using all this material, he referenced his earlier ideas pertaining to the stages of archetypal development in human consciousness, which he had published in his major opus, *The origins and history of consciousness* (Neumann, 1954). In a later, unfortunately unfinished book (Neumann, 1973), he presented strikingly coherent findings about the infant's state of mind and its continued development. His innovative contribution consisted in his drawing parallels between the earliest relationship of mother and infant, as well as the continued process of infant development, with myths, as phylogenetic stories, from prehistoric times, and then interpreting them accordingly. This served as a major contribution to the understanding of the symbolism involved in play, and is very relevant for child therapists. As far as I know, however, his analysis of adults never included the reconstruction of the "clinical" infant. Yet the attempt to equate phylogenetic findings with the ontogenetic is quite questionable up to a point; but I will take a clearer stand on this matter later in the book.

The attempt to gradually re-create the often broken bridges to the emotions of the "inner, often wounded child" for adult analysands is also considered essential by some Jungian analysts today (e.g., Asper, 1993). One tries to follow the feelings, dreams, memories, and stories of the client as unconditionally as possible, and above all to take into account the countertransference of the therapist. However, this can never happen completely unconditionally. Psychotherapists are human beings too, who bring along their "personal equation," their preferences and aversions, and it is important that this occurs as consciously as possible. In addition, therapists always finally have, by virtue of their training in psychology, a general picture of "normal" human functioning, which may serve as a sometimes questionable criterion for assessing the degree of psychological woundedness or vulnerability. Such concepts are composed of the experiences of one's personal life history, from one's own ideas about man and the world, from the hierarchy of values inherent in the respective cultural canon, and from the psychological theory of personality to which one best relates.

3

THE "CLINICALLY RECONSTRUCTED" INFANT IN THE DEVELOPMENT OF PSYCHOANALYTIC THEORY

Introductory remarks

Theories always come into play. What is important, however, is to be as conscious of them as possible, and to be able to question and critically analyze them. They are intended to focus the attention of the observer regarding the meaning of certain experiences. Theory, derived from the Greek "theorein," literally means "observe." But, as long as a theory remains in operation as unreflectively self-evident, that is, unconscious, there exists the danger that meanings can be bent to fit or constricted, even falsified, in order to correspond to the theory. In any case, the clinically constructed inner child inevitably takes on characteristics of the various theories and reconstructions of Fordham, Winnicott, Klein, Mahler, Erikson, Bowlby, Spitz, Kohut, and so on.

With this book I intend to add, to this nowhere nearly finished list, additional characteristics of the "observed infant," according to Lichtenberg, Stern, Emde, Sander, and others. I hope to be able to answer the question of what good there may be in this to some extent over the course of this book. What seems important to me – this is to be emphasized again – is to attribute such generalized theoretical interpretations to neither the analysand nor oneself, but rather to personally integrate only those theorems, which bear enough evidence and which suit one's own views, in a way which will assist in the integration of understanding and intervention.

Freudian drive-theory

It is not possible within the scope of this work to unpack the manifold theories and constructions of early childhood development one by one, and as they developed from the Freudian psychoanalytic view. In summary, it need only be said: for Sigmund Freud, the drives and drive conflicts signified the foundation of psychic life. In early theory, those were the conflicts between sexual- and ego-drives, later between sexual libido and aggression ("eros" and "thanatos"). The social and "higher" cultural concerns were derived from these original drives through processes of what was called "sublimation." Childhood development, starting with the newborn, was equated with the unfolding fate of the drive.

According to this view, the newborn first experiences an autoerotic phase, moving immediately into the state of "original narcissism in which the childish ego found its self-sufficiency" (Freud, 1922/1949, p. 69). This is followed by the dominance of the oral, anal, and genital impulses and their respective goal-directed drives. In any case, the infant is considered to be a creature of drives; one which seeks always the goal of releasing itself from tension. In the face of such "ruthless" determinism by the various drives, defense mechanisms must develop early on; otherwise social cohesiveness in the culture would be impossible. There are the parents who are perceived as objects of drive gratification and drive frustration. Conflicts between drive gratification and drive frustration can become so unbearable that they have to be eliminated by means of repression. Over time, such repressed conflicts make themselves felt again in the form of neurotic symptoms. This is where the work of therapeutic psychoanalysis is applied.

This is only a rough depiction whereby early psychoanalysis admittedly gets reduced to the simplest patterns of its drive psychology. Over the course of his life, Freud revised and restructured much of the theory, introducing considerable refinement. His work towers above others as an enormously pioneering achievement: the unveiling of a new territory of the psyche.

In 1937, Michael Balint, influenced by the approach of his teacher, Hungarian psychoanalyst Sandor Ferenczi, suggested a new interpretation of the psychology of the infant. Based on his experiences, he did not see a confirmation of the early phase of "primary narcissism" anywhere. Instead he speaks of "primary love," meaning that from the very beginning the newborn is oriented towards the "object." Balint is the first to interpret the earliest relationship as "mother–child unity." Even when he asserts that this object relation is still of a passive nature, in connection with the demand of the newborn – "I must be loved and looked after in every respect by everyone and everything important to me, without anyone demanding any effort or claiming any return for this" (Balint, 1965, p. 70) – one is still able to place his formulation at the very beginnings of so-called "object relations" theory.

Psychoanalytic theory of "object relations"

The beginning of the object relations perspective is usually attributed, however, to the theoretical advancements of the London psychoanalyst Melanie Klein (Segal, 1964). She postulated in the infant an already highly complex organization. Hence, in her view, the infant already experiences a representation of part-objects, like the "good" and "bad" mother's breast. These fantasies, according to Klein, belong to the genetic make-up, are innate, and express themselves independently of the individual experiences of the infant. Klein is therefore closely aligned with a biological viewpoint. Jungian analysts (e.g., Fordham, 1989) see a great affinity between her ideas about the "unconscious fantasy" and Jung's hypothesis of the archetypes. Personally, I have great difficulty in connecting them up. Archetypes are in no way hereditary ideas or images in the understanding of the later Jung; they are innate *dispositions* which, in the interplay with specific life experiences, serve as early foundations for the later elaboration of mental representations and images. Further, Klein's reconstructed baby is marked most notably by greed, sadism, jealousy, by "paranoid-schizoid" and later "depressive" experiences, all of which are far removed from Jung's ideas.

In contrast, Winnicott's reconstructed infant strikes one as very "observation-near." In his view, the mother is not only perceived as the object or goal of the infant's drives, but as the most important caregiver, who carries out a great variety of functions for her child, especially the "holding" and the mirroring of his existence. In interaction with the most important early caregivers, there develops a relation between the "true self" of immediate spontaneity and the "false self," which early on adjusts to the expectations of the environment and hence hides the direct and spontaneous expressions of the "true self" with intent to protect it (Winnicott, 1965). By observing the true and false self, and their respective function and meaning, Winnicott succeeded in articulating an extremely fruitful theoretical formulation, one which is also clarifying for Jungian therapists. This will be further elaborated later on (pp. 81–83).

Winnicott's ideas are important for the Jungian analyst because his main interest no longer lies in the vicissitudes of drives, but in the development of the ego in the interchange with the mother and other caregivers. He made invaluable contributions to the understanding of preverbal experience. His studies of the origin of human creativity in the context of the transitional object and children's play are extremely stimulating and compelling.

About psychoanalytic ego-psychology

There are still other classical psychoanalytic theories which concern themselves less with the drives and more with the developmental lines of the ego and its functions. "Ego-psychology" has its beginnings in the thoughts of Freud, where the term "ego" and its genesis was interpreted variously over the course of his research. Not until 1923, with the writings of his metapsychology (Freud, 1923), does the term "ego" get a thoroughly psychoanalytic meaning and is assigned a specific function within the "psychic apparatus." However, even at this point Freud also adhered to his lifelong position that the ego develops out of the conflict between the id (meaning the instinctive unconscious) and the demands of reality. In the face of the demands of reality, the id is forced into various modifications, from which the ego emerges. In other words, the ego can be defined as an "organ" that is principally concerned with representing reality for purposes of securing a progressive control of the drives (Laplanche and Pontalis, 1980, p. 197). Freud points out that the difference between the ego and the id can be compared to the contrast between reason and passion (Freud, 1923, p. 30).

Freud himself, however, did not pursue the topic of ego development in detail. This remained the task of the ego-psychologists who were to follow him after 1923. Anna Freud (1973), for example, worked out the defenses of the ego, and revised the theory of psychoanalytic technique insofar as she now devoted increased interest to the analysis of defense mechanisms, whereby the analysis of the id-aspects, namely, making the unconscious conscious, receded into the background.

The backbone of ego-psychology, however, was developed by the theses of Heinz Hartmann. What seems to me to be especially important in Hartmann's theories of ego-development is his explication of its inherent principle of organization, which does not necessarily derive from drive conflicts. Hartmann's infant is therefore not just a creature of drives. His behavior is also determined by neutralized energies that guide and organize ego-development. For Hartmann, ego-development therefore rests upon an inherent principle of organization.

It was also Hartmann who, in 1950, introduced the difference between the concept of the ego within Freudian structural theory (in contrast to id and super-ego) and the concept of the self in the sense of "myself as an empirical person." This double meaning was always contained in Freud's ego concept; it was, however, never explicitly differentiated by him. Hartmann thereby introduced the concept of the self into psychoanalysis. He understands this to be the "self-representation," meaning the more or less conscious ideas that I preserve with regard to my person; in other words, the view I have of myself. This is in contrast to "object-representation."

4

THE "OBSERVED" INFANT IN PSYCHOANALYTIC PERSPECTIVE

In this chapter, I limit myself to the key findings of two highly innovative and influential scholars, René Spitz and Margaret Mahler, although I am conscious that other scholars, for instance, Anna Freud, would have merited high consideration.

The research of René Spitz

It was René Spitz who, to my knowledge, was the first in his attempt to verify, through empirical research methods, core psychoanalytic assumptions. He initially researched hospitalized infants and discovered that neglect of their emotional care during the first year can lead to the most serious disturbances, even when nourishment and physical care are otherwise perfect. Emotionally deprived children show infantile depression, which manifests in vomiting, intestinal disturbances, insomnia, and above all in general passivity. Spitz also observed major developmental delays. In addition, the mortality of such infants, despite their receiving excellent physical care, was again and again found to be very high (Spitz, 1965, p. 285ff.).

With this, Spitz had empirical proof for the grave consequences of infantile deprivation. Thus he directed the attention of psychotherapists to the so-called "early damage." Related to this, the Jungian analyst, E. Neumann, in his own description of early relational disturbances (Neumann, 1973), referenced Spitz again and again.

Though Spitz articulated a very clear theory of unconscious organizing principles operating in the psyche (Spitz, 1965, p. 117ff.), I cannot enter more fully into that discussion here. Nevertheless, Spitz's theories should be of particular interest for all Jungian psychotherapists. He ascertained that infants possess a function which he called "coenesthetic" feeling (Spitz, 1965, p. 134ff.). This feeling moves at the level of the deepest sensibilities and is experienced as a global, overall impression, one which principally utilizes body sensations. It developmentally precedes later, more differentiated perceptions, although adults may maintain certain vestiges of this form of receiving and evaluating information, and may even have a particular gift in using it. It appears that this form of assimilating information largely corresponds to the function of intuition in the Jungian sense, and must also be taken seriously and cultivated by the analyst.

Results of the research of Margaret Mahler and associates

The research of Margaret Mahler and her associates has received widespread acceptance, both within the psychoanalytic community as well as more generally within the discipline of developmental psychology. This is understandable insofar as Mahler and her associates' contributions are also so well suited for furthering hypotheses regarding the characteristics of clinical borderline phenomena and their transformation in psychotherapeutic practice (Blanck and Blanck, 1981, 2nd edn). Mahler has based her conclusions on the most precise observations of the interaction between infants and their mothers.

Of course, Mahler also operates from within a theoretical perspective which impacts her understanding of the subjective experiencing of the observed infant. Above all, she stands on the theoretical foundation established by Heinz Hartmann (1964) and E. Jacobson (1964) in their creative explorations into psychoanalytic ego-psychology. According to these theorists, the infant is observed after birth to exist, first of all, in an undifferentiated matrix from which it gradually, in connection with the development of various ego-functions, differentiates self- and object-representations. Mahler, along with her research team, subjected the mother–infant relationship to detailed empirical study in order to better understand what life is like for the infant. Mahler distinguished between three main developmental phases, namely, the autistic, the symbiotic, and the separation-and-individuation phase (Blanck and Blanck, 1981). The latter leads, around the age of 4 years, to the development of a sense of identity.

In the first weeks of life, "the infant seems to be in a state of primitive hallucinatory disorientation in which need satisfaction seems to belong to his own 'unconditional,' omnipotent, autistic orbit" (Mahler et al., 1975, p. 42). According to Mahler, the baby therefore has no object, and is incapable of distinguishing between itself and its caregiver.

Next, around the second month of life, the infant becomes dimly conscious of the object which satisfies its needs. With this, the symbiotic phase is at its beginning. Regarding symbiosis, a concept originating from biology and used by Mahler in its metaphorical sense, she understands it in the following way:

> The essential feature of symbiosis is hallucinatory or delusional somatopsychic omnipotent fusion with the representation of the mother and, in particular, the delusion of a common boundary between two physically separate individuals.
>
> (Mahler *et al.*, 1975, p. 45)

At the center of Mahler's conclusions on the symbiotic phase stands the realization that if the needs for optimal symbiosis receive satisfaction, this is determinative in terms of the infant's development. If the communication between mother and infant is extremely disturbed it can result in psychosis or a regression to the autistic phase. Such a disturbance can indeed also be the consequence of an innate defect, which makes it impossible for the infant to adequately take in symbiotic linking. Mahler has, however, also observed the opposite: some babies have an unusual talent to wring from their environment everything they need for their development. It is worth pointing out that both of these polar possibilities often play a decisive role in later psychotherapeutic transference phenomena.

The gradual phase of separation and individuation processes begins by the age of 4 to 5 months: first with the *differentiation* subphase, followed by the *practicing* subphase by the tenth up through the sixteenth month. During this phase the actual *"birth" of the infant* as an individual occurs, insofar as it now reacts to the mother's signals and alters its behavior accordingly.

At the age of about 18 months, at the onset of the *rapprochement* subphase, there often begins a lengthy period of vulnerability; this period is therefore called the *rapprochement* crisis. Mahler distinguishes it primarily by the child's clearly perceiving its separateness from the mother. The infant realizes that the mother's wishes by no means always agree with its own, and vice versa.

To this subphase, and its corresponding developmental steps, Mahler has applied a whole host of highly relevant observations, which I cannot individually explore here. Only this much: when the infant is reminded of its separateness from the mother, this may result in increased fears of abandonment, and hence may lead to difficulties when the mother leaves, with a corresponding clinging to the mother. The mother's absence triggers heightened activity and uneasiness, which Mahler sees as an early defense against feelings of sadness. These reactions often continue into depressive irritability and an increased inability to play. On the other hand, there can be an increased capacity and readiness to connect with others available for a relationship (first of all, quite naturally, the father). Due to the beginning internalization of parental demands there now exists, however, the fear of the loss of the love of the "object," along with the infant's highly sensitive reactivity to approval and disapproval coming from both the father and mother in parallel lines. Infants in this subphase often show, occasionally in very dramatic forms, reactions to the discovery of anatomical sex differences.

Mahler assumes, interestingly, that there are essentially three unfolding characteristics of individuation, which appear to make it possible for the child to function at greater distance from the mother; indeed, without her bodily presence at all. Mahler pinpoints the following:

1   The development of language. The ability to name objects appears to strengthen the infant's sense of having control of his environment.
2   The internalization process, which follows from identifying with the "good," providing parents, as well as internalizing their rules and instructions.
3   The increasing ability to express wishes and imagination through symbolic games, as well as the experience of play itself serving to build a sense of efficacy.

These elements, which evidently have the effect of supporting one's autonomy, are therefore important, insofar as they possibly apply also to the analytical situation, where unhealthy dependency may need to be overcome.

Mahler speaks of yet a fourth, final subphase, which she calls *"consolidation of the individuality and the beginnings of emotional object constancy."*

> In the state of object constancy, the love object will not be rejected or exchanged for another if it can no longer provide satisfactions; and in that state, the object is still longed for, and not rejected (hated) as unsatisfactory simply because it is absent.
>
> (Mahler *et al.*, 1975, p. 110)

The most important requirement for emotional health is the so-called "object constancy," insofar as it deals directly with pre-Oedipal development. In other words, the internalized mother, i.e., the intrapsychic representation of the mother, is by the third year more or less available to provide the child with comfort in case of the mother's physical absence. Having attained object constancy, the infant also acquires the ability to maintain his self-esteem by trusting in the internal mother to restore it.

I have relatively comprehensively described the infant studies of M. Mahler, because they come close to describing the observed child of modern infant research, even if the author always tries to direct her observations to fit within psychoanalytic theory. D. Stern refers throughout his books to Mahler's results, especially where he subjects her findings to clear modifications.

Digression: individuation as understood by Jung and Mahler

The Jungian psychotherapist is inevitably reminded, through Mahler's application of the concept of individuation, of the individuation process from Jung's perspective. Of course the respective contexts, in which Jung's concepts find application to Mahler, could not be more different. Is there however, from a purely empirical observation, perhaps not an overlap all the same?

It was Jung's conviction that "the urge and compulsion to self-realization is a law of nature and thus of invincible power" (Jung, 1940, par. 289). The process of individuation is for him an experience, through which he – during the lengthy crisis following on his break with Freud – personally lived and suffered. He was 37 years old at the beginning of this crisis. As a consequence of this crisis there emerged for Jung's followers the idea that a genuine individuation process can only first arise during a midlife crisis, and is therefore an experience of a riper age.

This surely raises the question from a contemporary point of view as to whether Jung may have tailored his descriptions of a psychology of the individuation process too much to his own internal experience in order to claim any general validity for them (see Jacoby, 1990, p. 92f.). Yet in 1921 Jung gave a definition of how he understands individuation, which refers so clearly to generally acknowledged experiences that it would hardly contradict any open-minded observer. It states:

[Individuation] is the process by which individual beings are formed and differentiated; in particular, it is the development of the psychological individual as a being distinct from the general, collective psychology. Individuation, therefore, is a process of differentiation, having for its goal the development of the individual personality. . . . Since individuality is a prior psychological and physiological datum it also expresses itself in psychological ways. Any serious check to individuality, therefore, is an artificial stunting.

(Jung, 1921, par. 757)

This definition is a purely formal statement. It does not prejudge or oppose the countless, possible individual variations in this process, which aims at the development of the specific uniqueness of each personality. In Jung's view, therefore, the development of one's unique individuality is part of general human nature and is activated and guided by a genuine urge towards individuation. He described it further:

Individuation is practically the same as the development of consciousness out of the original state of identity. It is thus an extension of the sphere of consciousness, an enriching of conscious psychological life.

(Jung, 1921, par. 762)

So far, Jung's definitions can be applied with almost no difficulty at all to the processes of early childhood as well. If, however, Jung speaks of individuation as aiming to differentiate one's own individual nature from the collective psyche, or as evolving one's consciousness out of its original identity with the collective, we know that, by "collective psyche" and "identity," he understands something quite specific. "Collective psyche" can, on the one hand, indicate "collective consciousness," namely, the Zeitgeist, the basic unreflected and unquestioned assumptions of the cultural canon. What *one* does and how *one* behaves, in different social groups, rests ultimately upon the uncritically accepted validity of respective value hierarchies. "Collective psyche" can also mean, on the other hand, the "collective unconscious," with its archetypal, emotion-laden manifestations, with the numinous inspiration on consciousness, but which can also be accompanied by destructive hatred, compelling addiction, psychotic inundation, and so on. Therefore, in the process of individuation, there needs to be the gradual development of a critically differentiating consciousness, which enables one to question and confront collective phenomena. "Confrontation" (*Auseinandersetzung*) is one of Jung's favorite words. By *Auseinandersetzung* he meant the confrontation of ego-consciousness with the contents of the unconscious, namely, dreams and the imagination. Often certain contents, which emerge from the unconscious, point out that a process of integration is occurring, which aims at expanding one's consciousness and self-discovery. But this internal process is in need of accompanying people to which one can relate; people who understand, confront, encourage, make demands, limit, ground, etc. For, as Jung so aptly states, "nobody can individuate on Mount Everest."

In Mahler's understanding, individuation means the development of an initial sense of self-identity, which is normally reached by the fourth year. She also sees an innate, powerful driving force at work in the urge to individuation (Mahler *et al.*, 1975). She also speaks of a process of differentiation emerging from an originally undifferentiated matrix with the goal of distinguishing between self- and object-representations. Upon this distinction rests the sense of ego-identity: "I am I, and not you." This whole process exists largely in the internalization of functions, which were exercised first by the mother and other caregiving people in relationship to the child. In Jungian language this would be explained in terms of "withdrawal of projections." That is to say, unconscious contents are found first of all projected into the outer world and are, in the process of the dawning of consciousness, gradually experienced as one's own. Perhaps it does not appear evident to apply this knowledge from the psychology of adults to the psychology of the infant. Still, it needs to be said: if the ego-functions were not laid out already as potentials in the infant, it could not develop them or find them available at a given age. Of necessity, these ego-functions are delegated initially by the still helpless and unconscious infant to its caregiver. However, in the course of early ego-development the infant's own internal powers gradually begin to manifest. The whole process depends, in any case, on the interaction between archetypal readiness and a facilitating environment.

I mean here that individuation, as Mahler understands it, serves as a thorough precursor to the individuation process in the Jungian sense. The essential confrontation between the ego and the unconscious, in the process of the second half of life, presupposes at least an ego-consciousness, which both questions collective norms and discerns contents which emerge from the unconscious. This therefore requires a relatively stable, yet flexible, ego-identity.

One comes to the conclusion that, today, one can no longer define emotional life processes as pertinent to only the first or second half of life. A confrontation with collectively ordained structures or the onslaught of intrapsychic turmoil often occurs in adolescence or young adulthood. In our current crisis of the general decay of values, with all its dangers, but also opportunities, there are invariably gifted young people who search for a sense of meaning in life. Their despair with themselves personally, and with the world at large, is frequently based on extremely complex motives. It is not to be denied that the condition in which they find mankind may provide ample reason for occasioning despair. At the same time, however, such despair may also have subjective motivations, for example, feeling depressed or upset, lacking in self-esteem, intense anxiety, an internal void, and a complete absence of meaning. Such sufferings are often symptoms of so-called "structural defects," that is, disturbances which are rooted in the complicated separation-and-individuation process of early childhood.

In any case, the clinically reconstructed infant, as understood by Mahler, moved much more closely to the observed infant. All the same, the more recent infant researchers have felt obliged to modify certain reconstructions which Mahler unquestioningly assumed from psycho-analytic ego-psychology.

5

THE "OBSERVED" INFANT IN INFANT RESEARCH

Introductory remarks

Modern American infant research attempts, above all, to refrain from using psychoanalytic developmental theories to establish hypotheses about the infant's earliest experiences. Rather, it is based instead upon the most precise, often experimentally supported observations, with the least possible amount of presuppositions. In contrast, analysts have concentrated on developing their hypotheses in the context of the emerging clinical picture. Their early childhood theories are thus influenced by this point of departure. This is the case, for example, with S. Freud, M. Klein, R. Spitz, and also M. Mahler.

The infant researchers began by asking such questions as: What am I actually observing? Which patterns can I differentiate among these observations? What hypotheses can I formulate? How can I test these hypotheses? Their position seems to be arrived at more independently of preconceived theories than that of analysts; and their research work to date has maintained its reliance upon specially devised experiments, as well as evaluations of video recordings and computerized data analyses (see Lichtenberg, 1983, p. ix). But psychological theories of cognition and affect, as well as neurophysiological and neuropsychological research findings, are also taken into consideration (Piaget, 1954; Tomkins, 1962/1963).

It is therefore not surprising that the findings of infant research contradict some fundamental assumptions of psychoanalytic developmental theory. For example, they contradict the view that the baby is passive from the start of life and lives in an original state of bliss, an "oceanic feeling." (Although the idea of "passivity" was already called into question from within the psychoanalytic contingent given earlier. Winnicott (1965) comes to mind, with his interpretation of motility, and Fordham (1969) with his observation of early "de-integration and re-integration processes." Balint (1965), too, was in doubt about the "oceanic feeling" of "primary narcissism," instead positioning his observations of the "primary love" in the foreground. On the whole, infant research propounds that the principle of drives and tension reduction is inadequate to explain early developmental processes (Ludwig-Körner, 1993, p. 161 f.).)

I will report some findings of modern infant research below. That is, I will select those theses from the great abundance of contemporary findings that I consider relevant for the practicing psychotherapist or analyst. Even among infant researchers, there is a certain divergence in opinion with regard to how the many observed data are to be interpreted and classified. It is therefore important not to fall prey to the illusion: Now we finally know about the experience of the baby, know exactly how the human being develops, how he matures, and to which mistakes earlier developmental theories were subject. Infant researchers, especially Lichtenberg and Stern, are modest enough not to postulate absolute, self-assured knowledge. Rather, they always operate by means of hypotheses, acknowledging their interpretations as well as subjective appraisals of the data. They also consistently point out which areas are in need of further research. I believe, however, that their findings can enrich the therapeutic exchange in a major way, by introducing to the clinician innovative and more refined sensibilities.

The genetic make-up of the newborn

In contrast to the traditional psychoanalytic view – where the newborn, like a baby chick inside its eggshell, remains at the level of "primary narcissism" until his hunger forces him to pay attention to his mother as the need-fulfilling object – modern research considers the newborn child as an organism who is quite active and responsive to his mother, adjusting to, and centering around, affective perceptions and actual dialogue with her. Many more recent investigations have consistently documented the already established potential of the newborn which enables it to engage in fully mutual and direct, person-to-person contact with its mother (see Lichtenberg, 1983, p. 4ff.).

Thus it is that newborns react selectively and actively to those sound frequencies that are in the range of the human voice. Their gaze falls upon objects that are at a distance of approximately twenty centimeters, for the most accurate focus. This corresponds exactly to the distance of the mother's eyes while nursing (Stern, 1979). Newborns look at line drawings of human faces for longer time periods than they do at dots. Already, by approximately the second week of life, they tend to look at the face of the mother for longer periods of time than at other people's faces. Film recordings have documented the newborn's reactions, characterized by a special receptivity when the mother "babbles" to them. They react as if they were truly participating in a dialogue with the mother.

Furthermore, infant research offers strong evidence that autonomous, organizing, as well as orienting, and even controlling, functions are already in effect for the infant. For example, newborns turn their eyes quite correctly in the direction from where a noise originates. They react with uncertainty, however, during an experiment where the sound source is separated from the picture on which they see the mouth of the "speaker." This discovery leads to the conclusion that the localization for hearing and processing audio-visual cues represents inborn, autonomous functions. Another kind of system of steering is manifested in newborns' tendency to turn away from unpleasant smells, indicating that smells, as well as the direction from which they originate, are identified as unpleasant without any instruction.

This pre-programmed capacity quickly connects to learned reactions and preferences, as indicated in the following experiment. A bra is hung to both the right and left sides of an 8-day-old baby, one of which belongs to the mother and the other to an unfamiliar woman. The babies were able to smell the difference and turn towards the maternal bra.

Clearly then, from birth on, there is an existing need in the human being to generate hypotheses and expectancies, and to test them. This occurs, for example, based on the organizing principle of correspond-ence or non-correspondence of the results: Have I already come across what I am now coming across, or not? Based on this method, we ourselves, as adults, later structure very complex sets of facts.

Moreover, the category of cause and effect also seems to be geneti-cally pre-programmed; this is illustrated in the following experiment. Two-day-old children were taught that music would always play at times when they sucked slowly. When they sucked quickly the music imme-diately stopped. Next the music was played to them for several days, except now with pauses at times when they were not sucking. Following this, even when slow sucking was again "rewarded" with music, the expected behavioral connection was no longer evidenced (Köhler, 1990, p. 34). They apparently realized that the cause of the music was no longer their slow sucking. Such a causal connection is incorrect; rather, it is mistaken.

The observation that 3-week-old infants can perceive in a transmodal manner is also important. This means that they can coordinate different perceptual modes, such as seeing, hearing, or touching, and alternate back and forth between them. For example, pacifiers with special bumps were put in the mouths of newborns without their having seen them beforehand. Afterwards, they were able to visually recognize the particular pacifier, which they had previously had inside their mouth, from among many "normal" pacifiers (Köhler, 1990, p. 34).

In summary, one could say that the newborn is already endowed with considerable cognitive competence. Thus Dornes quite justifiably named his book (which is well worth reading) about the preverbal development of humans *The competent newborn* (1993).

The mother–infant "system"

Besides the aforementioned inborn competencies, a number of innate release mechanisms are observed in the newborn, which ensure contact with the indispensable caregiver who is necessary for his survival. The newborn is not able to remain viable by himself. He is, however, not merely on the receiving end of a relational system, but takes part in the dialogue soon after birth, and even activates it. For example, babies by 12 to 21 days of age can copy the gestures of adults with their faces and hands. They are capable of imitating an adult who sticks out his tongue, opens his mouth, or widens his eyes. Such "social" preparedness necessitates an inborn pattern that appears to be quite complicated. For example, to execute the tongue gesture, babies must recognize that this thing they see sticking out of the mouth of the adult is the same thing that they feel in their own mouths (yet cannot see). They then have to carry out quite complex muscle movements in order to actually accomplish the imitation.

Such observations offer powerful evidence that the baby, as well as the mother, is "programmed," from the very beginning, to take part in a social interaction and to enter into a bond which rests upon reciprocity. Babies almost immediately manifest the expectation that caretakers are quite occupied with their cycles of attention and lack of attention. In the course of one day, babies go through different states, conditions, or psychosomatic dispositions. These states are observed through non-REM-sleep (deep sleep), REM-sleep, alert inactivity, and alert activity, which can slip over into a cry of distress. Consequently, the child psychiatrist Louis Sander asserted the view that mother and child form a system, a dyad, in which they reciprocally relate to one another (Köhler, 1990, p. 35). The first weeks of life thereby serve to familiarize both partners of the dyad with one another, and to create a system of reciprocal exchange (Köhler, 1990, p. 35). In a successful course of earliest development, after about three to four weeks, we see an organization and sequencing of events which is familiar to both partners – for example a phase of awakening, nursing, and going back to sleep (ibid.). Emde (1980, p. 89) claimed that, within this interactive system, "each partner is viewed as someone who has separate abilities which affect the behavior of the other, and as someone who triggers the other's behavior and strengthens it." When the mother does something unexpected, for instance, when she does not move her face, the baby alters his interaction, and eventually "turns off." To what degree the mother–child system is capable of mutual adjustment and synchronizing has important meaning for the well-balanced development of the infant. Hence it is critical to achieve what researchers call a sufficient "fit" or "match." The mother thus has an important regulating function, and what matters is how capable and willing she is to adjust to the rhythm of the child. In this regard, L. Köhler writes something interesting: "If mother and infant are in correspondence with each other, neither of the partners feels that what happens to him in the sleep-wakefulness phase is caused by the other. It is as if, by chance, each wants the same thing" (Köhler, 1990, p. 35f.). Now there is the quite obvious question of whether these are not important experiences which have their value also for psychotherapeutic practice. By optimally and mutually responding to one another, a spontaneous permission to simply and naturally unfold is cultivated; something transpires in the mutual therapeutic field. In any case, through such experiences of confirmation by the mother, the baby comes to believe in the validity of his perceptions. This process serves as the foundation for the baby's trust, both of himself and others.

In summary then, one can say that the baby is endowed with a complex genetic foundation that to a great extent is "programmed" in reference to the environment. For continuing development, it is certainly decisive that this genetic foundation is synchronized as much as possible with the environment's reactions. Some infant researchers (e.g., Spitz, 1965) point out that these interactions with the environment must occur within the limits of the maturational timetable in order that the respective phase of development would not slip away without being fully actualized. Other researchers (e.g., Stern, 1985) relativized the importance of such sensitive periods. It was previously understood that a given impasse might directly correspond to specific disturbances in later development. For Stern, psychological disturbances are not necessarily related to specific biographical, or localizable, core conflicts and deficits, meaning that it is not, under all circumstances, the main task of therapy to reconstruct such fixation points.

Such ideas, which will be discussed later in more detail, are certainly familiar to Jungian analysts. They also bring to mind Jung's assertion in 1928, which is as follows:

The form of the world into which [a person] is born is already inborn in him as a *virtual image*. . . . We must therefore think of these images as lacking in solid content, hence as unconscious. They only acquire solidity, influence, and eventual consciousness in the encounter with empirical facts, which touch the unconscious aptitude and quicken it to life.

(Jung, 1928a, par. 300)

What we are dealing with here are central, intuitive observations by Jung. Understandably, they are, in accordance with the spirit of his time and his way of thinking, still very global in character. Today, infant research can describe for us, in a very differentiated and detailed manner, in what way these inborn "virtual" images have their effect. To be sure though, one needs to be careful when using the expression "images," in light of the fact that the newborn necessitates a period of maturation of at least twelve months before it begins to retain images of its caregivers under the condition of their being physically absent. Nonetheless, if one translates Jung's "virtual images" as the unconscious potential for "programming" the interactions with the people in the infant's environment, it is certainly possible to interpret or adapt this concept into a much more contemporary idiom.

6

DRIVES VERSUS
MOTIVATIONAL SYSTEMS

General remarks

In classical Freudian psychoanalysis it is assumed that human beings,
by virtue of their inherited disposition, are ruled by two drives: that of
sexuality and of aggression. Jung questioned this view long ago because
he thought that it too greatly narrowed the multidimensionality of human
psychic life. Thus he doubted its validity, already as early as 1912, in
his book, *Symbols of transformation*. He came to the view that libido,
or psychic energy, could express itself in any number of qualities, each
endowed with a particular intensity. Naturally, psychic energy manifests
itself in sexuality and aggression, but also in the power drive, in intellectual
and creative pursuits, and finally also in the drive towards individuation.
There is also libido, or energy, at the disposal of consciousness and the
ego. This libido manifests itself in the so-called free and controllable will.
The so-called free will was defined by Jung in a very experience-near
way, namely, as the sum of psychic energy which is at the disposal of
consciousness (Jung, 1921, par. 844).

Five innate motivational systems (Lichtenberg)

Today one speaks much less of drives, and more of motivations and
motivational systems; which, of course, are often experienced subjectively as drives or impulses of drive. Lichtenberg differentiated between
five basic, innate survival mechanisms, out of which grow motivations.
They are already active in the newborn (Lichtenberg, 1989a, 1992).
These are motivational systems based on:

1   The need for psychic regulating of physiological requirements
    (these needs are also experienced psychologically, of course).
2   The need for attachment and, later, affiliation.

3 The need for exploration and assertion.
4 The need to react aversively through antagonism or withdrawal (or both).
5 The need for sensual enjoyment and sexual excitement.

(Lichtenberg, 1992, p. 1)

This means, for example, that the caretaking environment either responds, or fails to respond, to each of the five different basic needs or motivations. Let us say, for instance, that the baby sucks, and after a while stops sucking and looks into the mother's face; the mother looks back into the infant's face. It is important that, in this making of contact, there is the right distance to the eyes of the mother. The mother says something to the baby, and the baby reacts to what was said, in mime and gesture, and this brings forth a new reaction from the side of the mother, and so on.

In this exchange, the infant will be satisfied, by the mother, in its *physiological* need for nourishment. In addition, the mother also reacts, based upon the need, which may be *mutual*, to form *attachments* and make contact. She becomes involved in the game of looking and being looked at. Before that, the mother was also alerted by the signal of crying, which belongs to the *aversive* motivation, and which announced the discomfort or hunger of the baby. (This may be communicated by a most unpleasant sound. There hardly exists any sound which is more displeasing than those certain sounds of crying and screaming of a baby. But I think this is organized by nature in a very meaningful way because it motivates the mother to feed the baby, care for it, calm its over-excitement, etc. "Stillen," the German term for this, means breastfeeding as the calming or pacifying of the child.) The need to *explore* will be satisfied whenever the baby puts its hand into its mouth. The mouth functions in this way as an organ of exploration, with the question: "How does it taste? Is it hot? Is it soft? etc." Or perhaps the infant will follow a mobile, which hangs over the bed, with both eyes. But sucking its thumb may also signify, for the infant, a wish to satisfy its need for purely *sensual enjoyment*. Such *sensual needs* may also be gratified by means of skin contact with its caretaker.

Of course, all of these motivations can take on a more or less intense degree of drivenness. We speak of the "thirst to know," or greed for new things (exploration), or of power and the drive to be someone in order to be validated (assertion). We often speak of greed with which the infant wants, in a certain way, to incorporate the breast which is giving milk (physical regulation). Of course, this could be a specific problem of Western civilization because there are too lengthy intervals between feeds. In archaic cultures, where the newborn is always carried every-where, mothers give the breast to their infants if they sense the slightest signal of discomfort. Empirical researchers show that to feed every half-hour would be optimal (Ludwig-Körner, 1993, p. 162). One has to assume that the intensity of drivenness, within the various motivational systems, correlates very strongly with tensions which are brought forth by respective frustrations.

The question of aggression

Which motivations are responsible for the drive of *aggression*? I think we must differentiate between aggression and forceful drives of destruc-tion, or even violence. Aggression is based on the motivation to explore the world and to assert oneself in the world. The word, from the Latin "aggressio," belongs to "aggredi," which means to get at something, to step towards something. When we speak today in therapeutic diagnostics of inhibited aggression, we mean the lack of the capacity, or rather an inhibited capacity for asserting oneself, for holding one's own without being intimidated or frightened by the smallest appearance of resistance.

But how do we understand destructive forms of aggression, the drives for destruction and violence, which manifest themselves in people at all times to such a frightening degree? Again and again, undomesticated drives of destruction are enacted on a huge scale; even in societies claiming lofty moral standards, aggression finds itself expressed in diabolical form. Thus Freud, Melanie Klein, and also Konrad Lorenz, speak of a genetically innate drive of aggression which belongs to the human species.

The question of whether humans are born with the drive towards destructive aggression, whether this belongs to our undomesticated natural endowment, is answered negatively by infant researchers. They find confirmations instead for the frustration–aggression hypothesis; that is, the motivation to assert oneself becomes destructive only when it meets with excessively negative reactions from the environment. On an individual level, this can take place under the most diverse circum-stances at each stage of life, and collectively, in a very crude form, in totalitarian states in society. It may take place whenever the infant's rights to live and truly express itself in the world are virtually disavowed, as are the infant's satisfaction of impulses associated with all major motivational systems. In a world where significant caregivers are them-selves dominated by various social taboos, narcissistic vulnerabilities, and authoritarian political structures, the infant's opportunity to make a place for itself in the world is severely impinged upon. When the infant feels powerless and oppressed, pent-up aggression can turn into rage, and may later break out destructively in the form of the so-called narcissistic rage, as Kohut termed it in 1972. The motivation for assertion gets mixed up with impulses which belong to the aversive motivational system and then may lead to destructive hatred against real or imagined oppressors, against people or institutions which humiliate in an unjustified manner. Of course, the destructive element can also express itself in self-hatred.

It is probably a question which cannot be solved: whether a destructive drive of aggression is really innate; in other words, whether by nature man himself has to be "the wolf of man" (*homo homini lupus*, as the old Romans knew!). If one considers the history of mankind, it is quite understandable that one might conclude that there is indeed an innate human proclivity to kill and devour. Yet Margaret Mead (1988) and ethno-psychoanalysts like Parin and Morgenthaler (1972) have found so-called "nature people" who live together in a very peaceful way. What is significant in these cultures is the fact that the parents are very loving and that they really care for the needs of their infants. The same researchers investigated other tribes which lead a strongly aggressive way of life; they found a connection between the aggressive way of life and the frustration to which they exposed their infants. It was proven that the intensity and the effect of aggressive drives are very much influenced by the environment.

Needs for attachment and sexuality

It is also interesting that the need to get involved in attachment represents an independent motivational system, which has to be distinguished from the need for sensuality, tenderness, and sexual arousal. Eibl-Eibesfeldt has differentiated, in his book *Love and hate* (1974), behaviors associated with caring for the brood from sexual motives. Freud's assumption of early childhood sexuality is also called into question from Eibl-Eibesfeldt's point of view. Clearly, in the best, so-called mature, adult love relationships, the motivation of attachment becomes fused and integrated with those of tenderness and sexual arousal. However, we know that this is not always the case because many strong attachments are not sexualized; and a great deal of sexual behavior is unattached to a specific person. Sexuality may be free floating; this is not necessarily to be seen as a kind of pathological split. In any case, this is a field in which quite powerful emotional misunderstandings often take place; for example, manifesting at times, in both literature and real life, as tragic love entanglements.

In a very general way, one has to see the motivational systems as organizing structures of human experience and behavior. Of course the question springs to mind: In what way could one see or describe them, from a Jungian point of view, as archetypes, the unconscious organizing structures of psychic life? Unfortunately, the discussion of this very important and difficult issue is not possible here.

7

THE AFFECTS

The categorical affects

Motivations can emerge in the most diverse gradations of intensity, correlated to the affects and the force which accompanies them. As far as the affects are concerned, they had been considered early on, because of psychoanalysis, primarily in terms of pleasure and displeasure, which were seen to be the sum of all affects. Yet Silvan Tomkins, in his extensive research of affects, which was initially highly influenced by Darwin, was able to differentiate a great number of innate, qualitatively diverse affects. These so-called *categorical affects* also express themselves physiologically; mainly in the form of mimicking certain movements of the muscles and certain patterns of reaction of the autonomic nervous system, like changes in the rate of pulse or the velocity of breathing or electrical resistance of the skin, etc. (Köhler, 1990, p. 37).

Tomkins (1962/1963) described nine innate categorical affects. These affects are distress (an expression of pain, desperation, or sadness), rage, disgust, contempt, joy, surprise, and interest. The affects of fear and shame are inborn, yet require a maturational period of a few months before they become visible. What is essential in the consideration of affects is their biological effect, and thus the part they play in psychosomatic problems and disturbances. Lichtenberg writes that some researchers suggest or suppose that there is a time plan for the first manifestations of the single affects in the process of maturation of the infant (Lichtenberg, 1983, p. 25). This is surely the case if we consider shame, and in a certain sense also, fear (Jacoby, 1994). If one also considers, as Izard does, the feelings of guilt as belonging to the primary affects (Izard, 1981, p. 46), there is, for their appearance, a necessary process of maturation.

However, as noted above, the categories of pleasure and displeasure are a great part of the diverse single affects. Pleasurable are surely joy and interest; and displeasurable are sadness, disgust, contempt, fear, and shame. Yet one also speaks of the "thrill" associated with fear, or even a certain kind of pleasure connected to experiences of anxiety or shame. Contempt can be accompanied by a certain satisfaction; surprise also has a pleasurable and also an unpleasurable side. In other words, affects are not necessarily felt only in terms of the polarities of pleasure or displeasure. The scale for "measuring" affects is thus "gliding," and never independent of the respective context.

These affects accompany and reinforce the various motivations. Surely the need for exploration goes together with the affect of interest; but it can also be the result of astonishment or surprise. The motivation of self-assertion is usually accompanied by joy, especially if it succeeds. But it can be disrupted by the affect of fear, and the result may be a conflict which mobilizes shame.

Lichtenberg has drawn attention to the fact that the psychological reinforcement of affects comes about through repetitions of certain experiences, and some repetitions may add to the respective affect's significance. For example, the mother smiles at her baby, the baby experiences joy; but as soon as the mother turns away, the feeling of joy disappears. The mother attunes herself again, smiling at her child; again she brings forth joy. If this happens two, three, or four times, the significance of this mutual smiling is reinforced to the point where such experiences become quite important, and are especially reinforced as a key aspect of emotional contact (Lichtenberg, 1989b, p. 82).

It is evident that the displeasurable affects are in the majority. They reinforce the aversive motivational system through disgust, rage, contempt, fear, and shame. These affects are able to emerge in all motivational systems; they are in the final analysis general signals of our human finiteness. It is as if nature would take care that, even if we are very motivated, that is, if we have needs for deeper knowledge, for self-assurance, for physical well-being, for so-called eternal love, and pleasure of the senses, we are still somehow reminded that "trees do not grow into heaven." Too much pleasure, for example, with food or sex, can occasion its opposite, namely, disgust. Longing for attachment may bring forth shame if it undercuts the motivation for self-assertion and autonomy. Such a longing may in fact become a kind of emotional slavery or addiction. The need for self-assertion can also bring forth attendant fears. We have to attribute a regulating function to the whole system of our affects.

It is evident that our way, and intensity, of expressing affect has a great influence on the environment, together with the response that respective affects will receive from significant caregivers. Whether our needs for attachment, affiliation, or sexual contact will be satisfied or rejected will of course bring out different affective responses in us. Later on, we will discuss how the habitual forms of fulfillment or denial of the child's strongly motivated needs imprint his affective life. From the Jungian point of view, we have to explore how the so-called "feeling-toned complexes" are similar to the previous dynamic.

The vitality affects

So far we have talked about the distinct affects, each with its own particular quality, and all of which have been observed among infants. Infants express clear and distinct affects which, as some evidence shows, are also accompanied by inner experience and not just acted out. In addition to these qualitatively distinct affects, the so-called *categorical* affects, something new and important must be added: what Stern has called the *vitality affects*. All the basic affects manifest themselves, as well, in the dimension of time. As in *sudden* joy, or a *slowly growing* sense of psychic pain, emotions can go on or off again quickly, rise to a sudden peak or slowly ebb away. "Ebb" and "flow" are images for this movement and express something significant about emotional states. Furthermore, the forcefulness of the growing and decreasing of affects is expressed in this image; the intensity which waxes and wanes.

Music and dance express emotions that have a temporal course. At the same time they may display a great palette of nuances, expressing distinct emotions, such as sadness or joy, where there are many modes and styles. But usually the whole work conveys a basic mood or atmosphere which shimmers through; and if one listens or looks at the performers, one can usually feel the overall intensity, the way they are gripped by their music or dance. What kind of intensity, what kind of temperament emanates from the performer can be distinguished from the discrete contents which he or she performs. One speaks, in certain cases, of a very strong (or deficient) "spell" which the artist has on the public. One may also speak of the artistic temperament and of incredible vitality; or of reservation, coldness, or a sense of feebleness, etc. Stern therefore makes a distinction, rightly so, between the distinct categorical affects and the more global vitality affects (Stern, 1985, pp. 53–61).

Likewise, the infant, interacting with its mother, experiences not only *what* its mother does, but also *how* she does it. Whether nursing, holding, changing diapers, or talking, she has her own particular style of doing what she does. There is something entirely personal about her behavior; yet at the same time, all personal styles are variations of the universal maternal pattern of behavior. It is, in Jungian language, the mother's personal way of living the mother archetype, together with her child, living it and giving it form. In the end, her style probably expresses her basic emotional disposition or perhaps her so-called temperament; though of course, the infant brings his own way, his inborn vitality, his or her temperament into relation with the mother. It is thus not only a matter of distinct affects, but also of the basic temperament of the mother and of the infant; and when the infant's inborn disposition is too much at variance with that of the mother, there is a blockage to so-called affect attunement or mutual tuning into each other. It is obvious that these vitality affects, which are part of the temperament belonging to one's own unique personal disposition, play a major role in the early mother–infant relationship. Too many discrepancies may evoke for the child a feeling of basically not belonging in the world; of not being accepted for who he is, or of fundamentally being "deprived of his birthright."

Stern is of the opinion that infants do not first of all perceive observable actions, as such, in the way that adults do. That is, the infant is impressed by the vitality affects which are implicit in the caregiver's behavior; hence the infant begins to try to "understand" those affective colorations. In other words, the infant experiences its world, first of all, as a world of vitality affects before it can develop the perception of formal actions. I think this more or less serves as the basis for our intuitive sense for what emanates from other human beings, and how we experience ourselves in their presence. Accordingly, we may experience ourselves as calm, or tense, or excited, or stimulated, or battered, or heavy, etc. Of course, in all of these feelings we may also run into our own projections. The question of what is projection and what is real perception, in terms of what others may be "sending out" consciously or unconsciously, is often quite difficult to answer. But Jung has already affirmed, rightly so, that there is always a hook on which projections are hung. In any case, the vitality affects also have a very important role in the therapeutic relationship and its interactive field.

8

THE SELF AND THE
ORGANIZATIONAL FORMS
OF THE SENSE OF SELF

Introductory remarks

So far I have described, from infant research, some important traits of
the innate endowment of the newborn. We have seen that the observed
child already possesses, from birth onwards, the capacity to perceive
its own body boundaries; thus it can distinguish itself from the mother.
Of course, all this is outside reflected awareness. But taken together,
the newborn has astonishing capacities of perception and reaction. In
addition, the specific human motivational systems and basic affects are
already in operation and are observable in various infant activities. One
can assume that they also express diverse rudimentary experiences of the
infant. In other words, there is an essential archetypal inheritance already
in place; but it needs, in order to become fully effected, the contribution
of the maternal caregiver.

Lichtenberg speaks about a "ground plan" for the infant–environment
system, which wants to be followed and realized. But he immediately
adds: "This ground plan is the same for all infant–environment systems;
but will be coped with in an individual way" (Lichtenberg, oral communication). Transposed into Jungian language, one would talk of a fundamental, archetypal reality, which is always being modified by one's
personal interests and needs. The opposite is also true; that is, the archetypal dimension influences the personal dimension as well. Disturbances
arise when there is too great a gap between the personal and the
archetypal.

In the Jungian view, the early processes of maturation and development are organized and steered by the self, which is the directing center
of the whole personality. In infant research there is also a lot of stress
on the term "self"; however, we have to differentiate what is understood
in the different schools by this concept of self.

Thus, for Lichtenberg, the self could be defined in terms of a sense of unity which remains stable in spite of all the various changes of emotional states which accompany human experience (Lichtenberg, 1992, p. 57). In other words, the self, as Lichtenberg sees it, is integrally connected with a sense of identity and continuity across time. Lichtenberg also observed that each of the various motivational systems has its own particular organization. Yet at any given time, the hierarchy or priority among the distinct systems varies. For instance, whenever physiological regulation is required, we may experience, as hierarchically dominant, such needs as hunger or thirst or physical fatigue. Or, in situations where the system of self-assertion is the focus, keen mental concentration may be in the foreground.

Needs which are at the center of one system may also shift or transition smoothly into other systems. But they may also come into conflict with one another. For instance, sexual excitement may intersect with aversive motivation, which then manifests as fear, disgust, and so forth. It is obvious that there is a superordinate organization which is responsible for compensating and adjusting between the motivational systems; and it is the center of this organization which Lichtenberg defines as the self, or self-organization. He also defines the self "as an independent center, for initiating, organizing, and integrating experience and motivation" (Lichtenberg, 1992, p. 58). The maturation and development of this integrating and organizing capacity is really the chief interest of infant researchers. It is this very capacity which is so specific to the human species, and which is at the same time highly prone to becoming disturbed or derailed. All psychological, and probably all psychosomatic, disorders are at one and the same time disorders within the self-organization.

In any case, the great significance which infant researchers attribute to the self could be of keen interest to Jungian analysts, even if the concept of the self is not completely identical.*

The development of the organizational forms of the sense of self

Daniel Stern has proposed an experience-near model for understanding the development of the sense of self. His model, derived from infant research, involves the emergence of a sense of self through developmental

---

*For the different views and concepts of "ego" and "self" in Jungian psychology and in psychoanalysis, see Jacoby, 1985.

stages from birth through the first eighteen months. From the very beginning, an essential characteristic of any person's sense of self is the observation that it necessitates other people (typically, at least, the mother). There is always a sense of "self with other."

This model of infant development differs from various other, popular psychoanalytic views, which are based largely on the findings of Margaret Mahler (Mahler *et al.*, 1975). According to Mahler, after the brief, initial phase of autism the infant passes through a stage of symbiotic fusion with the other (between the second and seventh months), after which it begins to gradually differentiate itself as a separate person. In contrast, Stern and other researchers have observed that infants are already able to distinguish between themselves and other people at birth. I want to sum up the most important conceptualizations of Daniel Stern.

The emergent self

From birth until the second month the infant lives in a world that Stern calls the domain of the *emergent self*. In this preliminary stage, particular events and perceptions are experienced as their own entities. But the newborn perceives them as separate moments with no cumulative relationship to each other. Observing such discrete, unrelated experiences, other psychoanalytic thinkers have concluded that infants live in a state of undifferentiation. However, according to Stern, the subjective life of the infant may consist of many distinct and vivid experiences. Of course, for now, we have no way of knowing whether the infant experiences a connection between these various experiences. It probably still lacks the understanding that any sort of coherence between different experiences might exist at all. But these single moments eventually begin to organize themselves into successively larger, more comprehensive structures. The infant experiences what Stern calls "an emergent self," when an inner, creative process begins that brings the infant into the first domain of organized self-experience.

> This global subjective world of emerging organization is and remains the fundamental domain of human subjectivity. It operates – of course, without the infant's awareness at first – as the experiential matrix from which thoughts, perceived forms, identifiable acts, and verbalized feelings will later arise. It also acts as the source for ongoing affective appraisals of events. Finally, it is the ultimate reservoir that can be dipped into for all creative experience.
>
> (Stern, 1985, p. 67)

In other words, from the Jungian point of view, one could say that this is the primal form of what in later life is called the emerging of contents from the unconscious. Those contents may, with time, transform one's sense of self and attitude towards the world, and may indeed enrich it. They are the source of any creative activity. (In Part II of this book I shall provide a relevant dream example with commentary.) In any case, an infant experiences here the earliest prototype of a creative process. And this process aims at generating the initial organization of the sense of self.

The "sense of a core self"

Stern called this first domain the "sense of a core self." He and other researchers observed that, by the second month, a sense of self has already developed. It enables the infant to experience its intention and motivation as indeed its own. If the infant could talk, he would now say, "*I'm* looking at Mother"; or, "*I'm* responding to her looking at me"; or, "*I'm* now reaching out to her breast (or to the bottle)." At this point the infant's sense of its own body's boundaries and its sense of coherence have also come alive. At the same time, the infant has the experience of togetherness in the presence of another, the caregiver. These are not, however, experiences of symbiotic fusion. Rather, according to Stern, they simply represent a way of being together with the self-regulating other. The infant experiences changes in its own internal state coming about via the other, the caregiver; for example, through nursing, bathing, and the changing of its diapers. But of course, the interaction with the self-regulating other is not always pleasurable. Aversive motivations and affects may also become activated. In addition, there is also a dependence on the caregiver for the infant's sense of self as it connects to its need for security; this manifests in various bonding behaviors such as mutual gazing, snuggling, and being held. In spite of the fact that the infant's sense of self changes along with the activity of the caretaker, the boundary between self and the other remains intact. This can be better described as relatedness to a self-regulating other, rather than as fusion. However, it is important to keep in mind that in this phase the infant's experience consists primarily of bodily sensations and various exchanges of physical intimacy.

The "sense of a subjective self" – intersubjectivity

Between the seventh and fifteenth month of life the capacity develops for actual interpersonal relatedness. Infants discover that they can share subjective experiences with someone else. Whereas in the previous phase the infant's subjective experience was still determined by the mother's regulation, now the focus shifts to the need for *common* experience. There are three types of inner states which are crucial to interpersonal relatedness, and which infants at this age can share without yet being able to speak.

First is the sharing of *the direction of one's attention*. For example, the mother points her finger towards an object. But she can only draw the infant's attention towards that object if the infant realizes that he has to shift his focus from the mother's hand and direct his gaze in the direction pointed to by her finger. By about 9 months of age the infant begins to point towards objects on his own. In addition, he is now able to allow his gaze to wander between the location of the object and his mother's face. He can also notice whether the mother is herself likewise attentive.

Secondly, there is the issue of *sharing intentions*. A most straight-forward example of intentional communication, before the onset of language as the chosen means of communication, has been provided by Stern (1985, p. 131). For example, the mother may be holding something that the infant wants, perhaps a cookie. The infant reaches out his hand, palm up, towards the mother. By making grasping movements and looking back and forth between his hand and the mother's face, there is an imperative communication. These acts, which are directed at the referent person, imply that the infant attributes an internal mental state to that person; namely, comprehension of the infant's intention and the capacity to satisfy that intention. Intentions have now become shareable experiences. In other words, inter-intentionality becomes a reality, though of course, the infant need not yet be self-aware.

The third and most significant factor for later emotional development is found in the emergence at this age of the need for *sharing affective states*. One group of researchers have described the phenomenon which they named "social referencing." Here is one example of social refer-encing, which I have taken from Stern (1985, p. 220f.). A 1-year-old infant is placed in a situation which is bound to create uncertainty; usually, ambivalence between approach and withdrawal. The infant may be lured, by means of an attractive toy, to crawl across a "visual cliff" (an apparent drop-off which is mildly frightening at 1 year of age). When infants encounter this situation and give evidence of uncertainty, they look towards the mother to read her face for its affective content; essentially, to see what they should feel, to get a second appraisal to help resolve their uncertainty (whether to climb over the cliff or not). If the mother has been instructed to show facial pleasure by smiling, the infant crosses the visual cliff. If the mother has been instructed to show facial fear, the infant turns back from the cliff, retreats, and perhaps becomes upset. The point is that infants would not check with the mother in this fashion unless they attributed to her the capacity to have, and to signal, an affect which has relevance to their own actual or potential states. We can also see by this example the influence which the caregiver exercises upon the sense of self of the infant, together with its future development of identity.

Furthermore, something which is also very relevant for the analysis of adults has been investigated. From birth onward, the mother entertains meaningful exchanges with the infant. She interprets all the infant's behaviors in terms of meanings. In other words, she attributes meanings to them. She provides, as Stern says, the semantic element all by herself at first, and continues to bring the infant's behavior into relationship with her own framework of created meaning. Gradually, as the infant is able, the framework of meaning becomes mutually created. One can see that the meanings which the mother creates do not lie only in her observations, but also in her fantasies about what the infant is; and also her fantasies about how the infant will develop, what kind of personality he will be in the future (Stern, 1985, p. 134). It is obvious that such maternal fantasies influence the behavior of the infant; and also influence, to a great extent, its own fantasies. This relationship between the maternal fantasies and the observable behavior of the infant was explored by Stern (1971). Thus Jung's thoughts and views become more understandable: that infants are at first just a part of, or fused with, their parents' psychology. Therefore – Jung concluded at the time – psychic disturbances of the infants would in fact be psychic disturbances of their parents.

In any case, the infant discovers in this phase – where the subjective sense of self and, interconnected to it, intersubjectivity, have been emerging – which aspects of its experience can be shared and which cannot. At one end of a hypothetical spectrum of infant experience in this stage would be the feeling of psychic connectedness. At the other end would be a sense of profound isolation, even a "cosmic loneliness" (Köhler, 1988, p. 61). According to Stern's model, it is only now that fusion with a significant other is possible, while, in the psychoanalytic view, the period of symbiosis begins to recede at age 7 to 9 months. The decisive factor at this stage is the so-called "affect attunement"; that is, to what extent are mother and child able to attune themselves to each other's affects? Such an attunement assures the continued development of the infant's subjective sense of self and the emergence of the domain of intersubjectivity. At best, the mother's sensitive, affirming attitude allows the child to feel: "I know that you know how I am doing" (Köhler,

1988, p. 64). Thus in this stage of human development, the human need to express oneself, to be seen, heard, and understood, becomes central for the very first time.

The verbal sense of self

The age of 15 to 18 months initiates a new stage in the organization of the child's senses of self and its relatedness to the other. This burst of growth, coinciding with the acquisition of language, could be likened to a revolution. It begins with the infant's capacity to take itself as the object of its own reflection. Thus an *objective* self comes into being next to the *subjective* self of earlier phases. The propensity of children of this age to look with fascination at their own reflection in the mirror, and to recognize themselves, is a clear indication of this phase; as is also the development of the capacity for symbolic play and the further differentiation in the learning of language. Through language, issues such as bonding, separation, and intimacy are practiced with the significant other at a level not previously possible.

But language is a double-edged sword. On the one hand, it enriches the field of common experience; on the other hand, it limits it. Only part of the original, global experience can be expressed in words. The rest remains inaccurately named and poorly understood. Many other realms remain likewise unexpressed, left to lead a nameless, but nonetheless real, existence. Language thus drives a wedge between two modes of experience: one that can only be lived directly, and another that can be verbally represented. To the extent that experience is connected to words, the growing child becomes shut off from the spontaneous flow of experience that characterized the preverbal state. Thus a child gains entry into its culture at the cost of losing the robustness and wholeness of its original experience.

> This state of affairs both integrates and fractures experience and leads the infant into a crisis of self-comprehension. The self becomes a mystery. The infant is aware that there are levels and layers of self-experience that are to some extent estranged from the official experiences ratified by language. The previous harmony is broken.
>
> (Stern, 1985, p. 272)

This crisis in self-comprehension occurs because, for the first time in its life, the infant experiences the self as divided, and rightly senses that nobody can heal this split. Stern says: "The infant has not lost omnipotence, but rather has lost experiential wholeness" (p. 273).

Stern thus described four organizational stages of the sense of self – the emergent self, the core self, the subjective self, and the verbal self. But he emphasized, quite importantly in my view, that these points of crystallization are not strictly bounded to distinct ages. The various structures comprising the child's sense of self may develop in succession, each having its own period of formation and vulnerability. However, the higher stages do not simply replace the previous ones. Once a particular quality in the sense of self has been established, it remains for the rest of one's life. In other words, there are four fundamental ways of being in the world. Over a lifetime these can develop, differentiate, and become renewed or enriched, but they can also remain undifferentiated, atrophied, or become split off to some extent.

In order to illustrate these four coexisting domains, Stern uses the experience of making love.

> Making love, a fully involving interpersonal event, involves first the sense of the self and the other as discrete physical entities, as forms in motion – an experience in the domain of core-relatedness, as is the sense of self-agency, will, and activation encompassed in the physical acts. [I would add that each partner also influences and alters the state of the other's bodily self-experiences, as the self-regulating other.] At the same time it involves the experience of sensing the other's subjective state: shared desire, aligned intentions, and mutual states of simultaneously shifting arousal, which occur in the domain of intersubjective relatedness. And if one of the lovers says for the first time "I love you," the words summarize what is occurring in the other domains (embraced in the verbal perspective) and perhaps introduce an entirely new note about the couple's relationship that may change the meaning of the history that has led up to and will follow the moment of saying it. This is an experience in the domain of verbal relatedness. [I would add that lovers tend to create an idiomatic language of interaction that may bear a certain resemblance to the dialogue between mother and child. This sort of language facilitates an instinctive emotional exchange, while a highly abstract language aimed only at the head would hinder such an exchange.]
>
> (Stern, 1985, p. 30)

The emergent self, and its field of relatedness, expresses itself, according to Stern, in the feeling, for instance, of losing oneself in the color of the eye of the other. It is as if the eye, for a moment, would not be a part of the core other. "At the instant that the colored eye comes again to belong to the known other, an emergent experience has occurred, an experience in the domain of emergent relatedness" (ibid., p. 31).

The origins of human patterns of interaction

The various experiences of the infant with the self-regulating other comprise a specific, lived episode which will be retained in memory. Most of the episodes which are lived together with a caregiver, for instance, the changing of diapers, the feeding, the various games, repeat themselves; they therefore become recorded in memory and may be internalized in a more general form. This means that there comes into being a sort of knowledge and expectation of how the episode, or event, will take place and what kinds of changes in self-experience will be created in it. As a result of many episodes, which are recorded in memory, initial representations and expectations will emerge; what Stern named with the abbreviation "RIGs," whose initials indicate "representations of interactions that have been generalized." These RIGs are not isolated images of mother and father, nor representations of self and object, but rather, they are fantasies and expectations about *interactions with significant others.* For the child, they form an inner knowledge garnered from experience about how activities of the caregiver affects the child's state, whether through stimulation, satisfaction, fright, or pain.

By the term "RIGs," Stern means flexible structures which form the average of several, real episodes and build a kind of prototype to represent all of them. A RIG is something which never happened in exactly that way; all the same, it does not contain anything that did not happen at least once. In any case, the RIGs are very important emotional elements of our interactional patterns and our attitudes or expectations. The memories which are contained in a RIG are evokable, as long as one of the attributes of a RIG is present. When an infant has a certain definite feeling, this feeling may evoke in the infant's memory the very RIG to which the feeling is associated. These emotional attributes are also related to memories, insofar as they represent reactivations of the lived experience.

At first sight it is confusing that Stern does not give much significance to the difference between the self-regulating other who is present versus the other who is absent. He feels that the infant has to deal in either case with its past, lived experience – up to this very moment – of togetherness with the other. Even if the mother is present, the infant lives at the same time in his subjective experience of being together with a regulating, historical other, with what happened before.

Stern speaks of being together with an evoked companion. I find the term "evoked companion" somewhat confusing, because it is not so much a question of an actual comrade as a person but rather the evocation of a situation which takes place together with the other. In other words, it is not necessarily another literal person; rather, it may be the fantasy about the situation with the other. It is about latent or activated representations or fantasies about interactions. The idea of the evoked companion serves the purpose of evaluating the present, "actual" circumstance by means of comparison. And this comparison addresses the question: what is new and what is different in the actual situation? That is to say, a type of criterion has been developed through the generalized memories of former interactions. And this criterion serves to measure the actual present situation. The new situation will now somehow slightly alter the RIG of the moment. The former RIGs will thus be gradually changed, and actualized, by the present experience. In this connection, Stern says something very important for psycho-therapists. He writes: "The more past experience there is, the less relative impact or change any single, specific episode will have. History builds up inertia" (Stern, 1985, p. 113). I feel that it is thus comprehensible why, in an analysis, so many new experiences and evaluations are necessary and why it may take such a long time for certain kinds of imprinted interactional patterns to be modified, especially when there is a question of impeding or interfering "complexes." These RIGs can be considered as the forerunners of what Jungians call the complexes. But we will return to the question of RIGs and the psychic complexes, in the sense of Jung, more fully below.

Each infant, without being consciously aware of it, probably lives all of the time in memories of former interactions. This is so whether the persons who took part in those interactions are present or absent. The evoked companions of different characters are thus, in everyday life, constant companions. Stern asks, quite rightly, whether the same phenomenon does not pertain also to adults whenever they are not concentrating on specific tasks. He writes: "How much time each day do we spend in imagined interactions that are either memories or the fantasized practice of upcoming events or daydreams" (Stern, 1985, p. 118).

Thanks to those memories, the infant is, during the first few years of life, very seldom alone. He is at all times in interaction, sometimes with real outer partners; and nearly always with evoked companions. Development presupposes a constant, usually mute, dialogue between the two partners. In any case, according to Stern, subjective experience is to a great extent socially conditioned, independent from the fact of whether or not one is in reality alone. But I want to stress again that the representations are always of a form which is more or less generalized and need not be restricted only to the evoked personal mother. From a Jungian point of view, one could say that our capacity to form a representation out of innumerable, distinct experiences belongs to a creative, organizing force which Jung has called the archetype.

One has to add here that Stern does not seem to be satisfied any more with his ideas of the generalized representations of interactions (RIGs). More recently, he has replaced this earlier notion with the term "schema of being-with." The difference between a "schema of being-with" and a RIG is, in Stern's opinion, that the former captures more precisely the interaction from the infant's subjective point of view, whereas the RIG is much more recognizable from the objective point of view of adults, who view the interaction from outside (Stern, 1996). This "schema of being-with" is composed of five further aspects which Stern analyzes meticulously.

It seems to me that Stern, whose lectures I have found to be astonishingly intuitive and sensitive to feeling, lately seems to feel the need to analyze in tiniest detail this feeling–intuitive mode of conceptualizing. He dissects it to such an extent that it becomes more and more highly abstract; and is attainable only by intellectual "sprain." In this book I shall remain with this earlier understanding related to the concept of RIGs, as this term is intuitively understandable and clearly differentiates the corresponding data; yet it remains near enough to experience. (For those interested, the "schema of being-with" is very well explained in Stern's more recent book, *The motherhood constellation* (1995; cf. Chapter 5).)

9

THE QUESTION OF
FANTASY IN INFANCY

Introductory remarks from the perspective of
Jungian psychology

From the standpoint of Jungian psychology, one has to say that infant research basically confirms hypotheses having to do with the archetypal organization of our experiences and behavior. I noted earlier that these results of infant research serve the Jungian therapist in further differentiating his view of archetypal processes involved in the maturation of humans. This contribution is, in my opinion, both most welcome and necessary. Yet there remains something which may be quite controversial: infant researchers were not able to ascertain a world of images during the first year of life, nor any fantasy activity (Lichtenberg, 1983). This would, of course, cast doubt on the Jungian idea of a primordial image, because it would indicate that it is not the *image* which is primordial in the individual psyche. We will return to this important question more fully in a later chapter.

In the Jungian view, the infant clearly finds itself, together with the mother, in the domain and field of the mother archetype (Neumann, 1973). But at the same time, from the findings within infant research, we see that the infant experiences itself as a separate being from virtually the very beginning of its life; recognizing, for example, the voice, or even the milk, of its personal mother. In other words, the infant already seems to experience much that is personal, even if this can only be rudimentary at this point. In any case, what is personal and individual makes itself known very early on, much earlier than had been previously assumed. All this shows how it is very characteristic for the archetypal species-specific organization of the human infant–mother dyad that it be lived in an individual, unique form of personal interplay. In other words, a unique, personally colored relationship emerges between a particular baby, with its own individual rhythm and temperament, and its respective maternal caretaker, also with her own, individual uniqueness. Thus we see that the archetypal, basic patterns are in fact modified by the personal; yet the individual, unique situation is in turn powerfully influenced by the archetypal patterns. This naturally means that what is archetypal personifies itself from early on in individual ways.

Now the question is: How does the child experience this archetypal situation that has given rise to so many imaginative myths? What do infants experience internally? Are there fantasies which are already alive within them? As we observed earlier, it was Erich Neumann who, in his books, described a series of archetypal stages of consciousness from a Jungian point of view. His method consisted primarily in using mythic ideas suggested by the various maturational phases, thus providing him with a mythological framework for interpreting the stages of development. He called the latter "archetypal stages." There is a primary relationship between mother and infant that he connects with his idea of "unitary reality," which he sees best represented in the myth of paradise (Neumann, 1973; Jacoby, 1985). There are also many other mythic representations of the "elementary character" of the mother archetype. According to Neumann (1955), these all symbolize the archetypal field of the primary relationship.

Nevertheless, we have to realize that no infant is really able to imagine, for instance, the myth of paradise or the mythical aspects of the mother-goddess in any of our elaborate, adult forms. It seems to me that the myth of paradise or of the mother-goddess are imaginings of adults which certainly express something profoundly existential that can, and often does, emerge in different life circumstances. These myths are symbolic forms of expressing basic human themes, which may also play a significant role in the emotional life of the infant, naturally without the infant's knowing or reflecting upon it. The infant may be affected by such experience, but it is not yet able to produce the accompanying imagery. For example, infants may experience states of bliss or anguish but they have no image or concept of those states. This actually makes the emotional experience, raw and unmediated as it is, much more intense and pervasive, and therefore in greater need of being contained by the caretaker. In other words, no infant lives in a fantasy world containing such sophisticated images as the myth of paradise. Rather, these are later, symbolic formulations of preconscious, prelinguistic experiences, which are subsequently given verbal and conceptual expression.

But myths, of course, express basic themes that may play themselves out in a whole host of adult situations as well. Paradise may be lost, for example, in a number of ways, depending on the specific type of painful separation or loss that transpires. In addition, the mother-goddess, as an image of the mother archetype, always plays a major role in our feelings, relationships, and anxieties, as well as our longings.

Thus in reading Neumann, we have to take into account that he described developmental processes and experiences of the infant by means of adult mythology. This material cannot be directly related to the subjective, experiential world of the infant because it presupposes the capacity to symbolize which only begins to appear and mature, according to the newer infant research, by the age of 15 to 18 months.

There is no doubt that Neumann's procedure represents a very important, profound, and fascinating endeavor. But we have to think critically about the level at which we should apply and analyze it. We must remember that our great and elaborate myths are indeed the products of adult imagination, even if children may also begin to invent mythologems at a certain age. Mythic ideas are produced out of the collective imagination, out of the collective need to give meaning to one's experiences in the world. They are the outcome of a universal attempt to integrate the dark, chaotic unknown into the realm of human comprehension.

If one reduces such myths to representing a certain phase of infantile maturation, one does not do justice to the inexhaustible richness of their possible meanings. The attempt to imagine or understand experiences of the infant and of its maturation through myths of adults surely constitutes an instance of psychological projection. This strategy might very well be interpreted as borne out of the need to explain or understand the experience of preverbal infants, in this case via the mythological world of images. Yet one still needs to acknowledge that Neumann, as mentioned earlier, has found some very interesting and provocative applications generated through interpreting the mythological world of images. Through these conclusions he was obviously attempting to better comprehend the experiential world of the preverbal infants. But, to summarize, this material cannot be correlated *directly* to the subjective experience of the infant, because it presupposes in the infant an ability to form symbols, a skill which only begins to emerge, according to the findings of infant researchers, around the age of 15 to 18 months.

About the fantasy of the infant

But what about the real fantasy of the infant? As is well known, Freud and the early psychoanalytic community attributed to the infant the capacity to hallucinate the gratification of its desires. According to Freud, the infant can obtain in a hallucinatory fashion a sort of satisfying experience of its mother's breast whenever the tension of its drives is mounting, but cannot be literally soothed and gratified by its mother. Freud's hypothesis presupposes that the infant has a kind of inner design which he can activate according to his needs or wishes. In addition, Melanie Klein attributes to the infant an inborn, unconscious fantasy. But Jung leaves this question open insofar as he did not deal much with the psychology of the infant.

In connection with the previous idea, according to which the infant is endowed with an innate, interior world of images and fantasy at birth, and which is connected with the function of memories, Lichtenberg critically explored two hypotheses:

1 One could presuppose that there is a phylogenetic heritage in which images are laid down as deep structures that are then activated by the reinforcing experiences coming from the environment (Lichtenberg, 1983, p. 70). This hypothesis had already been proposed by Freud (e.g., in "Totem and taboo" in 1913), who postulated that the phylogenetic inheritance propagates itself from generation to generation. At times, Jung took up this "Lamarckian" idea, but was simultaneously doubtful, and later dismissed it altogether. What is inherited, in his opinion, are exclusively structural elements, which form themselves to various archetypal images, only in a mutual or reciprocal interaction with the surrounding environment. The *images* of fantasy are never inherited or innate (see also Jacobi, 1959, pp. 59–62), and thus there is no reason to attribute to the infant an imaginative fantasy.

2 The second hypothesis is that the memory of repeated perceptual experiences builds up an inner world of images. But all the experimental evidence regarding the infant's capacity to construct internal images argues against this until the second year (Lichtenberg, 1983, p. 71). The infant does not yet have an evocative memory; in other words, he cannot evoke for himself an "objective" image of his mother independent of his interactions with her. Thus infant researchers have not been able to ascertain a world of images during the first year of life nor any fantasy activity. What they have found, however, is that the child does remember many things which have taken place in its *interaction* with the mother. The fact that it recognizes the mother when she is present does not imply that the infant is yet capable during the first year of forming an image or idea of her when she is not present. This is a phenomenon quite familiar to us adults as well: we may recognize people with whom we are only slightly acquainted if we actually meet them. But when we try to describe them based strictly on our memory, we are very often

unsuccessful. Interestingly, we may recall the affective quality of interactions with this person; for example, whether the encounter with this person was connected to agreeable or disagreeable feelings.

From a Jungian point of view, it is quite obvious that the mother archetype has its impact on the subjective experience of the infant, even when it cannot yet express itself in mythological images. But it has to be stressed again: according to the findings I have been describing (e.g., Lichtenberg, 1985; Stern, 1985), a strong case can be made that the earliest archetypal experiences manifest themselves in relation to rhythmically repeated patterns that regulate the physical and emotional state of the infant. The infant experiences a whole spectrum of body sensations; and with them, different patternings of psychophysiological rhythm, having to do not only with its own and its mother's heartbeat, but also with the cycle of biological and emotional states that the newborn goes through during a twenty-four hour period. If the mother functions as a good-enough self-regulating other, she mediates, through the regularity of her dealings with the infant, a kind of primary world order. Thus an archetypal pattern unfolds here, one which does not so much possess a quality of image or symbol, but rather is activated within the category of time, the temporal order and its processes, and associated affective states. These processes regulate tension and relaxation, they direct movements, perceptual stimuli, and bodily sensations. These are the basic patterns which express themselves later on in music and dance, but also in the need for affection, bodily contact, and emotional exchange. This archetypal domain precedes the later, highly creative encounter with imaginative ideas, the experience of images and symbols.

In the first year of life, creativity expresses itself in the form of activity which provides the child with an arena for expressing its need for discovery. Fantasizing cannot yet take place insofar as the inner world is still confined, according to infant research, to the following:

1   the memory of experiences with others;
2   the emotional experiences which accompany such episodes;
3   the expectations which arise from those experiences regarding future episodes.

Thinking and fantasizing, in the adult sense, would only be possible after the emerging of the function of symbolizing, which, as the infant researchers assert, occurs only after age 18 months. It has to be noted that the symbolizing function, as understood by infant researchers, is not identical with the psychoanalytic view, and even less so with the Jungian view, of the symbol. These are different concepts of what the symbol and the symbolizing function is supposed to be, though they may also overlap. But as they each have such a significant application for psychotherapists, I shall describe them in a more differentiated way in the following chapter.

10

THE SYMBOLIC
FUNCTION

Introductory remarks

By "symbolic function" most infant researchers mean the ability of the infant to imagine other persons or objects in their *absence*. With this capacity, thinking loosens its grip from being limited only to concrete perception and opens the way for free fantasy, which is independent of literal reality and can even stand in opposition to it. The infant now has the possibility to imagine, and wish for, another reality than the current one. Before this maturational phase is reached, perception is biased towards the actual current circumstance, for example., affective and cognitive needs; but with no ability to imagine that what is given could also be different from what it is (see Dornes, 1993, p. 193). Transforming its perceptions of concrete reality into a world of fantasy or imagination is not yet possible for the infant. This specifically human ability of fantasizing, on which our creativity rests, and ultimately our entire culture and civilization, first appears at the age of about 18 months in the maturational unfolding of the infant. Before this age there is "clearly for the infant, in its experience, the feature of inevitability: It cannot possibly be different than it is" (Ogden, 1984, p. 187). Thus wishful thinking is impossible for the "presymbolic" infant, since to wish is an intrapsychic construction, which is itself "constituted by means of the symbolic function." Here the observation of the infant researchers stands in contrast to classical Freudian psychoanalysis.

Cognitive symbols

It should be noted here that, by "symbolization," the infant researchers mean the pictorial evocation of an absent object. The respective caretaker, or as the psychoanalysts so unpleasantly say, the "object," has become a content within the internal world of imagination, and is accessible whenever evoked by the child. This is described as "symbolic representation," and is the precondition of any mental image or representation of the other or of oneself. It is this capacity which has usually developed by the age of 18 months.

As mentioned earlier, this concept of the symbol is not identical with what Jung and analytical psychology understands by symbol; also, within psychoanalysis, symbols have a more complex meaning. What infant researchers speak about are so-called "cognitive symbols" (see Dornes, 1993, p. 184), which represent, in our mind, persons, things, facts, which are either momentarily or chronically absent in the external world. Yet the represented content is fully known, and thus corresponds to actual perceptions. It can be named verbally, and we have an image of it in our mind. Through verbal designations we can communicate this content to the minds of other people. Language thus consists, to a large extent, of cognitive symbols.

Psychoanalytic symbols

"Psychoanalytic" symbols, in contrast, point to something which is repressed from consciousness and is therefore unconscious. It remains under discussion whether psychoanalytic symbols begin to operate earlier in infant development (at 6 to 12 months) than cognitive symbols (at 18 months). Infant researchers hold the view, however, that cognitive or semantic symbolism must be seen as a requirement for the psycho-analytically understood symbol (see Dornes, 1993, p. 105). In addition, the visual representation of repressed contents via psychoanalytic symbols assumes the existence of internal images. Otherwise it would not be possible, for example, for the penis to be symbolized by a snake, or the feminine genitals by means of a vase. The existence of cognitive or semantic symbols is therefore, with all probability, a prerequisite to psychoanalytic symbols.

But there is already to be found, in psychoanalytic theory, another variant of the concept of symbolization which serves as an alternative to the notion of a repressed content. Following Melanie Klein's earlier work with symbol formation (Klein, 1930) and Winnicott's theory of the transitional object (1965) comes the understanding of symbolization as the bestowal of psychological meaning. Symbolization is not absolutely equivalent to graphic expression or depiction. Every adult has the potential to express or depict something graphically, yet there are plenty of people who cannot "symbolize." Thus many people suffering from psychosomatic maladies are not able to experience their various body sensations, affects, internal images, or thoughts as a meaningful part of their psychic lives. Feelings and thoughts are for them isolated fragments of an only concretized nature. Although they are, ideally, capable of evoking in their "mind's eye" something not physically present, their ability to fantasize about such objects or even their own bodily sensations is peculiarly empty or stereotyped. For them it is *not* the capacity to reproduce images which has been lost, but rather the experience of vividness, fluidity, or meaning connecting to any image or affect. It is therefore not possible for such a person to integrate images or affects into any coherent, internal world. This lack thus manifests itself in their inability to ascribe personal meaning to experience, or to access any creative path to imagination. This is a deficit which will be discussed further in connection with issues pertaining to psychotherapy.

Jungian view of symbols

With these latter observations we have moved closer to the Jungian view of symbols. Jung distinguishes between the actual symbol and that which he calls a sign or allegory. Signs and allegories have a refererential character; that is, they point to certain facts which may be generally known and understood. The actual symbol, on the contrary, is for Jung "the optimal designation or formula for a relatively unknown . . . fact" (Jung, 1921, par. 814). In contrast to the earlier psychoanalytic view, Jung is interested here not only in that which has been repressed, but mainly in the symbol as a form of expressing the unconscious' own creative power. Thus the symbol stands, so to speak, at the threshold between conscious perceptions or ideas and the influence of processes emanating from the unconscious. As such, it participates in both areas, uniting in itself both conscious and unconscious aspects. Thus Jung speaks of the *uniting* symbol.

It becomes evident, therefore, to what extent symbols are an integral part of any religion. They may constellate experiences of a numinous quality by giving form or image to an otherwise imperceptible, "transcendent" realm. By pointing in the direction of a transcendent dimension, they may evoke a sense of awe in religiously perceptive people. Indeed, from a psychological perspective the realm of the transcendent cannot mean more than a dimension which transcends human ego-consciousness and is equivalent to the unconscious. Depth psychology recognizes that it is the power of the unconscious which affects our conscious realm, and may express itself in symbols of radiant numinosity. In other words, it is beyond the limits of psychology to pronounce declarations concerning the "truth" of any religious creed. However, beliefs and numinous experience can be open to psychological investigation. Thus it is as if symbols of a numinous character would function as an attempt to link us with the transcendent dimension. ("Symbol" comes from the Greek verb "symballein," which in English means literally "to throw together.")

As mentioned above, for Jung, a symbol, as long as it is alive, represents the "expression for something that cannot be characterized in any other or better way." It is alive, however, only under the condition that:

> It is pregnant with meaning. But once its meaning has been born out of it, once that expression is found which formulates the thing sought, expected, or divined even better than the hitherto accepted symbol, then the symbol is dead, i.e., it possesses only an historical significance.
>
> (Jung, 1921, par. 816)

It is, for that reason, completely "impossible to create a living symbol, i.e., one that is pregnant with meaning, from known associations. For what is thus produced never contains more than was put into it" (Jung, 1921, par. 817). Jung also knows, however, and this appears to me to be of decisive importance:

> Whether a thing is a symbol or not depends chiefly on the attitude of the observing consciousness; for instance, on whether it regards a given fact not merely as such but also as an expression for something unknown.
>
> (Jung, 1921, par. 818)

Jung expresses all of this relatively matter-of-factly, and it appears from his formulation as if the aforementioned attitude of the observing consciousness and its openness to the symbolic dimension could be chosen by a willful effort. This is understandable, as for Jung himself, being in his essence a *homo religiosus*, such an attitude was so evident. Insofar as he was entirely convinced of the deep meaning of richly symbolic language, he often generalized or assumed far too much for others. From this it follows that many classical Jungians also try time and again to convince their analysands of the meaningful importance of the unconscious and its symbolic language, only to impose themselves in a most counterproductive, didactic mode of instruction. The capacity to creatively symbolize cannot be taken for granted, as it may be underdeveloped due to conditions of early damage. (We will come back to this point later.)

Here we find ourselves facing the question: How does this specifically human ability of symbolic imagination come to be? In any case, it is a capacity which is connected inextricably to creativity. Although we do not know for sure the ultimate source of creative fantasy in the individual, such fantasy certainly remains unthinkable without the ability to symbolize. The fantasy process certainly necessitates full cooperation between the so-called cognitive-semantic symbolization and the capacity for symbolic imagination, the latter of which is postulated most forcefully in depth psychology. Put another way, reality must be depicted first of all as an inner representation. It must be represented in such a way that it can be evoked at any time as a mental image, even when in a given moment it cannot be perceived directly, or may not be available for actual interaction. At the same time, such symbolic-cognitive representations may take on continually new meanings. They become "pregnant" with meaning, as Jung used to say. For example, the image of the mother is often endowed with great powerfulness, her presence perhaps indicating all-embracing containment, security, and protection. Or she may assume the form of an intrusive, abandoning, or devouring figure. Over time, this imaginary depiction of the mother accumulates its own sense of history, shaped by the actual mother's many interactions with the child. Thus the "mother" becomes a symbolic image with a mulitiplicity of emotional ramifications and meanings.

Even if the baby has not yet developed the ability for symbolic fantasy, there are still his early emotional perceptions, which have coalesced into various RIGs and which serve largely as the affective background for later fantasies. Jungians do not necessarily find it so easy to accept the assertion that the individual appears to exist, at least in his first twelve to eighteen months, in a "presymbolic" phase. Only with the development of language, arising during the second half of the second year, does there even emerge the capacity for symbolic representation. According to Lichtenberg, this capacity serves to a great extent to build up organizing structures, in order to cope with turbulent, conflict-ridden, or "demonic" aspects of one's life experience (Lichtenberg, 1983, p. 130). That these aspects of the child's experience (indeed, of the experience of the entire lifespan) are later represented symbolically in dreams, slips of the tongue, free association, and in spontaneous play, he rightly maintains to be a truly unique discovery of psychoanalysis. Lichtenberg emphasizes that traumatic events may be organized, in these symbolically represented forms, from the eighteenth month onward (ibid.). Here Lichtenberg obviously joins together the cognitive-semantic concept (language) and the psychoanalytic.

A digression: cognitive symbols and the Jungian view of symbols

I would like to try to demonstrate here how language, which is made up of cognitive symbols, stands in connection with symbols in the Jungian sense. Language provides, as our means of communication, an agreed-upon designation for individual objects or facts. There is the assumption that, for both partners in the communication, this designation evokes the corresponding image; otherwise the word remains an empty sequence of sounds. The designation and that which is designated must more or less match, both in the mind of the speaker as well as for the one addressed. With this matching, language may become the means for communication and possible mutual understanding. Insofar as language deals with the designation of concrete objects, where there is congruence or matching between the designation and that which is designated, communicative exchange occurs. More complexity arises, however, with feeling-toned content, which is often difficult to grasp with words and which the other person may no longer find understandable. Thus the language begins to assume a more symbolic or metaphoric character. Somebody might say, for example: " I feel very despairing." The word "despair" designates a feeling state which is understandable only if one knows from experience how it feels. Even then, it is by no means certain whether both people share the same nuances, or mean the same level of intensity of the despair.

In any case, this sentence – "I feel very despairing" – points to a corresponding affective condition. Perhaps the one who expressed it has a hunch about what drives him or her into despair. Or perhaps instead he finds himself subject to a despairing mood which appeared to overtake him and for which he can find no explanation. Despair so often corresponds to a feeling of no longer knowing how to proceed from here. There seems to be no way out. In such a state there may also arise an image of a path; yet one is stuck with the question of whether to continue on it or to leave it. Or the path goes on endlessly, yet one's strength to proceed is suddenly lost. Should I go back in the hope of finding another path? What should I do? I cannot find a way out; I am in despair. Such images may be associated with the feeling of despair; and it may be possible that they would emerge in a similar fashion in dreams, again symbolizing this affective state.

But a whole cluster of images may be called forth by my sentence, "I am in despair." For instance, I may see myself as an infant who wants to joyfully engage or contact its mother. The mother, however, averts her gaze; perhaps she is preoccupied with her own despair. She scarcely takes notice of my need; she is not there. Today we realize, with special thanks to infant research, that we may have here an example of chronic deficits in the mother–infant exchange of emotions. Thus the infant may feel abandoned and rejected. Infants, when they are repeatedly un-successful in getting the mother's attention, eventually give up. They cannot tell whether the lack of love is due to the mother's limitations (e.g., her self-doubt or despair) or the infant's own limitations.

Perhaps there is also something else behind this condition of despair which remains in most cases deeply unconscious, but which is expressed in a famous collective myth of the Western world. Despair means, ultimately, the feeling that one has fallen out of harmony with God, the world, and oneself. In other words, we are dealing with the myth of a lost paradise. In this myth, doubt is triggered by questioning the perfection of God's world order. And of course it is the serpent, with its forked tongue, which sets itself up as God's adversary. The serpent symbolizes, among other things, the possibility built into human nature to cast such doubts. It poisons the self-satisfaction of simply being in harmony with world and self. Thus it represents a deep-seated human instinct to doubt time and time again the validity of taboos, articles of belief, and value systems. Seen from the old value system, the "conservative" inner order, it thus appears as destructive evil. On the other hand, as seen within the flux of life, such questioning can be both beneficial and necessary, as such doubts may occasion reorientation in one's life.

The feeling, "I am in despair," ultimately means, however, that I have lost the ability to cope fruitfully with my doubts. Not that I *have* doubts, but rather, I am completely immersed *in* doubts. These doubts preoccupy me; they undermine my self-worth and zest for life. I am left dis-believing in justice and values; they make no sense and offer no hope. The term "despair" expresses an inner state which is felt emotionally; and can also be rendered symbolically, for example, in imagery. When emotions are expressed in images, it is often easier to find a conscious attitude to deal with them. In this regard, dreams may be quite valuable.

In order to illustrate the meaning of the symbol from a Jungian perspective, I have intentionally not spoken of well-known religious symbols, nor of the circle or the Buddhist Mandala, which as a symbol of psychological wholeness played such a major role for Jung. I have also not chosen a picture in the literal sense, even if the idea of symbol is most typically associated with visual imagery. I took instead, as my point of departure, the phenomenon of descriptive language, accompanied by the question: To what extent does the designation symbolically characterize that which is designated? And, to what extent does the language fit with the ascribed symbolic meaning? As previously mentioned, it is of decisive significance for any meaningful processing of strong emotions and conflicts, whether the latter can be formed and arranged in a symbolic representation, and whether, by means of the cognitive symbol expressing the verbal description, the depth and richness of the symbolic dimension may resonate as well.

Towards the maturation of the capacity for symbolization

Infant researchers, who are primarily interested in healthy or normal development and maturation and only secondarily in the consideration of disturbances, assume that the capacity for symbolization, in which all fantasy finds its basis, develops spontaneously according to the maturational timetable. There is the requirement, of course, that the caregivers facilitate this development as best they can, or at least place no obstacles in the infant's way, whether consciously or unconsciously. The fantasies concerned with the infant may play a major role. In any case, development of a meaningful symbolizing capacity depends largely on a facilitating mirroring and an optimal dose of stimulation coming from the environment – a theme which we explore more in Chapter 11.

However, Winnicott's observation is still worth noting; namely, that the infant, in its mother's absence, may experience a piece of the bed-cover, or later a doll or a stuffed bear, *as if* it would contain a maternal aspect. With good-enough mothering the infant knows how to distinguish between the actual mother's presence and this "as-if" function, which Winnicott called the "transitional object." The bridging function of the symbol is also illustrated in the use of the term "as if" (Gordon, 1993). The actual world and the imagined world are moving into connection – though not fusion – whereby some awareness of the "as-if" character of the symbolic image does not get blurred. It makes sense to assume that a fruitful access to the world of symbols, in their "as-if" meaning, has its roots in the infant's undisturbed ability to create and make use of transitional objects (Winnicott, 1965).

11

THE INFANT AND ITS ENVIRONMENT

The influence of the unconscious background of the parents (Jung)

In 1927, C. G. Jung wrote the following: "We cannot fully understand the psychology of the child, or that of the adult, if it be regarded as a subjective concern of the individual alone; for almost more important than this is his *relation to others*" (Jung, 1927, par. 80; my italics). In Jung's opinion, children are "so deeply involved in the psychological attitude of their parents that it is no wonder that most of the nervous disturbances in childhood can be traced back to a disturbed psychic atmosphere in the home" (Jung, 1927, par. 80). Jung supposes that one cannot speak of an individual psyche, in any truly valid sense, until the age where the child begins to say "I"; and that is, as hypothesized by Jung, between the third and fifth years of life. The infantile psyche is, in a way, only a part of the maternal – and somewhat later also the paternal – psyche, due to the common, or shared, psychological "atmosphere" (Jung, 1928a, par. 106). As mentioned above, Jung concluded from this observation of psychic interdependence that the emotional disturbances of children, at least up until school age, are based exclusively on the disturbances of the psychic "sphere" of their parents. Jung came to this conclusion mainly by observing the dreams of children. For instance, he tells us of the case of the boy of 8 years old who "dreamt out the whole erotic and religious problem of his father" (Jung, 1928b, par. 106). The father could remember no dreams at all; so for some time Jung analyzed the father by means of the dreams of the 8-year-old son. Eventually the father began to dream himself and the dreams of the child stopped (Jung, 1928b, par. 106). This is the reason why Jung was so skeptical about all attempts to treat young children psychotherapeutically. More important in his opinion was the attempt to facilitate the self-exploration of the child's parents; because what has the most impact on children usually has to do with whatever aspects of life which the parents and their forefathers have not, yet probably should have, lived out (Jung, 1927, par. 87).

The views of Jung during that time of his life – views he seemed to hold all his life – leave no room for the individuality of the infant. They also support prejudices, which have at times come to be rigidified into dogma; namely, the prejudices that all psychic difficulties of the child are always a consequence of the mother's (or, less frequently, the father's) fault. Jung did not intend to overly promote or accentuate this prejudice; thus he also stressed that "the causal significance of parental problems for the psyche of the child will be seriously misunderstood if they are always interpreted in an exaggeratedly personal way as moral problems. More often we seem to be dealing with some fate-like ethos beyond the reach of our conscious judgments" (Jung, 1927, par. 90).

The question, to what extent infant and caregiver are emotionally interwoven, has occupied many theoreticians of psychoanalysis. From Winnicott, we have this famous saying, "There is no such thing as a baby; only a nursing couple." Very often one speaks in psychoanalysis of fusion and symbiosis (for instance, Jacobson, 1964; Mahler *et al.*, 1975). In contrast however, the Jungian analyst and infant researcher, Michael Fordham, already expressed in the title of his book – *Children as individuals* – a point of view in which he sees at the very beginning what he calls the primal or original self. This primal or original self is the basis of one's personal sense of reality, as well as the starting point from which individuation unfolds (Fordham, 1969, p. 29).

I consciously placed, at the beginning of this chapter, the quotation of Jung, where he attributes to the relationship between infant and caregiver the most decisive significance. But already by the next sentence, Jung does not differentiate between relationship and fusion. But relationship can only take place between two, at least rudimentarily separated, living beings. Thus it must be seen as different from symbiotic fusion. With fusion, in the sense of a symbiotic "interwovenness," those boundaries within the dual union are very unclear. It is due to the equation of relationship and fusion that Jung feels that one cannot truly speak of the individual psyche of the infant. Yet modern infant research has observed a sense of self from birth onwards, and investigates with fine-tuned subtlety how the relationship between mother and infant differentiates and transforms during maturation.

No one will deny that the interactions between the mother, as primary caregiver, and the infant are of utmost necessity for the psychic life of the infant. On this point at least, all of those who observe infants are in accordance, particularly since the results of the research by René

Spitz. But basically, the earlier research had to limit itself to registering in refined ways the *behavior* of infants; whereas, when it came to the *experience* of the infant, it was only possible to pose certain more or less plausible theories. Modern infant research is interested, therefore, especially in the infant's inner experiences. It deals intensively with the question: How are the exchange processes between infants and their primary caregivers really experienced by the infant? It also investigates or explores ways by which the psychic development of infants can be influenced, furthered, blocked, or misguided. Without a doubt Jung is at least partially correct in his observation of the unconscious influence of the parental psyche upon the child. But more differentiated individual analyses of this very significant phenomenon are urgently needed. I believe that modern infant research provides an important contribution to this question. I will therefore describe some examples indicative of the great variability of possible maternal or parental attempts at forming an intersubjective relatedness. The degree to which they are successful or not depends on the quality of attunement. In any case, they have a decisive influence – sometimes consciously, though very often unconsciously – on the experience and maturational processes of the infant. It is obvious that, through these interactions, certain patterns of behavior and experience are imprinted, and hence remain formative and influential in the life of the adult.

At the same time, those very subtle observations of mother–infant exchange processes also provide a general model for observing the phenomenon of mutual influence – which operates semi-consciously or unconsciously – in intimate human relationships, including the therapeutic situation. As the mutual influence between doctor and patient is inevitable, the observations of infant research can be of great benefit as well for Jungian therapists. Such findings may provide a valuable aid to refining therapists' sensitivity and their feel for the subtleties of therapeutic exchange.

To the question of maternal (parental) affect attunement

Stern (1985) has described in detail the influential effect of parental affect attunement. How does this effect come about? In order to try to give a tentative answer, I would like to return to the experiment mentioned earlier, in which the 1-year-old infant looks at its mother's face in order to determine whether or not it is safe to climb over what visually appears to be a "cliff." One draws the conclusion from such experiments as this that infants would not check with the mother in this fashion unless they attributed to her the capacity to both experience and signal an affect that has relevance to their own actual or potential feeling state; and that by this checking with the mother, their own orientation to the world is advanced. It follows that infants, from approximately 9 months of age, can register this correspondence of affects; that is, between their own affective state and the expression of affect on the face of another person. From this, one can conclude that the infant is able to construct a correspondence between its own inner experience of affect and a state of feeling which he or she observes in the other person. Stern has spoken here of interaffectivity. This interaffectivity seems to be the first and most influential – and in its spontaneity, most important – form of common subjective experience. At the age of 9 to 12 months, affective exchange is definitely the predominant mode and substance of communications with the mother. It is for this reason that the sharing of affective states merits primary emphasis in our views of infants at this age. In any case, one observes that the sharing of affective moods and states appears before the sharing of mental states that reference objects; that is, things outside of the dyad (Trevarthan and Hubley, 1978, cited in Stern, 1985, p. 133).

Three processes are necessary for the experience of interaffectivity, which is based on a necessary mutual affect attunement. First, the parent must be able to read the infant's feeling state from the infant's overt behavior. Secondly, the parent must perform some behavior that is not a strict imitation, but nonetheless corresponds in some way to the infant's overt behavior. Thirdly, the infant must be able to read this corresponding, parental response as being relevant to its own original *feeling experience*; but without the response somehow being only a simple imitation of the infant's behavior. It is only by means of the presence of these three conditions that feeling states within one person may be transmitted to another, and that they can both sense, without using language, that a transaction has occurred (Stern, 1985, p. 139). If such an experience could be "clothed" in words, it might perhaps be something like: "I am able to initiate a process in which my mother (and other people) perceive and mirror me – therefore, I am." This kind of interaction is the source of any experience of mutual emotional resonance. Together with empathy (which will be examined in more detail later), affect attunement is identical to emotional resonance, and is of decisive importance for the maturation of one's sense of self.

The affective attunement between the caregiver and the infant serves as the first and most deeply seated influence on its later maturation and development. It also comprises the beginning of the infant's socialization. Stern tries to differentiate the complexity of attunement behaviors by positing several important distinctions. He differentiates between non-attunement, selective attunement, misattunement, authentic attunement, and over-attunement. Because all these forms of attunement behavior are also relevant for the therapeutic situation, I would like to briefly elaborate on some of these observations.

Selective attunement

In reality, affective attunements between the caregiver and the infant are nearly always what Stern calls selective attunements. This selective attunement is one of the most potent ways for parents to shape the development of a child's subjective and interpersonal life. It helps us to account for "the infant's becoming the child of his particular mother" (Lichtenstein, 1961). Attunements are also one of the main pathways for the expression and influence of parental fantasies about their infants. In essence, attunement permits the parents to convey to the infant what is shareable; that is, which subjective experiences are within, and which are beyond, the pale of mutual consideration and acceptance. It is in this way that the parent's desires, fears, prohibitions, and fantasies structure and contour the psychic experiences of the child (Stern, 1985, p. 208).

In a sense, parents have to make a choice, mostly without reflected awareness, about what to attune to, given that the infant provides almost every kind of feeling state, covering a wide range of affect, the full spectrum of gradations of activation, and numerous vitality affects. There is an almost infinite number of opportunities to respond to the infant's behavior; some are taken, and some remain unobserved and unacknowledged.

I want here to include an example from Stern: the case of Molly. Molly's mother very much valued, and sometimes appeared to over-value, enthusiasm in Molly. This was fortunate in that Molly seemed to be well endowed with it. When they were together, the most characteristically made attunements occurred when Molly was in the throes of a bout of enthusiasm. This is easy enough to do since such moments are of enormous appeal; and explosive behavioral manifestations of infant enthusiasms are most contagious. The mother also made attunement with Molly's lower states of interest and arousal level, but less consistently so; because these lower states were not selected out or left totally unattuned to they simply received relatively less attunement. One could argue that parental attunement with states of enthusiasm could only be a good thing. When it is relatively selective, however, the infant accurately perceives not only that these states have special status for the parents, but that they may be one of the few ways of achieving intersubjective union. With Molly, one could begin to see a certain phoniness creep into her use of enthusiasm. Her own center of gravity began to shift from inside to outside; and the beginning of a particular aspect of false self formation could be detected. Her natural assets had joined forces with parental selective attunement, probably to her later disadvantage. Thus, if an infant will only be accepted as a subjective partner when it manifests a state of enthusiasm, then his self-experiences which may be more depressive may be disavowed and excluded from the realm of potentially mutual or common experience (Stern, 1985, pp. 208–209).

In being themselves, parents inevitably exert some degree of selective bias in their attunement behavior. In so doing, they create a blueprint for the infant's shareable interpersonal world. If certain experiences are excluded from the intersubjective union, then, as mentioned above, there is the danger that a false self will be created. We will return to this later.

Misattunement and tuning

What Stern calls misattunements and tunings are yet another way in which the parent's behavior – and the desires, fantasies, and wishes behind that behavior – act as a template to shape and create corresponding intrapsychic experiences in the child. But that can ramify in the child into ways of experiencing and behaving which are of a self-alienated nature. Misattunement and tuning are difficult to isolate because they fall somewhere between a communing, or matching, attunement and a maternal comment that is effectively a non-matching response. In fact, the main feature is that they come close enough to true attunement to gain entry into events that matter; but they then miss achieving an adequate match. It is the extent to which they miss that possible problems develop (Stern, 1985, p. 211).

Here I want to give an example from Stern (1985, pp. 211–212). (I will abbreviate his example a little.) A mother was observed to characteristically just undermatch the affective behaviors of her 10-month-old son. For instance, when he evidenced some degree of affect, such as looking at her with a bright face and excited arm-flapping, she responded with a good, solid "Yes, honey." Her absolute level of activation fell just short of his arm-flapping and facial brightness. Such behavior on her part was all the more striking because she was a highly animated, vivacious person. When asked, one could see that she was vaguely aware of the fact that she frequently undermatched him. But she did it anyway, because it was her fear that her son would lose his own initiative if she were to completely match his experienced affect. Finally, she stated that she felt that her son was a little on the passive side and tended to let the initiative move towards her, which she prevented by undermatching.

When the mother was asked to elaborate, she revealed that she thought her son was too much like his father, who himself was too passive and low key. She always had to be the initiator, the "spark-plug" in the family, and she did not want her son to grow up to be like his father in these ways. She was quite surprised then to find that this one piece of behavior, this purposeful, slight misattunement, carried such weight and had become a kind of cornerstone of her upbringing strategy and fantasy.

Stern provides this very striking example in order to illustrate the various ways that attitudes, plans, and fantasies of mothers or caregivers can be expressed in concrete interactional behaviors; and thus really "hit their target." In this way Stern stresses the possible consequences of such misattunement; he adds:

> One of the fascinating paradoxes about her strategy is that, left alone, it would do exactly the opposite of what she intended. Her underattunements would tend to create a lower-keyed side who was less inclined to share his spunk. The mother would have inadvertently contributed to making the son more like the father, rather than different from him. The lines of generational influences are often not straight.
>
> (Stern, 1985, p. 212)

Clearly, misattunements are not attempts at communion, or more straightforward participation in the experience. They are covert attempts to *change* the infant's behavior and experience. What then might be the experience of maternal misattunement from the infant's viewpoint? Stern speculates as follows. Successful misattunements must feel as though the mother has somehow slipped inside of the infant subjectively and set up the *illusion* of sharing, but not the actual *sense* of sharing. She has appeared to get into the infant's experience, but has ended up somewhere else, just a little way "off." The infant sometimes moves to where the mother is, in order to close the gap and re-establish a good match. The misattunement has thus been successful in altering the infant's behavior and experience in the direction the mother wanted.

With this, Stern describes a very common and perhaps, in part, necessary method of education. At the same time, one can also see the danger inherent in the whole realm of selective attunement and misattunement. The child has already, at this very early age, experienced the potential danger in letting another person come close to its own subjective experience. The mother may attune to the infant's state, establishing a shared experience, and then change that experience so that it is lost to the child. It is then as if misattunements could be used to alter an infant's experience and to instill in it what amounts to an emotional theft. This is probably the starting point of that long line of development which ends up in the need of older children to lie, to have secrets, and to look for excuses, in order to protect their own subjective experience.

After all, parents are at best only good-enough. That leaves room on both sides of the ideal or optimum for the infant to learn necessary realities about attunement. It can learn that it is a key which unlocks the intersubjective doors between people; that it can be used both to enrich one's mental life by partial union with another (in the sense of Kohut's self-object: Kohut, 1971; 1977); and to impoverish one's mental life by bending or appropriating some part of one's inner experience.

Inauthentic attunements

It is interesting to note the subtle differences, which Stern observes, between misattunements and so-called inauthentic attunements. Unlike most misattunements, inauthentic attunements are not motivated by some hidden intention, as it occurs, for instance, with the mother who attempted by her behavior to prevent her little son from becoming too passive, and hence too similar to his father. Inauthentic attunements, rather, are attempts at togetherness which, for whatever reason, do not succeed; but they have little to do with intentional attempts to change or transform the behavior of the infant in a systematic way. Probably in many cases of inauthentic attunement, what gets played out may be largely due to conflicts of ambivalence, narcissistic disturbances, and other relational problems of the caregiver. Inauthentic attunements have no consistent pattern; and a mother who behaves in an inauthentic manner will be experienced as not being very reliable, as having mood swings, etc. If inauthenticity is dominant in the intersubjective realm, the interpersonal orientation will be very hampered. Because it is not possible to rely on the other person, the development of trust will be disturbed in a decisive way.

In order not to burden mothers or caregivers with the ideal of authenticity, insofar as every ideal can be overdone and become limiting, I want to pinpoint some remarks by Stern:

> Attuning behavior can be quite good even when your heart isn't
> in it. And as every parent knows, your heart can't always be in
> it for all of the obvious reasons, from fatigue to competing

agendas to external preoccupations that fluctuate from day to day. Going through the motions is an expectable part of every-day parental experience. Attunements then vary along the dimension of authenticity as well as of goodness of match.

(Stern, 1985, p. 217)

For Stern, it is not a matter of division between authenticity and inauthenticity. We are dealing here with a spectrum, not with either/or. The question is: "*How* authentic is the behavior?" Very often the mother has several conflicting, yet simultaneous, intentions regarding the infant, whereas the infant may more often only have one intention in relation to its mother. The messages of the mother will be sent by various channels; and of course there will often be "double messages" (see Stern, 1985, pp. 214–218).

The inconsistency of inauthentic attunement, together with its double messages, can of course provoke many moments of danger for development – especially since the need of the infant for social referencing cannot be fulfilled. On what can an infant rely? Where can it orient itself if it sometimes experiences acceptance, at other times rejection, without real reasons? Also, what if boundaries which build structures are never transmitted because the same activities by the infant evoke opposite reactions, according to the mood of the caregiver? Here psychic disturbances, which unconsciously befall parents and other caregivers, can have a most damaging effect. As an example, Stern observed a mother with her 1-year-old son. This mother reacted with depressive signs every time her son did something indicating lack of coordination, such as overturning an object, or breaking a toy. Her reaction consisted of long sighs, falling intonations, and "Oh, Johnny!", which could be interpreted as "Look at what you have done to Mommy again!" Gradually, Johnny's exuberant freedom became more circumspect. His mother had brought an alien affective experience into an otherwise mutual or positive activity, which in time turned into a quite different kind of lived experience for the boy (Stern, 1985, p. 222). Stern suspects that, with this attitude, the mother really could "plant" inside her little son her own affective experience, at least in part. Through this process, the future of his active, exploratory attitude could be chronically inhibited. Stern's observations could also exemplify in a detailed way the more intuitive view of C. G. Jung: that the infant's experience and behavior are to a great extent the expression of the unconscious background and complexes of the parents.

The split between the true and false self

As mentioned above, language can force apart the child's self-experience into that which is lived and that which is verbally represented. It can separate them into two different realms because the spontaneously lived cannot find a complete verbal expression, one which could be shared in a spontaneous way. The lived experience, as it is retained in the episodic memory (the so-called RIGs), and the experience which is verbally represented: both exist next to each other, yet they cannot be completely integrated. The question arises: What are the origins of this separation between one's lived experience as opposed to verbally represented experience; and how, if at all, might this split be bridged?

Here we see the beginnings of the development of so-called defense mechanisms such as repression, denial, disavowal (Anna Freud, 1973). Stern stresses mainly disavowal as appearing quite regularly during the phase of verbal relatedness. With disavowal, one's perceptions continue to be registered in a way corresponding quite closely to external reality. But the emotional and personal significance of the perception is neither admitted by the self nor able to be shared with others. In other words, there is a splitting of experience, insofar as there are two different versions of reality which are held separate from one another.

The relationship between these two versions of reality is very decisive for the further development of personality, whether positive or negative. Winnicott has described two categories in which the personal experience of the self will split itself – the true self and the false self (Winnicott, 1965). The origins of the false self are advanced because certain self-experiences are selected and enhanced in order to meet the needs and adapt to the wishes of the environment. This occurs regardless of the fact that such selection processes may diverge significantly from the self-experiences which are more closely determined by internal design, that is, the true self. We have already seen how this process of splitting may begin before the seventh month, during core-relatedness, as a function of under- or over-stimulation. It is greatly elaborated during intersubjective relatedness by means of selective attunement, misattunement, and non-attunement on the part of the parent (Stern, 1985, p. 229).

At the level of verbal relatedness, language becomes available to ratify the split, and confers a privileged status upon that which can be verbally represented, thus leading to the false self. Through the co-operation of the caregiver and the child, the false self comes to dominate in the form of verbal expressions, which inform the child of who it is, what it does, and what it experiences. In other words, there comes to be an identification with what the mother loves at the cost of one's own impulses. But the true self is disavowed and becomes a conglomerate of self-experiences which one cannot grasp in a verbal way; thus, of course, one cannot share with others, as the words are lacking. Disavowal thus divides one's personal, emotionally significant reality from that reality which verbal convention and the environment have deemed solely valuable.

The motivation behind disavowal, which serves to divide the true self from the false self, has primarily to do with the need for attachment and affiliation with important caregivers. In other words, there is a development of the false self whenever the infant can obtain confirmation of its being by no other means than adapting itself to the expectations of its environment. But in the realm of the true self, the mother or other caregiver refuses, for whatever reasons, his or her availability. A parent may sometimes behave as if this realm of the true self did not exist at all.

Between the true and the false self in the sense of Winnicott, Stern introduces, rightly so, the realm which he calls the private self. The development of a private sphere, to which nobody is given access, is somewhat akin to the development of the false self. But there is a decisive difference, insofar as the private self has never been disavowed. Rather, it consists of self-experiences which have not been attuned to, shared, or reinforced; but, if expressed, would not necessarily lead to parental withdrawal. These private self-experiences do not cause interpersonal disengagements, nor do they provide a basis of experiences of being-with. The infant simply learns that they are not part of what one shares; and they do not need to be disavowed. These private experiences are accessible to language and can become well known to the self and undergo more integration than the disavowed self-experiences. Thus one can modify them much easier through later life experiences; and they are less cut off from consciousness. Therefore, the boundaries which surround the private sphere are more elastic, allowing for more flexibility in any given situation (see Jacoby, 1994).

The splitting into a true and a false self, because of imperfections in our ways of relating, is unavoidable, at least up to a certain point. This is how Winnicott obviously viewed it. Stern therefore tries to introduce another terminology. He suggests that the developing sense of self could be seen as divided into three different sectors or categories: a social self, a private self, and a denied or disavowed self. How "true" or "false" these different parts of the self are in any given circumstance comprises a very complex clinical – and not necessarily developmental – problem. In the most benign cases, those parts of the self may interact with each other and become more integrated over the course of development, and operate in accordance with the inner design of the personality. Such a process would be in line with Kohut's self-psychology, but is also of course similar to the process of individuation, in the sense of Jung.

I would like to end this chapter on a more optimistic tone, with a quote by Stern:

> The fact that language is powerful in defining self to the self [i.e., that humans are capable of turning themselves into objects of reflection and evaluation] and that parents play a large role in this definition does not mean that the infant can regularly be bent out of shape by those forces and they can totally be the creation of others' wishes and plans. The socialization process, for good or ill, has limits imposed by the biology of the infant. There are directions and degrees to which the child cannot be bent without the emergence of the disavowed self, which then makes claims on linguistic ratification.
>
> (Stern, 1985, p. 229)

It seems to me that this quote by Stern comes very close to Jungian views. The biology of the child – in Jungian terminology, one could say what is archetypally given – does not tolerate too great a "bending" of the infant, through its socialization, without a negative manifestation sooner or later, often in the form of symptoms such as disturbances of self-esteem, neuroses, or psychosomatic illness.

Part II

JUNGIAN THEORY OF THE COMPLEXES AND MODERN INFANT RESEARCH

12

ARCHETYPES AND COMPLEXES

There is an enormous amount of literature on the themes of archetypes and complexes by Jung himself, as well as by many of his followers. I therefore want to remain brief in this chapter, and pinpoint some of the literature which addresses the relevant issues: Jung, 1934; Dieckmann, 1999; Jacobi, 1959; Jacoby, 1994; Kast, 1997.

In my view, the observations and points of view of infant research are both revealing and important for the Jungian therapist, especially in their connection with Jung's theory of the feeling-toned complexes. An integrated knowledge concerning the interactions between infants and their caregivers, and about the resulting "imprinting" in the psyche of the child, provides a highly refined appreciation of the complexes, in the Jungian sense, and how they affect the psyche. Hence such knowledge is, for the psychotherapist, of a value which cannot be easily overestimated.

Stern speaks about the limitations of the process of socialization brought about by the biology of the child. It is apparent that, by "biology," he means the basic psychological and physical givenness of being human; in other words, the species-specific roots of our experience and behavior. In Jungian language, we can speak at the same time of the archetypal basis of our being human. As mentioned earlier, by archetypes we understand the basic species-specific dispositions which organize and regulate human behavior and experience. Jung was mainly interested in the ways whereby these basic dispositions manifest themselves in human imagination; and his research therefore focused on the "contents" of the unconscious. We can see them in dreams, myths, fairytales, and alchemy; that is, in symbolic pictures and sequences in which they express themselves. Of course, he also spoke of affects which are connected to the archetypes, but without investigating them in a particularly differentiated way. Much of the investigation of the affects has been accomplished more recently by researchers interested in modern affect theory and the interpersonal world of the infant.

Archetypal dispositions and needs in the individual are interwoven with the environment in an intricate fashion which has such a powerful, imprinting influence, especially in infancy. In this encounter between the natural disposition of the infant and the reaction from the environment, we find the origin of many psychic complexes, especially as the infant responds to his parents' various ways of attuning to him. In whatever way this encounter between "inner and outer" occurs – whether there is a preponderance of "good-enough" mothering or an overall climate of irritation, conflict, or abandonment – it will constitute the fundamental or "root" experiences in the unconscious, from which so-called feeling-toned complexes originate. Complexes therefore have an *archetypal nucleus*, or core; and it is around this core that one's personal experiences group themselves, giving to a complex its respective feeling-tone.

The word "complex" is based on the Latin "complexus," which means "connection," "enclosure," "linkage," and/or "knotting together." Thus a complex is made up of many parts which have become "knotted together" into a group or cluster, which in turn has its own kind of unity or wholeness. One speaks, for instance, of an apartment complex (of homes). The term, in its typical usage, was first introduced into depth psychology by C. G. Jung.* Jung discovered, in his association experiments, feeling-toned representations which appeared to revolve around certain themes and what was deemed important. The subjects of his experiments were in most cases either not fully conscious or even completely unconscious about the content and the implications of those basis themes. Thus Jung has discovered what he called "feeling-toned complexes," shortened later to the term "complex." This term was also used by Freud and Adler for certain of their discoveries. Freud used it mainly with regard to the Oedipal and castration complexes; and Adler, for the inferiority complex.

Today, the term "complex" has become popularized; for instance, one speaks quite commonly of an "inferiority complex," particularly when thinking of inhibited or shy individuals. Depth psychology has so much invaded collective consciousness that for many people it is not unusual to observe that, behind very grandiose ways of flaunting one's merits, there is simultaneously operating an inferiority complex, which is somehow overcompensated. A 40-year-old man, who is unmarried and living with his mother so as to care for her, is not typically well regarded,

---

*One needs to remember that the expression "complex," as indicating an idea in one's mind which is both impactful and unconscious, had emerged already in Breuer's studies of hysteria, dating from 1895.

though he is quite literally in compliance with the injunctions of the fourth biblical commandment. Rather, one will say of him that he is suffering from a mother complex. One knows, of course, that complexes are very common, yet one attributes them largely to other people rather than to oneself.

Many Jungian psychotherapists concentrate diagnostically on the way that complexes operate within the experience and behaviors of their patients; how they manifest in the background, as well as how on certain occasions they are "constellated," though they are usually unwelcome in the here-and-now. It therefore seems helpful, therapeutically, to try to undo the "knots" which hold complexes together, to trace back to their origins, and particularly to see how infant research may provide us with some important points of reference.

13

THE MOTHER COMPLEX

Archetypal needs for mothering

In order to exemplify the usefulness of infant research, I want to examine again the oft-mentioned mother complex. It is in the infant's nature to be related to, and dependent on, the mother and the maternal reaction. In other words, in the very first phase of life, the mother archetype is very strongly constellated in the child as well as in the mother – as one can see by her specific biopsychological functions during pregnancy and after childbirth. The question is to what extent is the mother able to open herself to the mother archetype operating within her – to what extent is she able to attain a certain "correspondence" with the needs of her infant? This question pertains to the mother's own socialization, her physical health, and those complexes influencing her.

What exactly are the archetypal needs for getting mothering? There are needs to be fed and cared for, needs for containment, for stimulation and comfort. Very often these are aptly referred to by the term "holding," which stems from Winnicott (Winnicott, 1965). Thanks to infant research, we are now able to perceive these basic archetypal needs in a much more differentiated way.

This is the reason why at this point I want to add some relevant conclusions from infant research. Sander, who observed infants during entire twenty-four-hour periods, noted the following. In a twenty-four-hour cycle the newborn goes through the following phases: deep sleep (non-REM), wakeful inactivity, wakeful activity, crying, due to not feeling well (i.e., so-called "distress crying"), REM-sleep, and then again, deep sleep. The environment (mother) has here of course an important regulating function; and it depends on how a caregiver is able to attune to, and empathize with, the child's own rhythm. It is also essential that the caregiver be sensitive to moments when the infant wants to be left alone, for it already requires a certain amount of "private space in time" to pursue its own interests without guidance (Sander, 1975). This "private space in time" occurs when the physiological needs have been satisfied (that is, whenever the infant is neither hungry nor sleepy, is not too cold, and is not lying in wet diapers) and also when the mother is not engaging in a playful manner with the infant (for instance, through eye contact, through mutual vocalizations, or through whatever other engagements might serve the motivation for mutual attachment). During the time when infants want to be left alone, they fill this private space with a spontaneous exploration of their environment. The infant pursues its own interests without guidance. In other words, an infant needs the opportunity to choose between a variety of possibilities, including setting activities into motion, developing initiative, and watching what happens. Here the motivation of exploring is awakened, along with the joy of experiencing one's impact on the outer world as a result of having developed and expressed one's own initiative (see Sander, 1975).

With this description, I have mentioned, at the same time, three of the five innate motivational systems (Lichtenberg, 1989a). They are in operation simultaneously during the phase characterized by the dominance of the mother archetype; in psychoanalysis, this is the so-called oral stage. But the sensual/sexual motivational needs also belong here; and one ought not to forget the aversive motivation which expresses itself in various ways, such as crying and whining. The infant wants to get the mother's attention, specifically in her function as the self-regulating other. There is the expectation that these very averse affects will receive comforting in the mother's presence, and that her activities of carrying, of feeding, of changing diapers, etc. will transform and change those torturing, aversive affects into a sense of being contained. There is also the expectation in the infant that, through affectionate displays of mutual attachment, sensual/sexual needs will be allowed to live.

Whenever an infant wishes to have some "private space in time," this has to be respected by the caretaker. As mentioned above, the infant already gives signs, mainly by averting its face, whenever it wants to be left in peace. This is sometimes very difficult for the mother to tolerate as she may fear being rejected by the child. Such fears may not allow her to relax away from her constant, over-controlling caregiving. Thus she tries, through especially intense caregiving, to counterbalance those anxieties, becoming, as a result, an intrusive mother for the infant. Often, the mother's disappointment may be hidden behind "fears" that something might be physically "wrong" with the child.

In addition to these periodically changing emotional states, and the effect of the innate motivational systems with their accompanying affects, another important factor must be added; namely, the sense of self in its consecutive "sensitive periods" of maturation. The above-mentioned senses of the emergent self, the core self, the intersubjective self, and the verbal self coexist alongside each other, and they all involve the mother in their own particular forms (Stern, 1985).

The basic factors, necessities, and needs, which deeply condition human beings, are inborn to an astonishing degree, and they appear to manifest themselves among infants in the purest form. Simultaneously, the acknowledgment of the decisive importance of the quality of the interpersonal factor for the infant's development may put an unattainable expectation and demand on mothers. Thus there is the danger that a mother or other caretaker expects to be constantly attuned to the infant and to always know what the infant needs. Obviously, such demands are simply impossible for any human being to fulfill. With good reason, Winnicott therefore speaks only of "good-enough" mothering, not of a perfect mother. Likewise, Kohut believes that "optimal frustration" will be the basis of a good prognosis for a child's development (Kohut, 1984). Kohut's followers formulated some of this in a different way as "optimal responsiveness" (Wolf, 1988).

The origins of the mother complex

Psychic complexes always originate in confrontation with the world. We have seen that the infant initially has memories of regularly repeated interactions. The infant does not so much remember specific episodes as it does the average "sum" of such episodes (for instance, discomfort, crying, getting fed, and comfort). An attitude of expectancy is at the same time connected to these memories. Such memories are expressed in the form of what Stern calls RIGs (see pp. 55–57). The infant expects that a given episode will repeat itself in the future in the same way as before. This generalized episode is "a structure indicating the likely course of events, based on averaged experiences" (Stern, 1985, p. 97). Insofar as those expectations are confirmed, there will be a resulting feeling of reliability, and a sense of trust within oneself and the world. The accompanying emotional experiences, as well as the accompanying bodily sensations, are retained in the so-called procedural memory (according to Lichtenberg, 1989a, p. 276ff.). In other words, in Stern's RIGs there are retained the memories of how the occurrences usually took place in each respective episode, along with emotions and bodily sensations which have accompanied each episode.

Verena Kast (Kast, 1997, p. 41) seems to agree with my view that the RIGs, which I discussed in 1994 as "patterns of interactions," are very closely connected to the Jungian model of complexes. She also feels that the theory of episodic memory could give an explanation for three phenomena which are connected to the manifestation of psychic complexes. First of all, this would provide a theory which explains how complexes are retained internally as remembered interactions. Secondly, there is now also an explanation of why the complexes are constellated or reactivated in certain specific situations which resemble the earlier episodes in which they were initially "imprinted." Thirdly, there is also an explanation of how complexes may be released by certain sensations or affects, which are associated with the emotions of the initial, imprinting episodes (Kast, 1997, p. 41).

In general usage, psychic complexes are understood to be "inner enemies" from the unconscious which stir us up, disturbing our sense of well-being, interfering also with our capacity to relate to others and to function the way we would like. This would mean that only those RIGs, or interactional patterns, in which difficult or disturbing episodes are generalized, would manifest as complexes. But one must also consider those RIGs which deepen and extend self-confidence or interpersonal trust. They are really the most essential building blocks towards establishing our ego complex; that is, the sense of ego-identity. According to Jung, "my ego is a complex of ideas which constitutes the center of my field of consciousness" (Jung, 1921, par. 706). Whenever we are at the center of this latter ego-complex, there are images and feelings filled with the expectation of being satisfied, feelings of being accepted and loved, feelings of confidence. Whenever, in the center of this ego-complex, these RIGs are dominating – namely, those which are connected to experiences of being loved and accepted, and to the idea of being able to meet others' expectations – the overall sense of self will be felt as one of confidence. This is the basis of what is called a "strong ego" or a good sense of self-esteem. Neumann spoke relatedly of an "integral ego," with its capacity to integrate positive and negative elements.

"Positive" and "negative" mother complex

In Jungian psychology one speaks of a positive or negative mother complex. This distinction has primarily to do with the question: Do I have predominantly good or aversive feelings, love or hate, towards my mother; or towards the motherly aspects of women in general; or towards the realm of the feminine and even the entire realm of the unconscious operating in myself? Yet things are rather complicated, as there is also the so-called positive mother complex, (meaning that there is love between my mother and myself; I am attracted to women who mother me; I may even be dependent upon a motherly, accepting environment) which itself can be experienced as negative. It all depends on the vantage point. A positive mother complex can have the effect of an indissoluble attachment to the mother, an ego weakness, or a lack of autonomy. Therefore, from the point of view of the inner strivings for independence and autonomy, the complex attachment to the mother is considered as negative. On the other side, the negative mother complex may, under certain circumstances, have a positive effect. It may, for instance, "loosen" one's attraction to the maternal and thus set free liberating impulses towards separation and autonomy. In any case, things in the realm of our complexes are truly complex; and Jungians who are attached to labels of "negative" or "positive" may not really be contributing towards an adequately differentiated perception of such phenomena.

Many people who seek psychotherapeutic help are suffering consciously or unconsciously from the effects of a dominating negative mother complex. This is reason enough to further differentiate this so-called negative mother complex in the light of contributions from infant research. It is a complex which tends to evoke feelings of mistrust and hostility. The therapist, in his or her own reaction, is often confronted with the sense that whatever he or she says, does, or tries is never acceptable or "right" in the patient's eyes. The motto of such patients is very often: "I hate you, but don't leave me, for God's sake." They are obviously prisoners of their aversive motivational system. Affects like hate, envy, fear, shame, or guilt seem to overshadow or suppress all good feelings, and poison all longings to be close, to experience mutual attunement with others. Thus there is no trust in one's significant others, nor, basically, in oneself. Such domination by the aversive motivational system pertains usually to early experiences of having been traumatically rejected, violated, shamed, or misused by previous caregivers and intimate relations. This "poison" fuses with one's self-experience and, in turn, takes the form of hatred against self and world; and also of needs to humiliate and devalue. It affects too many parts within the composition of the ego-complex. In Jungian language, one could say that the ego is dominated by the destructive mother image, and becomes what Neumann has called the "negativized ego" (Neumann, 1973, p. 2).

A negative mother complex, if it has grown to have a massive impact, is usually at the basis of certain grave pathological states. Of course, in terms of considering the sum of interpersonal activities between infant and caregiver, one may find innumerable combinations. For instance, there may be a "good-enough" amount of attunement in one sector of the developing personality, while other realms remain unattended or may instead be associated with traumatizing misattunements. A positive mother complex, for instance, may express itself in a narcissistic identi-fication, with certain physical features (like beauty) or special talents which have been especially loved, admired, and encouraged by the mother in childhood. As a consequence, the sense of self-esteem is based only on such merits, and it will stand or fall depending upon whether or not these gifts can be used effectively and are seen and admired by the environment. In a negative sense, the fear of losing all of this beauty or all of these special talents, for example, through illness, accident, or the natural aging process, may bring about severe crises of self-esteem.

In psychotherapy, some patients come filled with expectations which are connected to a positive mother complex. They expect, for instance, that the therapist should have the function of the self-regulating other, and would somehow magically eliminate all neurotic discomfort. What may be the fantasy behind such an expectation? Has it to do with the episodic memory of a mother who spoiled the child by "over-attunement," thus evoking a fantasy as a repetition of infantile expec-tations? Or do patients long for, in the therapeutic situation, what they have never experienced in reality? Both motives may be at the basis of such expectations. In the case of repetition, it is usually a sign of a so-called "malignant regression" (Balint, 1968). In other words, for whatever reason the patient cannot easily give up longings for the "good mother" who sets everything right. Consequently, there is a great difficulty and often also a strong resistance to growing up into responsible adulthood.

On the other hand, this longing for the good maternal may be the very motivation which is unconsciously in the service of the process of individuation and may lead to a new beginning. The new beginning (as understood by Balint, 1968) is of course dependent upon whether or not the therapeutic climate is experienced as facilitating and trustworthy. In such cases, Balint spoke of the therapeutic or "benign" regression (Balint, 1968). In a Jungian view, this is made possible insofar as the archetypal needs remain potentially available in the unconscious, even when they have not been allowed to be realized in life. These con-nections will now be made clearer by the following hypothetical example. Let us assume that, in the childhood of a client, the physio-logical needs were regulated in a "good-enough" manner by the mother; yet in the phase of intersubjectivity there occurred many misattunements and an overall deficiency in affective harmony. Later, when the verbal self began to emerge to the forefront, the parents valued it highly and did much to encourage its development. This form of interaction would probably result in a strong enough core self which could also be assertive in the verbal or intellectual realms. But the need for an intimate soul-exchange would be left without response, as it would not belong to the reality of this person's world. Consequently, needs for close relationships of a soulful nature become invested with, at best, ambivalent feelings. To feel such needs, or to express them verbally, is therefore associated with a strong sense of embarrassment or shame. Sometimes they are repressed from consciousness altogether; in particular, they may be viewed as unsuitable for a man and somehow unworthy of manhood, or frightening to a woman, because the inner structures to deal with this feeling realm were never fully developed. Such a constellation may result in suffering from a sense of inner emptiness from lack of fulfillment in one's love relationships; which in turn will often be compensated for by a frequent exchange of one's love partners.

Whenever, in the psychotherapy of people suffering from such problems, a longing for a good mother will emerge – in other words, when the positive mother complex dares to show itself in dreams or transference feelings – this must be welcomed by the therapist. It may mean that various key aspects of the mother archetype, which could not find entrance into the patient's previous personal experience, have yet remained alive in the unconscious, and may now come out into the open, insofar as the therapeutic field is experienced by the patient as a facilitating environment.

I want here, based on my professional experience, to turn my attention to critical differences in the impact and origins of the negative mother complex. The negative mother complex can express itself in aversive withdrawal, in a firm and thick wall of defense against every form of intimacy; also, in the splitting off of one's attachment needs and one's need to be acknowledged. The aversive affects (fear, shame, rage, contempt, etc.) are, in such cases, so dominant in the psychic economy that all the other emotional needs may be pushed away. Such an inner "tyranny" often sets up strong interpersonal isolation; but at the same time it serves as a protection against new injuries. In most cases which are dominated by sad negativism, one can find a strong infantile traumatization of their needs for attachment and affiliation; and sometimes the sensual/sexual motivational system has been heavily traumatized (see Kalsched, 1996).

Whenever the longing for the positive maternal can be relatively easily awakened, one does not typically find direct traumatization in the early history. Rather, there may be a more or less severe lack of affective matching and attunement. In other words, the aversive affects are not dominant across the board. There may still be room left for the longing for relationship and attachment. These are distinctions that play a large role in psychotherapy, as will be elaborated in a later chapter.

In whatever form the mother complex may operate, it nearly always tells the story of the early processes of emotional exchange between mother and infant; notwithstanding that in the psychological make-up of adults one will find in the foreground quite diverse genetic, cultural, and biographical factors, as well as a variety of defense strategies.

14

THE FATHER COMPLEX

The father archetype

But what about the father? Archetypally, the paternal-masculine stands for aggressive, penetrating, and differentiating logos, whose symbol is often manifested as a phallus and/or sword. Conquest and the spirit of adventure are associated with it, but also laws and ideals. It is actively impregnating, and decisive in actions. The motivations having to do with exploration and the pride associated with competence and assertive power predominate in the overall image of the masculine, and are easily idealized.

To avoid misunderstandings, I would like to point out explicitly that the father archetype expresses itself in representations and images which are not identical with real fathers, yet have for centuries served as models in virtually every culture. Today however, as is commonly known, the representations and ideals of the "partriarchy" have lost their previously unquestioned validity, especially because they have largely exerted their influence historically amidst the simultaneous oppression of women and the intrapsychic feminine. As a result, there is now a great confusion regarding gender roles, to the point where relationships and all other gender-related issues are having to be tested out anew.

Nonetheless, it is assumed that, in general, fathers especially promote in their newborns and children the motivational system of exploration and self-assertion. They are idealized with regard to these motivations, and thus seen as models. The "strong" father, who is versed in the ways of the world, is loved by boys and girls alike. But such idealized expectations are bound to result in disappointment whenever the ideal is not met. Such disappointment connected to the father-image may contribute significantly to the development of a neurotic father complex. In the following section, we shall discuss some ideas about the role of the father in light of observations from infant research.

The father in infant research

In infant research, which generally addresses the first two years of life, the father is scarcely discussed. The key word "father" is, for example, not found in such important books as Stern (1985) or Dornes (1993). At best, the father plays a more specific and active role when he takes over "maternal" functions for the infant. It is likely however that the child becomes aware early on of the special relationship between the father and the mother (Mahler *et al.*, 1975, p. 91). According to Mahler, at the age of 16 to 18 months, the infant moves into an expansion of its previous mother/child universe, primarily through the inclusion and incorporation of the father. This coincides with the beginning of a "verbal" sense of self (Stern, 1985).

However, Lichtenberg points out that the motifs of bonding between father and child are often of importance already by infancy. He refers to Greenberg and Morris (1974), who studied thirty fathers of first-born children and found a surprising level of engagement by these fathers with their newborns. They had the strong wish to touch the baby, to hold and carry him. Obviously this gave them an increased boost in their self-esteem. Certainly "fatherly pride" is a commonly observed phenomenon. It can however be rooted in a father's purely narcissistic fantasy, and need not necessarily be related to genuine involvement with the child. Nonetheless, I believe that we should not impose an overly puritanical standard when it comes to narcissistic needs. Fatherly pride does not preclude empathic involvement in the offspring's life. In any case, Greenberg and Morris, as well as other researchers, found that fathers may completely open up and come alive as a function of devoting themselves to their baby; and they often dedicate themselves quite earnestly to the child's continuing development. Thus it is that fathers love to play with the baby, and often show much skill in retaining the child's consistent attention by means of a whole host of creative ways of engaging. Quite often the father is actually preferred by babies, especially at times when he presents an opportunity for social play and companionship – an observation which surprised Lichtenberg, particularly in light of other, prevailing assumptions (Lichtenberg, 1989a, p. 107).

The mother is typically preferred when the child feels physical discomfort, whether due to hunger, wet diapers, discomfort, pain, or otherwise. Mothers, in general, feel responsible for the care, nourishment, and protection of the infant's welfare. Fathers consider themselves primarily as "playmates," and their ways of playing with the infant differ from those of the mother: they are more energetic, tactile, physically engaging, risk-taking, and are characterized by a greater variety of activities. Thereby, they contribute to the infants' willingness to take risks; and they stimulate new developmental possibilities. Thus understood, pleasures of intimacy with the mother are associated first and foremost with her empathic way of caring and her emotional attunement. With the father, such pleasures are associated more with his style of introducing invigorating and stimulating games. (For example, the baby is thrown into the air, allowed to suddenly fall, only to be caught safely into the father's waiting arms.) Such interactions between father and child thus integrate the satisfactions of mutual affection and bonding with the gratification of needs for exploration and self-assertion. Needs of the motivational systems of attachment and belonging, as well as those of exploration and self-assertion, therefore find their gratification.

As a result of these observations, Lichtenberg (1989a, p. 110) rightly concludes that the heretofore one-sided, mother-centered focus on attachment needs demands revision. One can see that the motivation to create healthy attachments may be activated by both parents during the infant's first year of life, at least when both parents are adequately present and available for the baby. The actual quality of intimacy, however, takes on a different affective tone depending on whether the mother or the father is involved.

To my mind, there are two further points that need to be noted here. First of all, we are dealing with generalizations – as is the case of most psychological statements – while in real life the pertinent family dynamics show up in a nearly inexhaustible array of ways in which parents participate in, or evade, responsible involvement with the infant. There are of course many fathers who are not interested in their baby, who are often absent, and who even interfere, in a destructive or pathological way, with any close mother–child relationship (perhaps out of jealousy, etc.). Secondly, the question arises as to whether or not the aforementioned findings – namely, that paternal bonding promotes exploratory and self-assertive strivings – simply correspond once again to the most commonly held and socially accepted images of masculinity. However, those images are collectively connected with the mode in which the archetype seems to affect conscious experience. Thus it makes sense to associate such images with the interactions between father and child; they are based in the father complex. Yet this does not necessarily mean that such images will, in every case, correspond to the actual facts of a specific case.

"Positive" and "negative" father complex

The father complex also expresses itself in a positive or negative feeling tone. I would like to give an example of how a negative father complex may come about and develop. Let us assume that the father, who for whatever reason cannot bear his offspring's self-assertion, gets into power struggles with his little son, showing him brutally "who the man of the house is." The child reacts with powerless narcissistic rage, which in the long run will become consolidated into real hatred of the father. For this to happen, though, the child must have matured to at least 15 months of age, at which time the "evocative memory" will gradually become available. That is, the father must have become an inner representation which can be evoked by the child at any time. Now if the father punishes each rebellion and "rudeness" in a rigidly authoritarian manner, the child is often left to "fight" his battles with his father in the form of fantasies. The inner representation of the father may became so indelibly stamped with aversive affects that it is nearly impossible to correct. If the father later attempts to forge a closer connection with his offspring, he inevitably fails. He is no longer able to gain his child's trust. The young son, and later the adult son, will interpret everything the father does in the most negative terms, according to the affects which are released by the workings of the complex: "Now the father is trying to flatter me in order to gain for himself the angelic halo of a generous father, when in reality he is not." Or: "He pretends to be proud of my achievements, when he is really only proud of himself." Thus there is no room for good feelings, which can be, simultaneously for both participants, a source of immense suffering.

Although, through maturation of the evocative memory, the father has become an inner representation which in fantasy may have perhaps accumulated even further, hated attributes, there still remains a close connection with the early childhood RIGs. Because as soon as the representation "father" has become a content of a complex, he is only imagined within the negative interaction pattern; namely, in the role of causing hurt and humiliation. A more comprehensive representation of the father – as a human being with both light and dark sides, plus his own, personal motivations – is not accessible, or is constantly pushed aside by the affects associated with the complex. This interaction pattern between father and son faithfully follows the motto: Hatred towards him who despises and degrades me – Anger towards him who does not recognize my authority and position as father. From the son's viewpoint, these negative expectations contained in the respective RIGs grow into a negative father complex. In other words, oversensitivity and irritability develop, and not only in relation to his personal father, for he will also be suspicious of any new "authority persons" whom he imagines would humiliate him. The personal father therefore becomes interchangeable, under the predominance of these internalized patterns of interaction (RIGs), with their corresponding affects. The "other" (father) does not have his own autonomous existence. Rather, there are these episodes of feeling oppressed and despised, which become engraved into the son's (episodic) memory, and thus constitute the core of the complex.

As mentioned above, the core of a complex usually corresponds to an archetypal situation, and that this father–son conflict must have its archetypal roots may, for example, be shown by the Greek myth of Uranos and Kronos. Uranos, because of fear that his son, Kronos, will at some point oust him from his dominant position, insists on returning his children to the earth from which they were born. Kronos succeeds – with help from his mother, Earth, who groans under this heavy burden – to castrate his father. This myth addresses – when one understands it symbolically – the conquest and removal of a powerfully destructive father complex (Jacoby, 1975). Something needs to be added here. We also have to understand that hatred and anger toward one's father, "the fathers," and against any dominant authority may unconsciously serve as a defense against having to feel small, devalued, or even annihilated. Unfortunately, the cost exacted for this protection is typically far too great.

A variant of the positive father complex for people of both sexes may be expressed in the unconscious yearning for the "father" – be it for the personal father, for another, more reliable father figure, and/or for a set of values which promises guidance. In such cases, the father has often been absent during much of childhood. Too often, even when physically present, he remained in the background, and left the child's upbringing to the mother. In any case, the child had no opportunity to experience having a strong, and at the same time understanding, father; one whom he could love and admire. Later on in life, such a deficit may quite possibly engender in such individuals the sense that there is nothing in this world capable of rousing their enthusiasm; and no cause worthy of their commitment. Thus transpersonal concerns or ideals do not exert a vital attraction and are not able to compensate meaningfully for this sense of inner emptiness.

These, or other similar, constellations are not without danger. The idealized and longed-for father-figure, as well as the corresponding need for attachment and belonging, are both maintained in an archaic, undifferentiated form. Due to a deficient relationship with the personal father, there is an important sector in the child's personality which cannot mature. This may be mostly in the realm of spiritual orientation and differentiated reality testing. As a consequence, such individuals may have the need to join a group, in adolescence and perhaps later, which is centered around a religious or political ideology. The more archaic the need for attachment, the more uncritically is assumed an identification with such fanatical ideologies that promise, in the name of high ideals, the fulfillment of the most primitive impulses. The hopes which are placed in such groups are usually twofold: they point to archetypal core elements of both the mother and father complexes. With regard to the first, there is a longing to find kinship and holding, whereby the group may be experienced as the "Great Mother" (Neumann, 1955). With regard to the second, the effect of the father archetype is felt in terms of the search for an ideal father and an authority to validate norms and help one find personal meaning in life (see Jacoby, 1990, p. 183f.).

The father complex, if associated with a strongly positive or negative feeling tone, is most often seen in a compensatory relationship to the mother complex. That is, positive feelings with regard to the mother-world often go along with negative feelings towards the father-world, and vice versa.

However important the basic mental states associated with the mother and father complexes, and however extensively they manifest themselves in specific transference feelings during a course of psychotherapy, it does seem essential to me that the analytical approach should not lose sight of the various elements and components contained in such universal complexes. A more differentiated approach, a more finely tuned understanding of their manifold implications and ramifications, serves empathic attunement to one's analysands. To this end, observations and findings from infant research are extremely helpful.

15

ABOUT THE INFERIORITY COMPLEX

Forms of expression and history of origin

The likewise colloquial, so-called "inferiority complex" is surely quite common in our society and may be associated with enormous psychic pain. Whenever it is activated, it may express itself through the feeling of "having the rug pulled out from under one's feet." The term was introduced by A. Adler at the beginning of the century in the context of his observation that people suffering from this complex tend towards overcompensation, by striving hard for validation and power. Today, in the more specialized psychological literature, the expression "inferiority complex" has largely been replaced by newer terms, such as "disturbance of self-esteem" or "narcissistic vulnerability." Psychodynamically, this complex is closely connected with the previously described experiences of the mother and father complex. In its many ramifications and manifold effects, it has a very global impact – one in which all motivational systems often play a part – because it involves the difficult question of how much value I am consciously or unconsciously attributing to myself; how I evaluate the person who is myself.

I have already discussed some aspects of self-worth in earliest childhood, together with risks related to its possible disturbance, in an earlier publication (1994). This allows me to be brief here. The inferiority complex manifests itself in countless variations that sometimes shed light on its specific history of origin. In my practice, for example, I often see people who have an intense fear of being exposed, seen, or heard. These fears can also show themselves in relation to the therapist, with transference feelings blocking or inhibiting some aspects of the patient's experience; for instance, whenever they need to take the initiative to expose certain topics, their fear may instead render them "speechless." In their private thoughts, they may have had many imaginary conversations with me between sessions in which they explain and justify themselves, report various occurrences, etc. But in my actual presence the words stick in their throats, and they are at a complete loss. This is usually due to a sudden feeling that anything they have to say would be completely insignificant, and would only contribute to further devaluing or degrading them. At the same time, they perceive their inhibited silence and feel just as embarrassed. The situation becomes so unbearable that they would wish to render themselves invisible by "sinking into the floor" for being seen in their inferiority. These are symptoms of intense shame-anxiety (Jacoby, 1994).

The momentary "loss of words" makes one think first of all about the "verbal sense of self," a realm which seems very susceptible to disturbance in such people. With that in mind, one should take into consideration that, together with the maturation of the sense of verbal self, there develops the capacity to form the first "self-representation." In other words, the perception of an inner image of one's own person together with the images of the significant caregivers has now formed and can be evoked at any time in fantasy. In psychoanalytic terminology, one speaks of a beginning differentiation between self- and object-representations (Jacobson, 1964). The sense of self does not just stay subjective, as it was up until now, because the representation or image of oneself has developed simultaneously (see Jacoby, 1994, p. 110). It thus becomes possible for the infant to see itself increasingly as "objective," to observe and to evaluate itself – even though "objectivity" towards oneself always remains questionable, insofar as the representation is always intermixed with subjective feelings and (pre-)judgments.

This image of oneself is of course to a great extent imprinted by the presymbolic and preverbal experiences. The interplay between the archetypally organized maturation processes and the respective responses of significant caregivers results in the corresponding, basic frame of mind, or predominant emotional state, of a person. Herein also early preverbal experiences and conflicts participate and show their influence. It is therefore extremely difficult to distinguish that which originates in the "true self" of the "spontaneous gesture" from those experiences or behaviors which specifically reflect the identification with the influence of parental responses, expectations, and evaluations. Therefore, a "facilitating" environment promotes development, while a "disturbing" environment gives rise to fundamental insecurities within self-perception and the sense of self-esteem.

An example from clinical practice

At this point, in anticipation of the following chapters dedicated to psychotherapy, I would like to present an example from my practice. I am thinking of an analysand who from time to time fell into the aforementioned "speechlessness," whereby all comprehensible and communicable contents unraveled so that she felt only an inner emptiness. As a middle child, she had been raised in a large group of siblings. During her early childhood, the mother was obviously far too stressed to devote enough time to intersubjective exchange, with the exception of attention to flawless physical grooming. Still today, in every meeting with her mother, the client gets the sense that the mother possesses hardly any antennae for perceiving emotional subtleties. As for the father, she experienced him as dictatorial and treating her achievements in a critically condescending way, so that she evaded him whenever possible out of sheer fear.

Upon commencing therapy, her most obvious difficulties were with regard to her fears of not measuring up to the expectations of the environment which she perceived as being placed upon her. She believed she was too dumb, too clumsy, too despondent, too inhibited, etc. Thus there were plenty of devaluations of her personhood, as part of her personal history, which were also greatly exacerbated by the slightest failure in whatever she was and did. Certainly, the fear of her incessantly critical father contributed in an essential way to the formation of this inferiority complex. Insofar as her academic achievements had been good during her childhood, it never became clear to her what achievements, values, or behaviors her father should even have expected of her; and it remained a riddle as to which way she would be able to satisfy him, to gain his approval. The analysand had the feeling of having to produce some specific achievement without ever knowing exactly what it was.

This constellation will often be encountered behind an inferiority complex. The affected individuals have many fears of failing expectations which have been placed upon them. However, what these expectations actually are can rarely be ascertained, even with closer questioning. One often discovers that it is not necessarily the environment that makes such demands and expectations, but more one's own, mostly unconsciously operating ideas which will be projected on to the environment. Ultimately, an unconscious expectation is operating which demands overall perfection in all that one is or does. This would be the only possible condition to render oneself invulnerable. In light of such expectations, one will of necessity always feel inferior, as it is quite impossible to ever fulfill them. And this is where the vicious circle of the many forms of the inferiority complex becomes most apparent. An unconscious perfectionism, the "grandiose self" in the sense of Kohut (Kohut, 1971; Jacoby, 1990, p. 83ff.), produces the idea: "If I am not perfect in everything, I am a complete zero." There is no middle ground for evaluating oneself in a realistic enough way. To come back to the case of my patient, it was the lack of emotional attunement by the mother, combined with the devaluing criticism of the father, which had made her feel so insecure and grew in time into a full-fledged inferiority complex.

Overall, I noticed she seemed to have the greatest difficulty getting in touch with herself, her needs, reactions, feelings, and values. It was as if she had no right to allow herself to feel or think her own thoughts, her authentic self-perceptions, not to mention expressing them and sharing them with me. She in turn perceived this difficulty as being a flaw, judging it as a further reason for self-devaluation. She is not even "capable" of doing something so simple that everyone else obviously seems able to do.

However, there was at least something she was capable of feeling very clearly, although it seemed to be unpleasant and quite embarrassing to her. She would be overcome with a mixture of anger, disappointment, and jealousy whenever she had to wait for me in the waiting room for a few minutes longer than usual. In spite of great difficulties, she was able, in response to my questioning, to own up to this "embarrassing" set of emotions over time. I tried, indeed, to uncover further relevant associations, but that was difficult. She believed it could have to do with the fear that I may have forgotten her, combined with the apprehension that she would once again, as always, get the "short end of the stick." It was even more difficult for her to share with me the tormenting thought that I, surely enough, must prefer her "predecessor" (from the previous clinical hour) by far, as compared with her. With him I can laugh, and certainly with him, I do not suffer from boredom as I do with her.

Hence the image came to me that she, as a baby, often had to wait to be changed and fed, and that her signals were not heard promptly by her overstressed mother. Thus she could never really rely upon the "self-regulating other," and experienced scarcely enough maternal presence to enable her needs for intersubjective exchange to be satisfied. Her effort to obtain enough attention when she was a baby was surely often in vain; hence she reacted aversively in the form of withdrawal. This is how her basic affective state originated: that something must be wrong in her world and with her because she remains unloved, rejected, and hence inferior.

It was obviously, from a therapeutic viewpoint, a promising sign that she had begun to claim her right that I should be there for her at the correct time, punctually. She was able to express, of course with difficulty, her dissatisfaction. For me, the therapist, it was certainly essential to offer her encouragement at that point, without somehow "patting her on the back" in a paternalistic manner.

Compensatory strategies

Generally speaking, the inferiority complex consists in the feeling, and its attendant fear, of appearing "unworthy" in front of oneself, as well as in the eyes of others. It impairs the sense of self-worth, whereby the early interaction patterns have usually carved themselves into the self-image and are at the bottom of the lack of self-esteem. The sense of self is too easily influenced by others; one feels exposed and judged by the environment. Too great an influence is usually assigned to others – in the "positive" as well as in the "negative" sense.

It is understandable that people seek to protect their vulnerable sense of self from devaluing, or damaging, judgments of other people. To this end, one can mobilize conscious, or mostly unconsciously operating, defensive strategies. From a Jungian perspective, the formation of the so-called "persona" is pertinent here. It denotes a kind of "soul mask" (Jacobi, 1976), which is intended to protect or hide those personality traits which we regard as our weak spots (see Asper, 1993; Jacoby, 1994). The persona is often an attempt to show to the world (and sometimes also to ourselves) the way we *want* to be, not how we *are*. Behind all of this lies the fear of being rejected, devalued, or excluded, which severely impairs the sense of self-esteem and negatively impacts the basic motivational need of wanting to belong (attachment and affiliation).

It is usually a long and slow process to therapeutically modify the inferiority complex, not least because it ultimately rests upon the early childhood/preverbal interaction patterns that have become a part of the sense of self. This complex consists of a basic conviction, difficult to influence, regarding one's own unworthiness, which at times may be compensated for by feelings of one's own grandiosity. It has solidified itself within the self-image, together with corresponding defenses and compensations. Therapy must seek to again "liquefy" this solidification. These problems of practical psychotherapy, however, will be reflected upon later.

16

SEXUAL COMPLEXES

The sensual–sexual motivational system

As is well known, classical psychoanalysis since Freud attributes fundamental significance to infantile sexuality for the successful or unsuccessful outcome of personal maturation or development. In contrast, Jung, as mentioned earlier, attributes to the infant a polyvalent predisposition; he could not accept sexual drives as the primary "motor" of our whole psychic life from early infancy onward. The observation of infant research – that there are five distinct, innate motivational systems which take part from early on in the development of the sense of self and later in the sense of personal identity – comes somewhat closer to the Jungian thesis. Sexuality, together with sensuality, is attributed to one of the five motivational systems (Lichtenberg, 1989a). Lichtenberg believes that it is important to differentiate sensual needs from more properly sexual needs. According to his observation, the sensual joy or pleasure of the newborn is released from an innate program and is normally a part of day-to-day occurrences, as reflected in the infant's ongoing dialogue with the mother or other primary caregiver. But sexual excitement, although it follows the same innate pattern, begins to operate later as a part of the regular, daily experience of the infant from the age of about 18 months.

Sensual–sexual needs belong to an independent motivational system, but in most cases they also fuse with needs of the other motivational systems. For example, thumb-sucking by the infant may be initially motivated by sensual needs; yet at the same time it also may serve to soothe the infant. It is thus important also for physiological regulation; that is, physiological regulation thereby fuses with sensuality in this situation. Similar behaviors may be observed in infants, at the age of 2 to 3 years, who very often play with their genitals. On the one hand, such play can be strongly connected with excitement. It seems as if children at this age, when they are in a good mood, already understand that playing with their genitals can lead to a very pleasurable, excited state. But at other times, for example, where fears of abandonment may predominate, children will often make physical contact with their genitals in order to receive some consolation or relief; and this latter experience is not particularly associated with pleasurable excitement. Physical self-stimulation can thus have different motivations; hence, different effects. The same behavior is sometimes primarily soothing, and at other times primarily stimulating or exciting.

Furthermore, infant research confirms the generally recognized fact that there is an innate program of sensual-affectionate needs which plays a decisive and important role in the mother–infant relationship. Those needs are much more significant than has generally been assumed up to now, and constitute a vital part of our total life cycle. In normal development we are very dependent on our parents' devotion to us, which expresses itself ideally, among other things, in the satisfaction of our needs for sensuality and affection. At the same time, such satisfaction also advances the cohesion of our sense of self and our sense of feeling secure and contained. Thus the wish for sensuality arises as an independent need; yet it can also be accompanied by other motivations (such as attachment or physiological regulation).

In the original drive theory of psychoanalysis, sensual-affectionate needs are seen only as preliminary to sexual coitus; or they are viewed as signs of a defense because, according to Freud, the goal of the sexual drive is always the release of excitement through orgasm. Infant research has, of course, also examined the origin and development of the need for genuine sexual excitement. Thus we learn from Kleeman's studies (cf. Lichtenberg, 1989a, p. 235) that male infants very often discover their penis for the first time around the age of 10 months. They play with their genitals, stroking them very tenderly in a way quite similar to how they touch their mother's breasts. But such behaviors are scarcely differentiated from other games which satisfy their infantile needs for exploration. Kleeman concludes from this that, during the first year of life, self-stimulation of the genitals and curiosity to look at them primarily serve the purpose of creating contact with the body. The satisfaction of erotic needs is quite secondary, in the sense that intentional self-arousal and the quality of self-absorption are not prominent (Kleeman, in Lichtenberg, 1989a, p. 235). Beginning at about the age of 18 months, boys as well as girls play with their genitals; and this genital play changes to a genuine physical excitation, now of a masturbatory type. At this point, one may more properly speak of a real awakening of the sexual sense of pleasure.

Needs for sensual affection versus sexual excitement

Although pleasures of a sensual nature and the drive for sexual orgasm are goals of the same motivational system, their differentiation in adult experience is important. I want to mention a few pertinent observations. One may often hear a complaint in intimate relationships: "My partner is not able to be tender or affectionate. He wants sex all the time, immediately, the 'whole thing.'" Usually, these are mainly women who feel that they are only loved whenever a partner shows, in a sensitive manner, both tenderness and affection. When he does not succeed in being tender enough to their satisfaction, they feel humiliated and used as a sex object; that is, they are needed only for the release of their partner's sexual drive. As a consequence, they often have difficulty in opening themselves up to their own sexual energies. This pattern may come into play, of course, in the opposite situation gender-wise, even if not as frequently as the aforementioned. A similar complaint is often registered within homosexual relationships. The differences between sensual-affectionate needs and orgastic sexual drive impulses have to account for these conflicts. They also show that it is not a matter of course that these two forms of intimate behavior are always integrated together into the sense of self. As mentioned earlier, the satisfaction of sensual, tender needs may serve, to a large extent, the cohesion of one's sense of self and self-esteem ("I am loved by the other, therefore I experience self-worth"). This does not exclude, of course, the possibility that one's orgastic potency can also definitely influence one's personal sense of pride in being a "real man" or "total woman." The infant's timetable is such that sensuality and needs for affection are operative from birth onward. Yet more distinctively sexual interests are only awakened after the eighteenth month; this gap in maturation may involve the potential risk that, due to specific disturbances in the interaction between the infant and its caregiver, the integration of tenderness with orgastic drivenness may in fact become blocked or impeded.

It is of foremost importance here that we question old clichés, or general collective ideas, in which tenderness is attributed to the female gender and orgastic drivenness to the male. Such collective prejudices can in a damaging way operate in parenting, too; for example, as parents perhaps attribute to their infants such stereotyped sex roles from very early on. Thus for the male child, so-called feminine needs to receive tenderness and affection are then devalued. Likewise, for a girl, orgastic excitement may be labeled as inappropriate.

It is probable that such rigid ideas about masculinity and femininity may guide basic sexual motivations from early infancy onward, steering

111

them in certain directions and not others, and thus exerting perhaps a problematic influence on the later development of sexual identity. Regarding the latter, one may see it evidenced in the development of feminine problems of frigidity or of a kind of personally unrelated male chauvinism, more preoccupied with potency than intimacy.

Sensual–sexual motivations and needs for attachment

Another result of infant research is of great interest psychologically. As mentioned above, the need for attachment belongs to its own motivational system; and needs for sensuality, tenderness, and sexual excitement are understood to originate from a separate motivational system. In many adult love relationships, attachment on one side and tenderness and sexual excitement on the other all operate together; the various motivations are thus more or less integrated. But this is not always the case, as is well known. On the one hand, there are many strong attachments which are not sexualized; and on the other, there is much personally unrelated, or non-intimate, sexual behavior. Thus it is that many people, typically men (though not exclusively so), believe that various sorts of sexual adventures represent no break in faithfulness to their life partner, insofar as in their experience they do not touch and, even less so, basically question their deep-seated motivation for "belonging together." *This of course raises the question of whether the expectation of absolute sexual faithfulness really belongs to a fully integrated sexuality, or whether it may not have more to do with possessiveness or narcissistic vulnerability.* It becomes necessary to examine this on an individual basis.

Origins of sexual complexes

As experience shows, it is the sensual–sexual motivational system which, in connection with the caregivers, may be especially vulnerable to various disturbances; and thus is often at the basis of the development of a complex. The conscious or unconscious attitude of caregivers towards their own bodily sensations and sexuality influences from earliest childhood onward the ways in which those awakening sensual and sexual pleasures are integrated, first by the infant, then later on by the adolescent.

Dealing with sexuality certainly belongs to one of the most difficult themes of humanity. Each society, beginning from native peoples up to Western modernism, has created its own codified laws, customs, and taboos; and much has been written about the cultural and spiritual history of Eros. Throughout the history of humankind there was and is always the attempt to cope with the tremendous power of sexuality by an attitude that is based on a collectively held belief system. This is necessary to serve the purpose of integrating sexuality into the overall context of a society in order to assure the organization of a certain social coherence. Of course, the infant's caregivers are also influenced by, or even identified with, the norms which are valid in their surroundings, their social class, or their culture. These norms concerning the sexual sphere are by necessity mirrored in the caregiver's approach to the infant. Thus, already in earliest infancy, there are key attitudes of some belief system that are transmitted and which then become internalized; thus it is that these core beliefs get passed down from one generation to the next.

As mentioned earlier, infant observers tend to agree that, between 18 and 24 months of age, both boys and girls experience an increase in genital awareness and sensation (boys at this age already experience erections in REM sleep, while girls experience vaginal sensations). Relatedly, one finds at this age an increased interest in masturbatory activities (Lichtenberg, 1989a, p. 238). The infant's caregivers may show a great variety of reactions to these first signs of sexual awakening. A whole palette of attitudes towards sexuality may come into play here. At one extreme, caregivers had over centuries invented the most malignantly destructive methods to control their infants and prevent them from ever playing with their genitals. Children always had to keep their hands outside of their bedcover. At the other extreme, one can cite instances where the caregivers actually participated in playing with the infant's genitals.

Nowadays, many modern parents, with their liberal attitudes, don't want to make a big deal about the infant's masturbatory practices; indeed, parents may think that it is best to not even notice or pay any attention to such behavior. But even this attitude has its problems; and Lichtenberg noted, with some accuracy: "At the time when almost every other activity of the child draws attention, positive or negative, and labeling is a prominent mode of exchange, not to notice – to avert the eyes, or to see and then grow tense and ignore all – signals to the child that this activity is special in the sense of being beyond the pale" (Lichtenberg, 1989a, p. 240). In this way, sexual activity will now remain outside any form of overt and mutual communication. Such rather helpless reactions by caregivers are not particularly facilitative for a dawning integration of early sexual impulses into the whole of the infant's lived experiences.

The influence of sexuality on other realms of life

It would take us too far astray at this point to really delve into the question of why we humans so often have such enormous difficulty in experiencing our sexuality as something natural. It is nonetheless a fact that sexuality is frequently related to the central problem of many clients coming for psychotherapy; though not of course to the exclusive extent propounded early on by Freud. In any case, we understand today that the phenomenon of sexuality cannot be considered in isolation. Indeed, sexuality reaches into many realms of life and may even insinuate itself, albeit unconsciously, into virtually any experience. In this latter case, we speak of "sexualization."

I wish here to return to the innate motivational systems. In most cases of disturbed sexual functioning, it is first of all a matter of the incursion of the aversive motivational system, mainly in terms of the affects of fear, guilt, shame, and contempt. These aversive emotions are chiefly released by unconsciously operating conflicts. Conflicts around the motivation of attachment often play a major role; for instance, the conflict between longing for closeness, on the one hand, and fear of becoming dependent, on the other. Such a conflict centers around a sense of profound personal vulnerability, and may impair sexual functioning. In other cases, some will worry about not meeting the expectation of the partner, being disappointing and thus feeling devalued. Or in yet another possible scenario, there may be a fear of failing in one's sexual functioning. Hence there arise fears of impotence or frigidity which have, in most cases, less to do with sexuality *per se*, and more to do with problems in self-esteem.

The various sexual difficulties often have to do with a failure in integrating the various motivational systems, with their respective affects, into the sense of self. Normally, during sexual activity, the ego is dominated by the sexual motivational system and its driving force. Insofar as the overall love-making experience is satisfying, the remainder of the motivations, together with the various senses of self, operate alongside the sexual motifs in a supportive manner (Stern, 1985, p. 30f.). If certain sexual problems arise however, it may indicate that the various motivations are in too great a conflict with each other. We may therefore view sexual complexes as, in most cases, symptoms of personality disturbances of a more general nature, with their deepest roots often in failures of infantile exchange processes with significant caregivers.

Of course, all the experiences and conflicts due to the maturation of sexuality later in puberty are also of great consequence for optimal sexual integration. In puberty, sexual maturation is but one aspect, though crucial, in the overall development of personality. Sexuality is certainly a key force behind development, yet so are all the other motivations. This makes for the multi-dimensionality of the psychic crisis of adolescence.

Sexual complexes of various kinds thus serve, in most cases, as a symptomatic reflection of more generalized psychological disturbances; that is, other motivational systems are also typically implicated. For instance, compulsive masturbation in adolescence, as well as adulthood, is often an attempt to get in touch with oneself, and also to compensate for, or defend oneself against, fears of fragmentation or unbearable feelings of inner emptiness. A general lack of sexual interest may be connected with repressed guilt feelings, a pronounced type of disgust, or a depressive state. Sexual voyeurism might well be connected to the motivation of curious exploration; and exhibitionism linked to the genuinely existential need to be seen, to experience "the gleam in mother's eye" (Kohut), an essential way of self-confirmation.

From a therapeutic point of view, I want to say the following. It is a rule-of-thumb for therapists to focus less on the symptom and more on the exploration of dynamics that may lie underneath it. But of course any given rule may prove, in the analytic dialogue, at times to be inadequate, if not even counterproductive. As therapists, we must take care that we do not, out of eagerness to "follow the rules," inadvertently repeat neuroticizing attitudes of parents and other caregivers. Thus, for instance, to avoid dealing with the client's sexual symptoms may come to mean for patients that their sensual–sexual behaviors, and related suffering, will once again remain untouched and excluded, as it was in their infancy. Such an evasive attitude may be endorsed, consciously or unconsciously, by many analysts, depending upon their personal attitude towards sexuality. Related here, one may observe in the behavior of some therapists an only partially hidden, sometimes unconscious, aversion to sexuality. Very often, in such instances, what is at stake is some sort of personal fear on the therapist's part that he or she may be seen by the patient as an indiscreet voyeur who in fact not so secretly lusts after the sexual experiences of his or her client.

As we reach the conclusion of this chapter, I want to stress again that, generally speaking, the sexual realm, as it is understood most broadly, is especially prone to the formation and sustaining of disturbing complexes.

17

THE DOMINANCE OF
AVERSIVE MOTIVATIONS
AND THEIR INFLUENCE
ON THE FORMATION
OF COMPLEXES

General remarks about the aversive
motivational system

It is characteristic for the aversive motivational system to exert some influence over all the basic needs. At its best, it serves us as well in terms of promoting our survival (for example, with signal anxiety) as well as supporting our self-regulation. Any kind of perceived threat naturally evokes fear, and over-satiation, for example, after too much food or sex, may evoke aversion or disgust. Too much curiosity will become inhibited by means of shame. Too much symbiosis in intimacy may with time be interrupted by impulses to withdraw. An aversive system which is to a "good-enough" extent integrated into the self will function, if necessary, in a compensatory way that serves to maintain the balance of our psychosomatic economy. However, the aversive realm can also play a critical part in the origin and maintenance of disturbing complexes, whenever aversive emotions such as fear or shame predominate in a dysfunctional manner.

It seems to me essential therefore to first of all investigate the nature of aversive reactions as they manifest in infancy. The aversive system can be released by the simple fact that the infant grows tired of sucking, or that he cannot quite reach the mother's nipple. If he actively rejects the nipple, or perhaps turns away and firmly clasps his mouth shut, it is imperative that the mother be responsive to such aversive behavior; that she understands this signal as being in accordance with her infant's needs. Such a positive response to the behavior of the infant is a vital part of the regulation of the physiological needs of the infant. But aversion is important not solely for the regulation of physiological needs; it provides a system of signals which are in the service of the optimal functioning of attachment needs, but also of the exploratory–assertive and sensual–sexual motivational systems.

Probably the most powerful and recognizable instance of an aversive reaction in infants is found in the newborn's loud screaming. Its quite forceful protests against having to adapt to its dramatically altered environment is for everyone around ample proof of the newborn's healthy vitality. From the very beginning, infants are resistant to all things tedious or frustrating to them. This becomes quite evident if we consider, for example, an experiment (Emde, 1981) in which a lightweight cloth was tossed over the face of a 3-week-old infant. Some infants used their arms or head to get rid of the cloth. Others closed their eyes and retired into a light sleep. Some sank into even deeper sleep. Already at this early point in the infant's life, it was observable which ones reacted with aggression or active countermeasures, and which ones reacted with passive withdrawal. But one does not really need experiments such as this; just by observing everyday experiences with caregivers, one can see quite tellingly that infants from birth onward do indeed possess aversive patterns of reacting against annoying or frustrating experiences.

Further observations clarify how children will react with disappointment whenever their expectations to enjoy intersubjective closeness are not met. In this connection, the following experiments are instructive (Lichtenberg, 1989a, p. 175):

> In an experimental situation a ten-week-old infant girl was approached by her smiling mother. The baby immediately responded with interest; her full body eagerly moving forward. Instead of the mother's voice, however, the infant heard the recording of another woman speaking. The little girl's interest turned to startle. The look of joy on her face dissolved into distress. And she averted her eyes from her mother's face.

In another experiment (Papousek and Papousek, 1975, cited in Lichtenberg, 1989a, p. 175), the mother of a 6-week-old boy was instructed to keep her face expressionless. The infant increased his effort to activate his mother. When she failed to respond, the infant's efforts became more hectic and disorganized, until finally he lapsed into a pained immobility. A similar example is found in another experiment in which mothers left their 4-month-old infants in darkness for three-second intervals, in a manner unfamiliar to the infants. After this was repeated several times, the infants turned away from their mothers and resisted their attempts to re-establish contact.

These previous examples tellingly represent observations of aversive reactions such as antagonism and withdrawal. They are evoked when the infant experiences what appears to be a painful interruption in the constant and predictable interactional patterns (RIGs) between mother and child. Such interruptions have to be taken quite seriously, as they may with time undercut the infant's trust in the reliability of self and the world.

In general, infants are remarkably well prepared by means of their innate capacities and their accompanying learning abilities to take part themselves in the regulation of their physiological needs, as well as striving for satisfaction of their needs for attachment, exploration, and self-assertion. But they are quite noticeably helpless when it comes to devising effective means for getting rid of the various sources of aversive affects. They may scream, be startled, kick about, fall asleep, turn away their head, avert their eyes, or even refuse any sociable attempts to get close to them; but all these activities, taken just by themselves, have little possibility of "getting things right" in their environments or to protect themselves from further injury. Whenever the intensity of its aversive reactions are not too intense, the overstimulated, crying infant can usually calm itself. This transpires primarily through sucking its thumb (activation of the sensual system) and/or through moving its attention towards the exploration of a visual or auditory stimulus (that is, through the activation of the exploratory–assertive system). Yet the entire function of the inborn aversive pattern of reactions is limited to giving signals to the caregiver that something must be done. The capacity of the caregiver to have an adequately attuned responsiveness towards signals of suffering, fears, frustration, or rage, as well as the ability to address or to remove, if possible, the cause of suffering by calming, soothing, or re-establishing closeness, is probably the key factor in keeping alive the attachment between the caregiver and the infant. Yet here, where the infant's greatest vulnerability is located, lies also the root for future developmental disturbances, foremost in cases where physical or psychological abandonment are predominant.

Of course, the close parallel to the psychotherapeutic situation is obvious here. It is, to my mind, necessary that psychotherapists likewise be aware of the signal function behind a patient's various aversive behaviors and experiences (Asper, 1993). This signal function, as confirmed also by Lichtenberg, remains active well after infancy throughout the whole course of life. Naturally, in the adult it expresses itself in a much more complex, often hidden, form.

Aversive reactions in connection with needs to explore and assert oneself

Aversive reactions may at times also invade the need for exploration and self-assertion. One can observe that infants, towards the end of their first year, demonstrate reactions of anger or rage whenever those needs are met with frustrating inhibitions. Lichtenberg (1989a, p. 178), for instance, has observed that an active, energetic "toddler" was pushing a toy back and forth across a wooden floor until it was stopped by a tiny rock. Continuing to hum, he gave the wagon a push, but with no success. With a look of mild anger, he gave the wagon a more vigorous shove, sending it flying over the impediment. His expression turned to joy, and with mounting excitement he began to push the wagon back and forth over the carpet.

In this case, the aversive reaction of anger has given the infant the necessary strength to successfully overcome an impediment. Self-assertion, connected with anger or rage, can also be a source of power, and may even have a genuinely intoxicating effect. When they are thus interconnected, it may be difficult to determine whether it is the assertive motivation or the aversive motivation which is dominant. Beginning in the second half of the first year, along with the sense of power which comes with greater freedom of movement, infants learn as part of their growing subjective awareness that anger may add a vitalizing ingredient to exploratory–assertive efforts to overcome obstacles (Lichtenberg, 1989a, p. 178).

Infants often encounter dangerous situations, particularly in connection with their greater liberty of movement and their increasing need for exploration and self-assertion. Yet they do not have at their disposal innate reaction patterns for their protection. Many dangerous objects, like fire, knives, and electrical sockets, inevitably attract them. Whereas chasing a ball may captivate their complete attention, the danger of a street will garner none. In such instances as these, the indication to the caregiver is the child's eagerness to enter into a dangerous situation, rather than a signal of aversiveness such as fear or distress. These dangers must therefore be recognized by caregivers in situations for which the child is obviously unprepared and even oblivious. The parents' actions provide not only for the infant's security, but also create a learning opportunity which the child may utilize for its own self-regulation. In other words, it is crucial that caregivers truly support the aversive reactions of the child when it encounters physical or emotional situations which are dangerous. Of course, the emotional state of the parents also plays a decisive part. How do they judge, and react to, the dangers which the child encounters? A mother who is over-anxious will abrogate her infant's needs or drives for autonomy, which manifest themselves in his exploratory and self-assertive behaviors. Ideologies of a *laissez-faire* education may induce parents under certain circumstances to suppress their instinctive fear reactions; hence they would less likely interfere in the face of real dangers. What is at issue here is finding some optimal criterion for helping parents to restrain their children from engaging in dangerous situations without at the same time somehow discouraging the child's normal and necessary needs for exploration and self-assertion on a more global level.

The pathologizing of the aversive motivational system

Observations indicate that the aversive motivational system can react in a pathological manner from early infancy onward. There may be signs, for instance, which point to the child's being incapable either of defending itself or of effectively motivating the caregiver to liberate it from its personal distress. Fear and suffering bouts of rage may simply become a matter of course and thus be incorporated into the developing sense of self; that is, such affects become the dominant state of the infant. In most cases such developments are based upon disturbances in the relationship between infant and caregiver. Fraiberg (1982), for instance, has published a noteworthy study concerning pathological defenses in infancy. She writes about twelve children, with ages spanning from birth to 18 months. These children were referred to her hospital ward because of severe neglect or likely abuse. With the exception of one mother, who was diagnosed as being schizophrenic, all the other mothers were seriously depressed. They had obviously been psychologically absent for their children most of the time, but occasionally a sudden rage might break through the maternal depression which of course deeply frightened the children. It was characteristic for all these children to manifest grossly avoidant behaviors towards the mother. They avoided looking at her, smiling at her, vocalizing towards her, attempting to catch her or crawl over her, or to show that they wanted to be consoled or comforted. At least they made some eye contact with their fathers or perhaps with a stranger.

In most cases of traumatization there is a predisposition of the child towards a pathological organization of its aversive motivational system. Subsequently, all the other motivations will become secondary to a tendency towards the dominance of antagonism and withdrawal. The angry, fearful child, who is also prone to feelings of shame and guilt, therefore experiences its environment as non-empathic, even hostile, with little understanding of its needs and wishes. This constitutes a grave risk for the development of stability in the infant's sense of self. Instead of being able to rely on constant, mutual experiences, the developing infant begins to expect, or even provoke, reactions from its caregivers which are associated with feelings of helplessness and accompanying narcissistic rage.

Hate complexes

According to infant research, one cannot equate reactions of avoidance, defensiveness, or rage with hatred. The child is only capable of hatred when it has matured into a state that allows it to evoke, or retain in its memory, the offending individual, physical object, or circumstance; that is, when the latter are recalled independently from their literal presence in a given moment. As mentioned above, the initial representation of the other and of self comes about only around the age of 18 months. This ability enables the infant to differentiate itself from its representation of objects in its environment. Thus an inner dialogue, between the infant's self and its representation of that which it hates, may now evolve. In such inner dialogues the violation which one has experienced, and the reactions of rage and vengefulness towards the offending individual, can be replayed again and again, and may also be amplified by other affective states. Hence the intrapsychic confrontation with the hated individual will become ever intensified, which of course influences the actual relationship to a great degree. The relationship will either become suffused with hatred or perhaps be avoided, if not totally broken off. In an infant, of course, such a breakdown in relationship, here in the case of latent hatred, leads to dire feelings of isolation. Note that this rupture in relationship, based upon hatred, may become concealed by over-friendliness or extremely compliant behavior.

Lichtenberg makes a great effort to stress that the aversion of the infant cannot be equated with hatred. As long as the attachment remains stable in the relationship, and emotional intimacy is able to be re-constituted by the caregiver's consoling and calming behaviors, the extent and intensity of screaming, negativism, anger, or rage in infants does not necessarily lead to hatred. But whenever intense aversive antagonism provokes the parents to respond by rejecting that so-called "difficult child," perhaps because they themselves feel so unloved, there is a genuine risk of the infant's developing hatred as a kind of reciprocal rejection (Lichtenberg, 1992, p. 68).

Fully formed complexes of hatred, some with a more or less paranoid component, are very difficult to treat later on in the psychotherapy of adults. This is due to a fundamental mistrust which is also transferred on to the therapist, and which obstructs the necessary development of trust within the therapeutic relationship. In such cases, there will often persist a profound suspicion that the analyst will simply be just like the hated parental figure; will never take the analysand seriously; or will invariably use interpretations just to humiliate him or her. The prognosis is much better when, in spite of this mistrust, conflicts can be negotiated openly as part of the therapy sessions. It all depends on whether the therapist can be seen not only as the source of all aversive fantasies and feelings, but also as an ally, helping the analysand to deal with and work through such poisonous emotions. A working alliance is necessary for the mutual exploration of the background of the hate complex. Under certain circumstances it may be possible for the exploratory needs to be freed up to some extent from the domination by the hate complex. Yet one must always remember that, in cases of hate complexes, the danger is never fully vanquished that, through whatever kind of misunderstanding, there may still arise powerful impulses within the patient to temporarily withdraw or even terminate the therapy altogether.

An example from clinical practice

Prior to Part III, the primarily practically oriented portion of this book, I would like to discuss some issues related to a course of psychotherapy with a young woman who was filled by intense hatred of her father. This hatred also included persons in authority, like her teachers or bosses. She had experienced her father as a very moody and aggressive tyrant, who could even become violent and abusive during his frequent and uncontrolled attacks of rage. Apparently the father was unable to tolerate his daughter's typically siding with her mother. This, according to her, had been the main cause of his rage. In any case, the analysand all along felt very humiliated by his behavior. As a consequence, it had become her main concern to make sure that "no man would ever again get the better of her."

This had already been her chief motivation to complete a course of academic study, which was in fact not difficult for her in view of her high intelligence. It gave her much satisfaction, by gaining an academic title, to surpass her father, to leave him far behind. She was also quite successful in building for herself a career in which she could be independent and her own boss. In this way, she did not have to tolerate any boss or other individual wielding power over her. In addition, she already had a brief Freudian analysis behind her, and was very well versed in the psychoanalytic literature.

Her wish to undergo an analysis with me was triggered by her reading one of my books. This led her to the conclusion that I was probably not a fanatical Jungian, and that I also seemed quite well versed in the principles of Freudian analysis. She also thought, since I apparently focus on the use of empathy in my analytic work, that I would be less likely to intentionally take advantage, or need to "get the better" of her. In addition, she really needed analysis in light of her constantly recurring depressions and fears.

Early on in this analysis I came to anticipate our analytic sessions with a steadily growing discomfort. This patient tended to prescribe to me how I should treat her. She believed that I should focus on analyzing her defense mechanisms. Since she had read a lot in the psychoanalytic literature, she assumed that she too must be full of defense mechanisms. Of course, she was quite right. Nonetheless, she understood by this term something quite different from myself; that is, she ascribed her depression and various inhibitions to defenses against certain sexual impulses. Of course, that is possible; but for me, it seemed much more obvious that her hatred served more fundamentally as a defense against any needs for closeness, trust, and love; that it was basically due to this lack that she really suffered.

My discomfort before and during the sessions was actually caused by several different factors. Certainly, in view of her specific problems, the young woman was relatively cooperative with me. In her fantasy she considered me as an exception among the men she knew. I was someone who, thanks to my psychoanalytically gained capacity for insight, would recognize all the manipulativeness and brutal power struggles of the man's world. Therefore, in her eyes, I would have to support the correctness of her viewpoints. As a result, there were countless sessions filled with themes concerning her hatred of men. In addition, her dreams also often featured themes having to do with rageful confrontations with assorted male figures. In contrast to such hateful outpourings, she informed me at the same time of her racing heartbeat and her fears which she experienced prior to our sessions. She was fearful due to the expectation that I would be incapable of tolerating her aggression and would react by scorning and humiliating her. All this did not prevent her suspicion that in my very scarce and careful interpretations there was a critical undertone directed against her. It was primarily this undertone which remained indelibly etched in her memory and which had the effect of distorting the intended meaning of my words. On many occasions, after a lengthy delay, she would reproach me for what I had said negatively about her.

Thus, to begin with, I came to realize that my discomfort was primarily a reflection of her ambivalence. On the one hand, it was of great concern to her to protect me, as an empathic exception to her father, from all the affects of hatred. On the other hand, there was a visible fear that I might humiliate or devalue her, as had her father; and there was always the risk that this fear could at any time also turn into hatred of me. Altogether, my discomfort had to do with the fact that I felt almost completely paralyzed in my therapeutic function. She seemed to be looking for a kind of collusion with me, hoping that I would confirm the justification of her hatred; also of her paranoia-tinged suppositions. This would have comprised a repetition of her collusion with her mother, who apparently hated the father as much as the patient. Yet her mother had never been able to stand the test; she always became too weak in decisive moments and switched to the side of the father. This had disappointed my client to a most traumatizing degree. At the same time, her wish to acquire me as her accomplice was certainly also connected with her need for intimacy and her motivation for attachment.

Thus I had to face the difficulty of maintaining an empathic attitude towards the experiences of my patient without at the same time confirming all of the fantasies tied into her hate complex. It was obvious to me that her hate complex had really originated out of repeated rejections of love, and had over time become consolidated into an integral part of her ego-complex. It was therefore evident that her absolute right to a world-view filled with hatred was not at all open to direct questioning, not even by me as her therapist. It would have meant at least ripping open the floor beneath her feet; and, as a defense she might have turned me into an enemy worthy of her scorn and hatred, to the possible detriment of the analysis.

In my countertransference reactions I mainly felt uncomfortable and helpless. I thought that, in this state, it was best to keep quiet and simply allow for her tirades of hatred and suspicion of the various people in her environment. She herself considered my behavior – of my remaining so quiet – in terms of my supposed psychoanalytic neutrality, thus defending herself against the fears that it might be a sign of my rejection. But whenever memories of her father's (or other authority figures') cruelty emerged, then I could be more active and engaged with her. Depending on the content, I could comment briefly on her feelings which she must have had at the time and her feelings in the here-and-now. But otherwise, on those numerous occasions when she was ensconced in paranoid fantasies about hostile manipulations, I remained fairly silent. Of course I could be very discontent with myself for just quietly accepting and letting pass her suspicious fantasies; yet I realized that casting even the tiniest doubt on her attributions would have a most counterproductive effect. I tried to find consolation for my own passivity by the reminder, accurate in my estimation, that it might be very helpful for her to freely express, in a protected therapeutic frame, her hatred and her suspicious fantasies in hopes that they might become attenuated.

I had also observed for quite some time how gifted she really was in gaining an awareness of her inner states, emotions, and fantasies, at least as long as they were not overly contaminated by her paranoid hate complex. As she could not expect much help from me in analyzing her defenses (as she understood them), she had begun to follow her associations at home by herself and to construct more or less conventional interpretations in the way she had learned in her Freudian analysis. I also became more and more aware over the course of therapy that even my feeling of helplessness had significance in our specific therapeutic field; that it was a reaction of my "syntonic countertransference" (Fordham *et al.*, 1973). It was obviously quite important for the confirmation of her self-esteem that she was able to find important psychic connections all by herself. (This would be an example of the satisfaction of her motivation for exploration.) But at the same time it was of decisive importance that she could feel "mirrored" by me and that I did not undermine her own findings and realizations through an attitude of "knowing better."

After about two years of our working together, she surprised me one day by telling me how good it felt that whatever was inside of her could now emerge in my presence. She added that she had felt better lately, could sometimes get rid of some of her most terrifying emotions, had less fears, and was a little more balanced . It was the very first time that she could offer a word of recognition. In addition, in two of her dreams I had appeared in a helpful paternal way, and that was very much in contrast to her earlier dreams, in which I had been depicted as a persecuting figure who always devalued and antagonized her. In another dream it was her father who needed help from her because he could not deal with an important issue. She also began to remark on how difficult life must have been for her father, and noticed that his behavior could be better comprehended in light of his own childhood and the various other vicissitudes of his life. In other words, she had begun to get in touch with the empathic stance within herself. Overall, she noticed that she got much less agitated and hostile upon encountering other people's intrigues. Everyone was the way he was; and as he had to be.

On the whole, the analysand became significantly more tolerant and accepting of herself and other people. It had obviously become possible to liberate to a certain extent her ego from its previous identification with aversive, hateful emotions. The question remains of what had brought about this change. To my mind, she could consolidate her sense of self-esteem (her ego) by getting in touch with (1) her needs for intimacy (in the analytic situation, there was my relative reliability in "being-there," my so-called "neutral" tolerance for her hateful tirades, my empathy with her wounded feelings), and (2) her needs for exploration and self-assertion (in therapy, I had taken part in the outcome of her self-exploration and had abstained from acting as if I knew better). Thus it was no longer necessary for her to identify completely with the hate complex in order to compensate for her deep lack of self-esteem. I have to acknowledge, though, that I did not attain these results by employing conscious technical strategies. I can in no way brag about therapeutic success as if it were due to my cleverly implemented therapeutic skills. It was more a matter of my accepting innumerable feelings of discomfort, helplessness, doubting my own attitudes and capabilities, and trying to gradually understand them in connection with the interactions within the therapeutic field. There are many therapeutic questions which present themselves at this point, which also arise out of the incorporation of infant research, and which will be reflected on further in Part III.

Part III

THE SIGNIFICANCE OF INFANT RESEARCH FOR ANALYSIS AND ANALYTICAL PSYCHOTHERAPY

18

SOME BASIC PRINCIPLES
OF JUNGIAN ANALYSIS

C. G. Jung's viewpoints

Since I am referring primarily to the Jungian school of psychotherapy, the following briefly articulates a few key principles. Psychotherapists of the Jungian School continue in various degrees to incorporate into their own approach most of the ideas, findings, and therapeutic attitudes which were acquired by Jung himself. In view of the wisdom and depth of Jung's work, its continuing appeal to contemporary analysts is understandable, perhaps even more so, as he tended to formulate theoretical statements in as broad and general a manner as possible in order not to obstruct, through theories or techniques, the therapeutic necessities of each individual situation. A very typical quote of Jung's, and one that could stand for many others, is as follows:

> Since there is no nag that cannot be ridden to death, all theories of neurosis and methods of treatment are a dubious affair. So I always find it cheering when businesslike physicians and fashionable consultants aver that they treat patients along the lines of "Adler," or of "Künkel," or of "Freud," or even of "Jung". . . . When I treat Mr. X, I have of necessity to use method X, just as with Mrs. Z I have to use method Z. This means that the method of treatment is determined primarily by the nature of the case.
>
> (Jung, 1926, par. 203)

It is therefore the task of the psychotherapist to understand and pay as close attention as possible to the intentions of "nature" – meaning the nature of the psyche. To accomplish this, a therapist has to learn to understand the "language of the unconscious" as thoroughly as possible. Hence, Jung considered the direct experience and understanding of manifestations of the unconscious, especially through dreams and imagination, to be a core requirement for the psychotherapist. His own lifelong research studies, which provided a key to disclosing deep realms pertaining to the "reality of the psyche," were devoted to such understanding. Jung's life work – as far as psychotherapeutic endeavors are concerned – consisted predominantly in his constant struggle to find the deeper meaning hidden in the symbolic contents of dreams and fantasies. In his view, these contents of the unconscious accompany and stimulate – but sometimes also inhibit – the process of individuation, which emanates from the self, the directing center of psychic wholeness.

The psychotherapy originated by C.G. Jung, amidst all its great diversity, stands primarily upon two pillars which are basically in relation with each other. The first one, as previously mentioned, has to do with his discovery that there are of necessity various organizing factors operating in the unconscious, like everywhere in living nature. This had led to his hypothesis about the "collective unconscious," along with its structural elements, the archetypes. The latter largely express themselves in symbolic sequences of imagery, as found, for example, in myths, fairytales, visions, alchemy, etc.; and can also appear in the dreams of modern humans. Therapeutically speaking, it is thus of crucial importance to establish a connection with these factors operating "in" and "from" the unconscious, and to learn to comprehend its symbolic language as expertly as possible. To this end, it became necessary for Jungian therapists to develop familiarity with diverse symbolism from mythology, alchemy, the history of religion, fairytales, ethnology, folk beliefs, etc., in order to enrich, that is, to "amplify," the dreams of their clients as necessary. Jung viewed this as the most important aid to interpretation. Also very essential, as well, for the analyst as for the analysand, is the experience of the spontaneous creativity of the unconscious psyche. A vital openness towards experiences of the so-called "numinosum" often belongs also to the deep needs of the human soul, which may be revealed in certain dreams. Yet in this realm there flourish many pseudo-religious superstitions. Thus, in order not to become their victim, Jung always stressed, rightly so, the importance of the discriminating, conscious mind. With this sketch, I have tried to provide – though in necessarily simplified fashion – the original model for Jungian analysis, which is in the end really derived from Jung's own personal confrontation with the unconscious. In his *Memories* he gave impressive examples of such an experience (Jung and Jaffé, 1963).

At the same time, and this is the second pillar of his contribution, Jung was also a pioneer of the actual practice of psychotherapy. Here he was the first to take notice of the unavoidable mutual influence taking place between analyst and analysand. With this insight, he anticipated modern therapy models of transference and "syntonic" countertransference, of the "therapeutic field" and systemic analysis, etc., whereby he freed approaches to psychotherapy from the rigidity of the Freudian school of his day. (Freud himself deplored this rigidity as well; cf. his letter to Ferenczi in 1928.) Thus Jung writes: "By no device can the treatment be anything but the product of mutual influence, in which the whole being of the doctor as well as that of his patient plays its part" (Jung, 1929b, par. 163). About twenty years later he still expresses this thought in a more focused manner:

> We could say, without too much exaggeration, that a good half of every treatment that probes at all deeply consists in the doctor's examining himself, for only what he can put right in himself can he hope to put right in the patient. It is no loss, either, if he feels that the patient is hitting him, or even scoring off him: it is his own hurt that gives the measure of his power to heal.
>
> (Jung, 1951, par. 239)

These two pillars, on which Jungian psychotherapy rests, seem at first sight to correspond also to the difference between introverted and extraverted attitudes (Jung, 1921, par. 710, 769). On the one hand, the primary focus seems to be on turning toward intrapsychic reality; on the other hand, the stress is placed on relating to other people, that is, to the outer world. However, these two realms are not so easily or antiseptically kept apart. Indeed, they are interwoven with each other in complex ways. That is, the archetypal potential of the unconscious needs to encounter the surrounding world in order that it incarnates into life, hence to become actualized. At the same time, the outer aspects of our various interactions are always interconnected with our subjective ways of perceiving and experiencing, and may, under certain circumstances, impress themselves deeply upon our psyche. Jung rightfully spoke of the process of individuation as being "in the first place . . . an internal and subjective process of integration, and in the second . . . an equally indispensable process of objective relationship" (Jung, 1946, par. 448). Therefore, in analysis or psychotherapy, the quality of the relationship between patient and therapist plays a decisive role, greatly influencing the inner lives of both participants. As a consequence, the therapist needs as refined a sensitivity as possible in order to be alert to the subtleties of this mutual influence. In other words, what we are dealing with here is something that can be described as the mutual "therapeutic field," in which the so-called transference and countertransference takes place. The "self-examination" of the physician, which according to Jung consists in about half of the treatment, plays a decisive role here. Thus it becomes evident that both of these basic pillars are related to one another, and are vitally important to therapy.

However, one must add that – despite Jung's many fruitful (and for his time, modern) viewpoints about practical psychotherapy, about transference and countertransference, and about what today is called the "interactive field" – his suggestions were neither greatly heeded nor really further differentiated by himself or the first generation of his followers. Their interest lay almost exclusively in the *contents* of the unconscious and its symbolic messages, whether in therapy or in the exploration of the realms of cultural or religious phenomenology. The few illustrations of practical analyses that Jung and his early students published restrict themselves primarily to interpretations of the patient's "material from the unconscious." They concern themselves with enhancing one's understanding of the symbolic language of the unconscious, through which the relationship of the conscious ego to the contents of the unconscious is to be promoted. Explorations which center around the question of how the unconscious manifests itself in the here-and-now of therapeutic interaction, with its concomitant emotions, remain relatively incomplete and undifferentiated. Hence, what is lacking most is the microanalysis of what is occurring in the intersubjective field.

That this gap needs to be filled in, in order that a bridge be found between both areas – to the benefit of a more differentiated psychotherapy – is something that more than a few Jungian analysts are aware of today.

Development since Jung

At first, during the 1960s if not earlier, the work on studying developmental approaches was initiated by analysts of the so-called "London School," as later referred to by Samuels (1985). Michael Fordham and his colleagues, who worked at the time with children, made the attempt to apply Jungian ideas in the analysis of children as well. Over the course of this work they considered it necessary to incorporate, in addition to their own self-devised psychotherapeutic approaches, ideas and methods that stem from the school of Melanie Klein and/or were inspired by Winnicott. In this way they created their own analytical "technique," in which infantile components of the adult in treatment are also accessed (Fordham *et al.*, 1973, Fordham, 1969; Gordon, 1993; Lambert, 1981; Plaut, 1993). However, this particular method, coming out of the

"London School," did not spread widely despite their many stimulating publications. Many of Jung's supporters perceived in this method too great a deviation from, and "Freudianization" of, his more "spiritual" standpoint. On the other hand, it should not be forgotten that it was Jung himself who suggested that Michael Fordham should be the editor of the English version of his collected works. He must therefore have thought very highly of him.

Since the early 1980s there arose the necessity to elaborate, in a more differentiated form, the process in the interactive field of analytic practice. In the USA, as well as in Europe, there were quite a series of publications which incorporated some stimulating ideas from contemporary psychoanalysis (for example, from Balint, Erikson, Kohut, Winnicott, etc.), but which sought also to explicitly integrate these ideas into the specifically Jungian emphasis on the encounter with the psyche. In this current and ongoing development of diverse models of Jungian psychotherapy, the focus is chiefly on refining the analyst's sensitivity to nuances in the interactions within the therapeutic field, and understanding their meaning in the client's psyche. Put another way, there is now much concern about accessing the experiences of the "inner child," its development and woundedness, to the extent that they are relevant to various disturbances in the *here-and-now*. None of these authors, however, ties himself or herself to "reductive analysis" or has devised or even suggested a specific treatment "technique" in the psychoanalytic sense. Spontaneous interactions and the free forming of relationships within the therapeutic frame are not to be hindered by any fixed theory – an attitude which has remained valid and alive since the days of C.G. Jung. The individual authors from this school of thought, of which I consider myself a part, differ among themselves in many ways concerning the details of their viewpoints. (See, e.g., Asper, 1992, 1993; Jacoby, 1984, 1990; Kalsched, 1996; Kast, 1991, 1992; Schwartz-Salant, 1989; Spillmann, 1993; Stevens-Sullivan, 1989.) But what is essential is that all the aforementioned analysts – in addition to providing the best possible observation of the contents of the unconscious and its symbolic language – seem to keep at all times a sensitive focus on the intersubjective process within the analytic situation.

The instrumental function of the analyst and the interactive field

As mentioned above, Jung pioneered the idea that in depth analysis or psychotherapy, there is a constant mutual influence between therapist and patient. Since then, one speaks technically of a mutual therapeutic or interactive field (Schwartz-Salant, 1989), in which the so-called transference and countertransference occurs.

In a practical sense, the process in Jungian analysis or psychotherapy rests upon the assumption, born from experience, that an innate disposition – the self – normally organizes and directs our emotional equilibrium and unfolding process. It is therefore a central intention of analysis and psychotherapy to trace the impulses of this unfolding process of becoming conscious and to clear away as much as possible any impediments. This process is credited to a "facilitating environment," to again use Winnicott's highly descriptive term. Many patients, from childhood on, have experienced a primarily hindering, instead of a sufficiently facilitating, environment. The therapist is therefore confronted with the question of if, or to what extent, he is capable of providing the "space" in which a facilitating environment operates. However, what is experienced by individual analysands as a facilitating environment can only be perceived from within their own inner process. As an analyst, I have to prepare for being the "instrument," and as such be available to the inner process of the analysand. The idea that the analyst serves in a kind of instrumental function seems to me to be appropriate, or at least useful, because it tends to promote an optimal way of therapeutic engagement. In my opinion, it refers primarily to the idea of a musical instrument, which provides resonance within the style and manner in which its strings are touched by the player, thus providing a resonance in answer to how it is "spoken to."

The problematic nature of the metaphor "The analyst as instrument"

Of course, there are certain problems connected with this metaphor. When I say therapists should make themselves available as an instrument in the process of their patients, I am primarily thinking of the impulses that originate from within the self. An instrument that lends resonance to the hearkening of self-unfolding is also subject, however, to possible misuses, whether through conscious or unconscious manipulations. To become aware of any misuse and to respond adequately within a therapeutic attitude is often not without difficulty; yet it belongs to the craft and art of the work which analysts do.

In any case, there remains a question of whether the idea, that the analyst should at all times be available as an instrument to the concerns of the self, does not itself represent an overly idealized view of the profession, and therefore places too unrealistic a demand on those in practice. In addition, there is the experience of many patients who often seem unable to really make any "use" of this "instrument." This poses, for the therapist, the lingering question of whether he may in fact be an unsuitable instrument for the client, or if perhaps rather it is the client's inability to make proper and productive use of what is offered. Certainly there is also the additional realization that I, as the therapist, am not only an instrument, but also first and foremost a human being with my own subjective reality, difficulties, and needs. How do I manage this paradox that one's own fullest potential as a human being is precisely the crucial prerequisite for being at the same time most accessible as an instrument for emotional processing with other individuals? It is a fact that, only by virtue of the radius of their own human experience and their access to their own vulnerability, analysts may be able to provide a truly resonant "sounding-board." Yet their own subjective needs, conflicts, and weaknesses are also present and want to have "their say," and are thus on the verge of coming into play. In addition, their needs for autonomy, the realm of their personal freedom, will at times intrude into the professional domain, in which they are required to serve as an instrument for others in the therapeutic process.

Nevertheless, the metaphor of the instrument is helpful in attempting to articulate the most adequate approach to being a therapist. As mentioned, I imagine such an instrument above all as a kind of sounding-board. For the analyst to really be able to convey resonance, he must have a keen "ear" for the vibration of those strings which are touched upon within himself. Having a keen ear is essential to perceiving how this specific "music" sounds: is it in tune or out of tune, here in the therapeutic field?

At this point, Jung's requirement for the "self-analysis of the doctor" must be invoked. This analysis of the analyst, the so-called "training analysis," consists chiefly of a profound experience of getting in touch with and working through his or her own unconscious conflicts, complexes, prejudices, but also potentials. I shall return later to this critically important requirement. Besides this, I also consider it necessary for the analyst to have available to him different clinical models, as have been constructed within depth psychology over the course of a century of psychotherapeutic endeavors. Some of these models may be too divergent from any Jungian approach, yet others may be helpful in order to enrich the palette of one's clinical understanding and therapeutic treatment. Specifically, I am thinking of certain, more recent developments within Freudian psychoanalysis, which are at times amazingly similar to Jungian approaches, and which may supply many helpful nuances to enhance therapeutic finesse and understanding. Here, for example, belong the publications of Searles (cf. Sedgwick, 1993), Balint

(1968), Winnicott (1965), Kohut (1971, 1977, 1984), etc. And here is also the place where findings from American infant research – especially the contributions of Daniel Stern and Joseph Lichtenberg – may be capable of contributing innovative and relevant entry points for furthering our understanding of the archetypal bases of human relationships, and thus enriching and refining analytical practice. As they represent the key issues in this book, I will come back to their therapeutic importance later in much greater detail. In any case, I believe that an analyst should never cease to question himself and his methods, trying out new ideas, and implementing constructive self-criticism.

As mentioned earlier, the self-examination of the analyst is therefore of utmost importance, and requires the most profound analysis of his or her own unconscious background. This analysis should enable the therapist to both experience his or her more or less pathological complexes, as well as deal with them more consciously. Individuals who have not experienced the intensity of neurotic phenomena within themselves, and have not tried to come to terms with them, are poorly suited to practice this profession. To acquire a truly empathic understanding of my patients, I need to have learned, at least to a certain degree, how much psychic suffering can hurt. Furthermore, an analysis should also provide the future analyst with a more conscious perception of his or her "personal equation," including one's own vulnerabilities, as well as the emotional roots of one's world-view. Patients often have an instinctual "knack" in picking up on the analyst's particular vulnerability, and then either circumventing it like a kind of taboo, to the detriment of the therapy, or, on the contrary, directly provoking the therapist by actively engaging with his particular weakness. The therapist will also of course project on to the analysand those needs, internal representations, and expectations he is unconscious of, and, in his own countertransference, misjudge his patient in an "illusory" manner. Thus a good self-analysis may open a therapist's continual awareness – and this in my view is very essential – that he is constantly exposed to the risk of letting an illusory countertransference interfere with an adequate empathic perception. Therapists may certainly never become totally conscious or invulnerable as a result of their own depth analysis, and thus must curb any unrealistic expectations of a given analysis. Optimally, one's own analysis should nevertheless sensitize one to the ever-present potential danger of falling prey to the projections of illusory countertransference. Finally, it is no doubt desirable that an analyst will "know" from his or her own experience that being consciously in touch with oneself and facing one's complexes can lead to a process of emotional maturation.

An example from clinical practice

I do not want to end this chapter without presenting at least a brief example concerning the process within the therapeutic field. I recall a female client who somehow knew how to perfectly set my "inner strings" vibrating. Over the course of our work, I was cognizant that these were not primarily "vibrations" of an erotic or sexual nature. In her presence, nevertheless, I always felt highly stimulated inside, and was attuned to her in the most acute manner imaginable. I was often quite surprised myself by the absolute precision of interpretations which came to my mind, and then landed on such fertile soil for her. The synchrony of our mutual "wavelengths" was very apparent; hence the therapy process was itself extremely satisfying for us both.

However, it is exactly amidst such seemingly fruitful exchange processes that self-critical questioning is so appropriate. First and foremost there is the question: On what specific motives is this ideal and mutual therapeutic concordance based? In the case of this particular client, I had to call into consciousness my awareness that she had, in her own childhood and adolescence, developed the most refined "antennae" for adapting to environmental expectations. This had been, and now persisted as, a very necessary survival strategy for her. She always "tuned into" the interests and needs of others with tremendous instinctual precision. In this way she succeeded in making herself likeable, all the while sacrificing her own standpoint, and eventually being used by others. Thus it was clear that she tended in the analytical situation, above all else, to avoid in any way "being a burden" by adapting and, as much as possible, bringing up topics that from her perspective might be of greatest interest to me. So I asked myself whether I, due to my own projections, was not perhaps falling into a trap of sorts. Did she know just how to animate me, evoking my "anima," so that I might feel inspired, and somehow wonderful and great in her presence; hence I would love her in turn? It seemed very important for me not to forget to keep an eye on this aspect of our interactions.

It was no less essential, however, that I be careful as a therapist not to become fixated exclusively on her arts of seduction, born out of an inner distress, insofar as it would have been a mistake for me to prematurely devalue our relationship by invoking such an interpretation, possibly shaming the analysand in the process. This all-too-apparent repetition of her pattern represented only half of the truth, for I became aware that our mutual fit really was based on a common wavelength – or, to use Stern's expression, a deep encounter in the "intersubjective domain." Within this domain there lies the creative potential for emotional development;

more specifically, the sense of being validated and mirrored for one's own way of being. Had I instead, on the heels of my skepticism, simply interpreted the patient's repetitive pattern, a crucial opportunity for a therapeutic breakthrough would have probably been missed. Yet, at the same time, had I not recognized the connection between her subtle seduction and my grandiose fantasies, we would have quite possibly persisted in a "folie à deux" of mutual idealization and/or narcissistic collusion. Such a collusion might be, from the patient's viewpoint, put into the following words: I adore you so much in hopes that you might love and value me. And, as a reaction from the analyst: You inspire me to my fullest potential; thus you are special, and I therefore love and value you.

This example may illustrate how helpful some familiarity with the findings of infant research may be. It was especially the knowledge of how crucial the respective qualities of intersubjective transactions can be to further increases in maturation which was influencing my approach. Thus the question arises, very generally, in which way the findings of infant research may be of decisive significance for the analysis or psychotherapy of adults. In discussing this question, I will deal in some detail with several specific insights gained from infant research, as they apply to adult analysis, in the following chapters.

19

THE CORE SELF IN THE PSYCHOTHERAPEUTIC FIELD

The "self-regulating other" in therapeutic practice

In order to introduce the reader to this theme, I will first present three brief vignettes:

Mr C

A young student, who consulted with me, initially complained that he found it difficult to sit in the university auditorium because he suffered from fears that everyone could hear the noise he made when swallowing. This prevented him from concentrating on the lecture. All he could think of were his swallowing noises, which made him feel horribly embarrassed. So he was clearly feeling exposed, observed, and even annihilated by the other students, in terms of his own self-esteem.

During the first few meetings we worked mostly on his chief difficulty, namely, the trouble he had marking out the boundaries of his own domain. After I informed him that psychotherapy should help him to gain a greater sense of what it feels like to be himself, he was able to repeat to himself: "I am what I am." It really helped to liberate him in an astonishing way. Above all else, he ascribed his transformation to a sort of magical power that I, his analyst, apparently had at my disposal. His recollection of our encounters in fantasy helped him to hold his ground – his "I am what I am" – against the annihilating effect of the "others." He believed that he needed only to remember our encounters, and that would suffice to reactivate the phrase which was so vitalizing to him: "I am what I am." This proved to be a decisive aid against the influence of the "others" who really oppressed him.

Of course this liberating effect did not last for long, insofar as it belonged only to the initial "honeymoon" phase of our analytic encounter.

Mr D

An academic of about 30 years old, Mr D used to experience what felt like falling into so-called narcissistic "holes" (his term), from which he suffered greatly. This meant that all of his self-confidence suddenly disappeared. It was as if he had lost the ground on which he stood. He simply felt terrible, unable to live up to what was expected of him; or, more accurately, what he really expected of himself. His sense of self-esteem was undermined to such a degree that he believed he was just a complete "zero." As a consequence, he felt completely devalued and was ashamed to appear at all at his workplace, where he carried considerable responsibility. But such self-devaluation obviously had less to do with his current, external reality. Rather, it seemed to be much more connected to his unconscious grandiose and perfectionistic expectations of himself which gave him such "hell." From a therapeutic point of view it was very important not to leave him feeling alone in this awful "hole," but to empathically provide some words expressing what torment he must have been cast into by this radical and sudden loss of self-esteem. I said how frightening it must be to lose temporarily any connection to his positive human or professional qualities. I sometimes also dared to temper his grandiose expectations, making them appear less absolute. By the end of such a session he usually felt much better, with his self-esteem returned to near normal; at least, that is, until he fell into the next "hole." During, or after, such a session it typically did not take long before he could again view, experience, and evaluate the world and himself more realistically. But in the following session he would often express his shame about having been such a "cry-baby," and about having needed me to help him get out of his agonizing state. Of course, in the long run, it became very important to work through the historical background of these disturbances in his self-esteem.

Mr E

Many years ago I saw a patient, Mr E, aged 30, who badly needed therapy because of his suffering from a severe case of agoraphobia. He was placed in a shelter run by a religious charity, but he could not leave his room or home because he was so afraid of major panic attacks as soon as he was outside. In order for him to receive any psychological help, I had to visit him at his shelter. His main and constantly repeated complaint was about a severe lack of "safe-containment" (*Geborgenheit*). He had never felt safe, accepted, and contained in his infancy nor, as might be predicted, in his current experience with the pious "brothers" in the shelter.

After a while he trusted me enough to leave the home together with me and thus we could hold our sessions while taking a walk. With time, he was even able to leave the shelter all by himself, as long as he was sure that at some point during his "risky" undertaking he could find a telephone to reach me, in order to simply hear my voice. He needed to hear my voice, he believed, in order to restore trust in his own autonomy. After about a year he had become capable of riding in a streetcar, and thus would come to see me in my consulting room.

All the above examples show some similarity to each other insofar as, for each of these patients, the sense of self had been severely undermined by various fears. As a result, willpower at the disposal of the ego had been paralyzed; hence the entire activity of the ego was deeply derailed. In each case, there were major disturbances in the sense of a core self; that is, for each of these patients, all four components of the core self were compromised to a greater or lesser degree.

The four components of the sense of a core self

Daniel Stern (1985) differentiates the following four components of the sense of a core self:

1 The sense of *self-agency*, that is, the experience of authoring one's own actions and having volition or control over self-generated behavior, which for each of these patients was impaired.
2 The sense of *self-coherence*, or having the experience of being a whole physical entity with boundaries, and a locus of integrated action, whether when moving or when stationary; this was a source of deep insecurity for all three patients.
3 The sense of *self-affectivity*, namely experiencing the patterned, inner qualities of affects which are connected to virtually all experiences of oneself; this was almost completely undermined for these patients, due to their extreme fears.
4 The sense of *self-history*, that is, maintaining an experience of continuity with one's own past, the sense that one goes on existing and remaining somehow essentially the same individual, even after various changes; this was at the very least jeopardized for these patients.

Because none of these patients suffered from a real psychotic fragmentation (severe forms of core self-disintegration can actually be psychotic), it was possible for all three to discover, over time, the means to access their own sense of a core self, at least temporarily. Obviously, one could ascribe each patient's own recovery of sense of self to their respective therapeutic encounter, yet in my opinion, in each case, such recovery appeared to have little to do with a specific skill around giving interpretations. Or for that matter, it also had little to do with any particular thing I *did* or even *was* as a person. Rather, what was important, at least to my mind, was that I should *not stand in the way* (by interpreting, challenging, etc.) in order that the patient might be able to experience the therapist as the "self-regulating other." All I could do was to try to be fully present and to be empathically in touch with each patient's particular subjective experience by listening and trying to understand how their personal anguish affected each of them.

Some hypotheses concerning the infantile background of disturbances of the sense of a core self

Only after a certain period of time in my therapeutic encounters with these patients did it become possible for me to formulate some more differentiated hypotheses about their infantile wounds and experiences of deficit, which served as the basis of current, subjective states involving the loss of self. In part, one might also deduce these hypotheses from the various presenting symptoms.

Concerning the student, *Mr C*, his transference behavior was dominated by a profound ambivalence. He needed and wished to have closeness with me, to have me nearby as a magical source of energy. But at the same time, he had to close himself off in front of me because he feared that I could endanger his sense of autonomy. This may offer a clue to the hypothesis that, as an infant, he was looked after and held in an intrusive and over-stimulating way, with the likely effect that he would have chronically felt very hemmed in. On the one hand, since he was the only son, he was the admired center of his family. On the other hand, his mother was quite often absent due to her taking an active role in supporting the career of his father. Thus there were fluctuations from one extreme to the other, from exaggerated parental attention to his experiencing sudden abandonment, all of which still remained at least vaguely in his memory.

Here is not the place to describe in detail his possible conflicts of ambivalence between longing for fusion (which led so quickly to his feelings of oppressive discomfort), on the one hand, and, on the other, his needs for autonomous independence (which were accompanied almost immediately by fears of abandonment). Nor can I articulate in detail the psychotherapeutic process. In any case, it was most certainly a therapeutic "tightrope" in our sessions: he would not allow me to be like his father, who was and still is, in his mind, overly "interested" in him and "concerned" about his well-being. Yet he also became easily depressed whenever he sensed the slightest disinterest or abandonment from me. However, despite everything, a very gradual process of differentiation and separation began to unfold step by step. His regulation of the sense of self grew increasingly independent of his transference relationship to me.

Mr D, the academic, must have as an infant experienced his mother's gross incapacity to attune to him in any way. There was evidence to this effect reported by third parties. From the earliest time he can recall, the mother–child relationship was always somehow poisoned by a kind of toxic, mutual rejection and "allergy." He also disclosed that he was dangerously malnourished during infancy, which may also be an indication that he quite likely refused nourishment from his mother. In any case, whatever the reason, for his mother to function as a "self-regulating other" seems to have placed too great a demand upon her. His father had apparently been very proud of his first-born son from birth onward, but he also tended to expect too much from him at too early an age.

Notable here was the patient's tendency to make himself unassailable by attempting to be perfect in all matters. As a result, even the slightest critical attack on his supposed perfection had immediately annihilating consequences, and threw him deeply into a state of disintegration and self-loathing. To my mind, it was prognostically a positive sign that he could at least accept my input as the "self-regulating other" in our therapeutic field; and that this began to have an impact on him within our relationship. The fact that this latter experience was quite impossible without accompanying, intense feelings of shame, which in fact used to overwhelm him after such encounters, was in his case understandable. Even when he used to experience strong feelings of relief – for having been freed from such a fragmented, earlier state – he found it extremely difficult to tolerate within himself that he had presented to me in such a vulnerable, even pitiful, condition. It was important to him that I repeatedly interpret the general psychological significance of such episodes in order to somehow relieve him of personal shame. Over time, he learned to understand and even tolerate these experiences, at least to a certain degree.

The patient with agoraphobia, *Mr E*, had been an unwanted child. It was due to his conception that his parents, albeit reluctantly, felt compelled to marry for so-called "religious reasons." That his mother had cared for him in only the most minimal way was very apparent. As far back as he could remember, she always let it be known how superfluous he was, and what a burden he had been to her from his birth onward. Consequently, his RIGs consisted primarily of disappointments, fears, and expectations of being rejected. He was also abnormally mistrustful. For instance, in my initial visits, when I knocked on his door, it typically took him a long time to open the door a little way, and even then with great hesitation. He would just stare at me, full of fears, as if he were expecting the devil himself. But if I was ever late, even by a few minutes, he became overwhelmed by fears that I might not come at all, thus majorly letting him down; or even worse, that I could even have been in a lethal accident in transit.

At the same time he was highly needy, with a tremendous longing to be contained by a "good mother." This latter need was for him quite powerful, despite all of his previously tragic and negative experiences. *Geborgenheit*, "to be contained," was his favorite word. But he was able over time to allow me in as a "self-regulating maternal figure."

These three examples demonstrate the manner in which the function of the "self-regulating other" may be implemented in the analytic situation. Thus it may happen that clients experience, at least momentarily, considerable relief from fears, tensions, or states of confusion; and find themselves to be calmed, for example, by hearing the voice of their therapist on the telephone. In addition, the experience of an empathic presence, for example, as expressed in a certain phrase by the therapist, or sometimes even by experiencing sensations associated with the physical ambience of the familiar consulting room (i.e., the "surrounding mother"), may evoke similar responses, though they are usually only passing. These may all be equivalents of the child's wish for a certain kind of loving attentiveness from the mother, which would facilitate for most infants an optimal measure of well-being. Yet one must remember that, for particular reasons, quite a few analysands experience such regressive needs for dependency to be frightening or shaming, and therefore cannot tolerate them.

The effectiveness of analytical psychotherapy

As mentioned earlier, no therapist can truly substitute for the mother; nor can he really repair what was missing for the patient during infancy. Yet in the above examples, my presence early on in therapy was indeed experienced by my patients *as if* I were functioning as the "self-regulating other" in the therapeutic field.

Analytical psychotherapy has the potential to be effective, insofar as the patient's mental representations in association with their accompanying emotional qualities are to a great extent open to being influenced by the environment. A helpless analysand, for instance, may evoke, in the therapist, impulses to intervene and support him in a comforting or affirming manner. Of course, the analyst is not supposed to act out such impulses concretely; rather he should register them and, if possible, inquire into their meaning with the analysand. I personally have noticed in myself that certain impulses to "help" the patient, together with their related fantasies, will definitely influence my approach or therapeutic attitude, including the pitch of my voice, even if I do not tend to fall literally into "baby talk."

It is of course extremely critical that interventions within the therapeutic exchange always remain oriented towards the patient's growing capacity to help himself. The danger associated with the analyst's trying to satisfy, in a literal or concrete form, the patient's infantile needs consists primarily in risking that the latter may become fixated in a so-called "malignant regression" (Balint, 1968). This means that the patient will unconsciously remain "fixated" in infantile dependence and become "addicted" to always seeking gratification from his or her significant other, often the analyst. Thus the development of self-help skills will not be facilitated. In fact, to the contrary, the infantile needs may, in an addictive manner, win the upper hand.

As long as the helpful self-regulating functions of the analyst are operating primarily within a symbolic frame, there is the opportunity that patients may use this satisfactory experience in a progressive way. In connection with Balint (1968), one speaks in this case of "benign regression," which represents a chance for an at least partially "new beginning" in the progressive unfolding of development.

Getting back to the description of my three previous analysands: one could say that there were at least two with whom I could be helpful right from the outset, by simply being fully present and maintaining towards them "good-enough" empathic attentiveness. I could, in other words, be instrumental for enabling them to reconnect to their sense of a core self, operating as if I were the "self-regulating other." The third patient, who suffered from agoraphobia, needed more concrete or literal activity from me. I was engaged with him not just through my empathy towards his experiential world, but also quite concretely in my visits to his home. I accompanied him not just symbolically during his first steps outside his shelter, but I also permitted him to reassure himself through telephone calls, again very concretely, to reinforce that I was still there for him in a caring way. All of these measures are, from a strictly analytical point of view, quite unusual, and certainly deviate from the typical frame of the therapeutic field in which exchange processes are engaged and explored in a symbolic way. I was conscious, of course, of posssible risks.

But it was this patient whose suffering from early damage was most pronounced, and whose emotional and cognitive maturation were most stunted. We will come back to this case at a later point. For now, suffice it to say that he had very little possibility of accessing the capacity of symbolic expression; and therefore I had to meet him, literally and figuratively, where he was. This meant offering him very concrete help. If I had not dared to break the therapeutic frame, to transcend its limits, then it would have been quite impossible for him to have received any psychotherapy at all. Yet, in spite of this, he found it possible to experience me in the therapy as the "self-regulating other." Thus it also became possible over time for him to gain enough confidence and trust in his own sense of a core self in order to eventually, step by step, inhabit more fully the experience of "standing on his own two feet."

"Holding" in the sense of Winnicott

Winnicott has described certain similar phenomena in connection with his term "holding." He observed that, for patients with very early devel-opmental woundedness, the establishment of an "analytic setting" is more important than any interpretation (Winnicott, 1958, p. 220). The analyst's behavior needs to be "good-enough" in terms of adapting to the patient's needs in a way similar to what the mother was asked to do in the patient's childhood. This process allows the patient to perceive the therapist's presence as "something that raises the hope that the true self may at last be able to take the risks involved in its starting to experience living" (ibid., p. 297). Understandably so, Winnicott also notes that this kind of work is highly demanding, "partly because the analyst has to have a sensitivity to the patient's needs and a wish to provide a setting that caters to these needs" (ibid.). Winnicott, as he always admitted himself, had some difficulty actually defining the "true self"; yet he circumscribes it vividly, for example, when he formulates that if "the infant starts by existing and not by reacting here is the origin of the true self. The spontaneous gesture is the true self in action. Only the true self can be creative, and only the true self can feel real" (Winnicott, 1965, p. 148).

The emerging of the sense of a core self in the infant, with the sense of being the center of one's own impulses, corresponds to the "true self." The "false self," which functions as its protection and adapts to the environment, develops only later, depending on the specific influence of the caregivers. Likewise in psychotherapy, an empathic attitude towards the emotional needs of clients is of immense importance to their gaining some access to experiences of the true self.

"Wearing" the attributions which are delegated to the therapist

It should be mentioned in this context that Lichtenberg *et al.* have recommended a list of very useful therapeutic principles (Lichtenberg *et al.*, 1996). For instance, they think it is important that the analyst should listen to his client in an optimal, empathic mode; and that he accepts the various images and attributions which are delegated to him (projected on to him) by the client. He needs to accept those attributions, and sometimes even to embody them. Whenever a patient needs me, the analyst, in a way, as if I were his "self-regulating maternal other," it is usually not very wise to reject this role which has been delegated to me, by interpreting it as merely an illusory wish. In so doing, I would risk devaluing the feelings of the patient, and under certain circumstances, would actually injure his extremely fragile sense of self-esteem. It is therefore crucial to take with utmost seriousness such attributions, and to understand them from the point of view of the patient's needs. As mentioned above, it can even be facilitating to the patient's growth for the therapist to take on certain ascribed roles in the analysis. In a Jungian sense, this can be understood in the following way. The activity of the self (in the Jungian sense), as the organizing center of psychological development and equilibrium, often includes a projection on to the analyst as "wearing" an instrumental function in facilitating the patient's individuation process (see p. 133–4). For this reason, the analyst may take on various fantasized roles in the patient's unconscious, which may be of considerable significance in the therapeutic process. Therefore my own experience in this regard leads me to agree with the recommendations of Lichtenberg.

However, I would also like to warn against a possible misunderstanding, namely, that the therapist should actually *be* as much as possible the early mother, and should participate by actively enacting this role for the regulation of self. Instead, as I see it, it is more a matter of not rejecting certain *functions*, for example, of the maternal, which may be unconsciously expected (and deeply needed) by the patient. It can be potentially harmful for the developing sense of self if such needs are, based upon principle, simply discarded by means of an interpretation; it is often a matter of a function, delegated to the analyst, which may later be taken on by the patient himself, as soon as his striving for increased autonomy is allowed to bear new fruit.

The above are thoughts pertaining to the theme of the "core self," and to the question of how the function of the "self-regulating (maternal) other" may become effective in the analysis of adults.

20

THE ORGANIZATIONAL
STAGE OF
INTERSUBJECTIVITY
IN THERAPY

Affect attunement

From time to time, clients may complain about being greeted by me in a friendly manner; they claim that this prevents them from directing their anger at me. That is, they feel disarmed in such an interaction; and the aversive affect with which they came to the session has apparently dissipated in the moment. Sometimes they may feel badly and even reproach themselves for having had any hostile feelings towards me, the one person who is so obviously warm-hearted. A female analysand once complained that I had seemed to be in such good spirits, at least while she was sitting in the waiting room. She had overheard me laughing with the patient scheduled immediately before her. With her, however, she observed painfully, I never laughed. She believed that she had simply become nothing but a burden to me in light of her constant depression.

These are two, commonplace examples showing a lack of affect attunement between analysand and analyst. The second example in particular has apparent "overtones" of emotional hurts that originate from repetitions in the transference (in this case, sequelae to the patient's earlier experiences of severe sibling rivalry). In any case, a temporary hiatus in affective attunement has emerged and is experienced as a disruption in the relationship, a momentary "estrangement." Nevertheless, both clients were able to bring up their acute discomfort, which certainly speaks to the openness and sense of mutuality within the therapeutic relationship.

As mentioned earlier, based on Daniel Stern's observations, "affect attunement" between mother and baby is of great significance for the maturation of self-perception. Affect attunement first manifests at the age of 7 months as a pressing need. It is, however, also of major importance in the analytical situation; therefore having a keen ear for subtle "over-tones" within the therapeutic exchange belongs, in my judgment, to the true art of being an analyst.

Milder interruptions of affect attunement are unavoidable in every human relationship. Two people can never be in complete accord with one another. Whether we are dealing with a romantic partnership, mother–baby relationship, friendship, or even therapeutic relationship, two people always have their own individual needs, their different temperaments, as well as their respective strivings towards personal self-formation and/or individuation. At the same time, however, the need for bonding and the yearning for a sense of belonging are an innate human motivation (Lichtenberg, 1989a). We are fundamentally social beings and, as such, are ever in need of the experience of "resonance" regarding our individual expressions of life.

Affect attunement and empathic resonance

In Kohut's self-psychology, and also in Winnicott's work, there is much discussion of "mirroring," which we – whether in infancy, adulthood, or old age – are always to a certain degree in need of (Jacoby, 1985; Kohut, 1971). We need a certain "resonance" in response to the expressions of our being in order to feel acknowledged as real and as part of the human family. Kohut spoke of "empathic resonance" (Kohut, 1977), which he also deemed to be a key factor in the success of any analysis.

To what extent is affect attunement synonymous with empathic resonance? Affect attunement is surely based on emotional resonance, which carries approximately the same meaning as reverberation. Without emotional resonance, genuine empathy is impossible. Yet, in the case of empathy, there must be the inclusion of certain cognitive functions. A deliberate, conscious decision must be made by us if we are to attempt to actually place ourselves into the subjective world of other people, and to try to comprehend not only their feelings but also their many thoughts and viewpoints. In contrast, affect attunement most typically happens spontaneously and is predominantly unconscious (see Stern, 1985, p. 143ff.). It is nonetheless an essential foundation in the intersubjective dimension of the mother–child relationship, and may be most aptly viewed as the prototype of empathy.

Vitality affects in the therapeutic situation

The question of affect attunement is initially posed more globally in the analytic situation: Are we, as the analytic "partners," adequately matched with one another in terms of our essential ways of being, including temperament? Or are we instead, right from the outset of analysis, in a kind of therapeutic misalignment? In other words, what are the human limits within which affect attunement may in fact succeed; and when is it obviously impossible?

We know that there are mother–infant couples, who – due to fundamental differences in their vitality affects, that is, in their temperament – cannot come together; where no "fit" or "matching" between them seems capable of developing. This applies similarly to the therapeutic relationship. Therefore, the keenest attention must be given early on to this question of foundational matching.

A great deal of what constitutes the earliest contact between the therapist and the patient, during the very first clinical session, revolves implicitly around the question of initial "first impressions" (in which hunches are formed about the "climate" emerging in this coming together): How does the other person come across throughout this meeting? What gets stirred up in me? Which feelings get set off? How do I experience the presence of the other? Is there any "chemistry" between us? Or, are we from "different planets"? There may be a "spark" of mutual attraction between us, or perhaps no common "wavelength" at all. I can also feel "run over," "pressed up against the wall," "paralyzed," "put right to sleep," "inspired," "fully absorbed" by and in my therapy partner, or very attracted for some reason. What comprises the overall climate in the first encounter often seems quite difficult to pin down. It may be projectively attached to a side remark, a simple gesture, the office arrangement, the therapist's physical appearance, even the way one wipes one's nose. Spontaneous sympathy versus antipathy certainly plays an important role. But what is it, lastly, in all its particulars which is evoking these feeling qualities? Analytical psychotherapists, due to their clinical experience, may have more refined antennae to become aware of the various kinds of evoked impressions and may be able to more easily generate intuitive hypotheses concerning their origins and possible meanings. Ultimately, however, such experiences are not fully explainable down to the last detail.

Let us say that the feeling of a certain incompatibility would emerge in this early encounter; this would bring with it, first and foremost, the practical question: To what extent is this apparently fundamental incompatibility a function of basic differences in temperament and personal character between analysand and analyst? Or, as another possibility, to what extent does this seeming mismatch represent analyzable transference/countertransference feelings, with corresponding resistances which are perhaps being concealed? Even in the case of an especially ideal emotional harmony, where the cooperation may result in very deep mutual understanding, one must ask oneself the question: To what extent might this represent a mutual illusory or idealizing transference, a "folie à deux," whereby therapeutic "blind spots" are potentially being concealed?

About the question of matching between the therapy partners

In any case, the question of matching is extremely significant. In light of all we understand today, the success of the therapeutic process depends substantially on whether the partners in analysis or psychotherapy are able to form a good-enough "match" with each other. Experience shows that therapeutic misalignments at this basic level end up only rarely being of benefit. Infant research, for example, has consistently pointed out that too gross a deficit in emotional or temperamental harmony between mother and infant may lead to all kinds of early developmental disturbances. A basic, inner sense of not being quite right, for instance, of being unacceptable, and therefore excluded from the rest of the world, may have its deepest roots in just such an early misalignment.

Such an all-pervading negative sense of self may be more or less operative in certain individuals but, understandably so, is defended, perhaps through various sorts of overcompensation. Yet it may be the deepest source that motivates people to seek a therapist. Inevitably then, such a negative basic sense of oneself will sooner or later crop up in the therapeutic field, making itself known, for example, in the patient's transference to the analyst. In any case, even though it initially exists outside of conscious awareness, namely, in the unconscious, it will powerfully shape current interactions, projecting itself on to one's closest partner in the relational field. Applied specifically to analysis, this dynamic operates in such a way that, no matter how the analyst might naturally behave, he will feel himself forced into such roles as being "untrustworthy," "possessive," "intrusive," "abandoning," "rejecting," etc. This gives rise to some critical questions: Is this relationship pattern we are in an outcome of transference? Is it, in other words, based on repetitions of what may have originally gone wrong with the parenting figures? If this is the case, then a working through of these early wounds could be of some benefit in the long run. If, on the other hand, we are dealing with a fundamental incompatibility in the vitality affects and the essential character of both therapeutic partners, perhaps the entire undertaking needs to be freshly evaluated, while a possible change in therapists should never be automatically excluded.

It must be taken into consideration that, behind a so-called "negative" transference – made up of earlier wounds, fears of rejection, intense disappointments – there are often deeply buried wishes for closeness, mutuality, and a harmonious relationship which want to come alive. In other words, deep inside the patient's psyche, there exists a profound yearning for paradise. However, access to such concealed desires may be blocked by defenses or compensations of various kinds (Asper, 1993). I have already claimed that analytic psychotherapy produces its greatest effect in the "interactive field" (That is, in that arena of the unconscious in which both therapy partners take part, wherein mutual influence occurs) (Jacoby, 1984, p. 53). It is here, it seems, that the unconscious calls forth both its creative and organizing, as well as (like everything else in nature) its destructive and chaotic possibilities. This marks the "potential space" for a creative "new beginning" (Balint), by means of which the old, pathological schemas and patterns may be relativized: thus losing another portion of their destructive hold on the patient's life. Especially then, in this arena organized around the context of early childhood intersubjectivity, it is absolutely vital that there be a satisfactory "chemical bond" between the analytic partners.

The selection of therapy partners

Yet how is it possible to really know from the initial session whether or not one's choice of a therapeutic partner is mutually satisfactory? I would like to address this question first from the viewpoint of a potential patient. Ultimately it really is up to him to somehow figure out if he can trust this previously unknown individual whom he has selected as a possible therapist. For many people, this process may be quite challenging. I have however experienced analysands who, already in the initial intake interview, even after the first half-hour, seem to "know" that they are in exactly the right place with the right therapist. This often proved to be true as time went on. It is as if they, from deep within themselves, receive an intuitive "signal" from the unconscious – that is, from the self, which operates as an unconscious organizing factor within our total personality, and which therefore virtually always seems to "know" what would be beneficial to us.

Such "instinctive" knowing is to be taken with the utmost seriousness. But to what extent is it trustworthy? A certain skepticism may be in order here. Because if potential analysands could reliably trust that they were always making the right choices, we would undoubtedly experience fewer bungled "entanglements" within therapeutic partnerships – not even to mention the more complicated processes involving our choice of romantic partners. In spite of it all, "instinctive-emotional" knowledge is of primary importance as far as questions about relationships are concerned; while rational reasons, even when they are emphasized, remain for the most part secondary. This in no way excludes the possibility that such confidence in one's intuition for choosing the "right" therapeutic partner may in fact be chiefly motivated by various illusions, complexes, and unconscious wishes – all of which are fully capable of erasing or minimizing opposing perspectives.

The initial meeting between the potential therapy partners may very well be perceived in many different ways. One patient, for example, will feel so immediately understood as a result of how the therapist listens and reacts that he or she already experiences trust, and awaits the mutual therapeutic undertaking in an optimistic frame of mind. In another case, however, the client seeking help may feel so humiliated early on by what appears to him to be coldness and indifference on the part of the therapist that he immediately discontinues the treatment, or at least remains very much on guard for further injury. Or perhaps he concurs that the therapist may in fact be correct in not taking all of the patient's "minor aches and pains" too seriously. It is the analyst, after all, who is the expert authority here; hence he must really know what is for the best therapeutically.

In any case, it is difficult for some individuals in search of help to know for sure if they are in the right place with a given therapist. For example, how can the patient be sure that his therapist is not accurate when he interprets the patient's mistrust and doubt, regarding the therapist's competence, as a resistance phenomenon which should be worked through for the sake of the analysis? Thus it is most difficult for the one seeking help to really trust his own feelings, especially insofar as it is exactly in this area in which he feels least secure. Nevertheless, being in touch with such feelings can be a good indicator for certain patients, as they usually have less to do with the "objective" reality of the analyst than with the emotions, fears, expectations, and yearnings that are released by the encounter in the analysand. If such feelings could be empathically understood by the analyst and interpreted accordingly, some meaningful clues about the emotional impact of this initial assessment of the therapeutic relationship would possibly come to light for the potential patient. Usually however, such first impressions are not so easily accessible, because few potential analysands already have the capability or freedom to perceive and verbalize such subtle impressions during or after this initial conversation. However, I personally attempt, during the first dialogue, to be in touch with my own countertransference feelings. This helps me to form a first, provisional picture of the general climate in the interview and also a hypothesis about what may have been evoked in the client by his or her encounter with me.

The question remains of how such a selection takes place from the vantage point of the analyst. First of all, one thing is not to be taken lightly. It is an essential part of an analyst's professional ethics not to use the potential analysand's helplessness and disorientation to one's own advantage and manipulate him into analysis based on one's own interests, for example, financial, narcissistic, or even erotic (see also Jacoby, 1984).

For analysts, then, it is about assessing in a responsible manner, based upon their professional experience, if collaboration with the prospective patient is advisable and could indeed "provide help" in the therapeutic sense. There are a number of factors which must be taken into consideration in this regard; I can only address a few in what follows.

The decision to accompany a specific analysand into this work rests upon diverse motives. Perhaps the therapist selects that patient with whom he already senses an emotional connection. I believe this may be quite justified, insofar as such a connection is often accompanied by a shared entry point into understanding the specific conflict areas experienced by the patient. Personally however, I repeatedly require of myself, in my clinical practice, to avoid falling into the too-comfortable habit of only accepting people into therapy who may be on the same "wavelength," whose problems I readily understand, or with whom I most easily empathize. There are always potential analysands who present a challenge to the analyst; people with whom he must venture into emotional realms which are less familiar to him. Of course, this may actually enable him to expand his own horizon, and to discover within himself regions which had heretofore remained unexplored. Jung rightfully referred to this in suggesting that the analyst who engages himself fully in the analysand's process is also always in analysis himself.

In any case, no analyst is capable of somehow creating therapy-enhancing harmony with all individuals who seek him out. Should any analyst fall prey to the former illusion, he will soon find himself thoroughly over-extended. Certainly it may serve the purpose of his own individuation process to ever expand the boundaries of his understanding, and to deepen and further differentiate his realm of emotional experience. Yet the question has to be asked: Might this not also entail a possible misuse of the patient if his therapy is expected to somehow promote the analyst's own individuation? In any case, notwithstanding the obvious sharing of the therapeutic field and the utter mutuality of the therapeutic partnership, it ought never to be forgotten that psychotherapy is intended first and foremost for the well-being of the patient.

Sympathy and antipathy

Furthermore, there is also the question regarding to what extent sympathy and antipathy may even be viewed as a helpful 'yardstick' for clarifying this issue of match or fit between two people. Based on my clinical experience, it is clearly much more difficult to turn down a potential client who is perceived sympathetically. Although sympathy in its literal translation means "agreement of feeling," the phenomenon of matching is in my judgment something far more complex. Surely, fitting together emotionally without sympathy is difficult to imagine. In contrast, it is possible to feel considerable sympathy, for example, for people with lots of charm or sex appeal, yet without being deeply touched by any sectors of common wavelength.

Still, it seems to me that it is nonetheless important for analysts to take note of their spontaneous reactions of sympathy and antipathy, especially during initial sessions, even when this may appear in some way dissonant, or unethical, when compared with their stated purpose to help. At least subliminally, these feelings almost always carry some weight in deciding if therapeutic cooperation is in fact desirable. It is therefore highly advisable to gain an awareness of them. Based on my experience, there is a wide gamut of intermediate feeling tones between the two opposite poles of sympathy and antipathy into which the feel of a conversation can move, only later to shift and change tonality. In a given moment, say, when I have been successful in acquiring an empathic understanding of the experiential world of my potential patient, antipathy will understandably play a much more minor role. Finally, however, the patient is not there solely for the purpose of my liking him, or to evoke sympathy in me. Another consideration is important: If I have difficulty in finding some feelings of sympathy towards him, this may be a sign of an important issue for him which I pick up by my "syntonic" countertransference reaction. It may belong precisely to a problematic area for him, one which not infrequently consists of unconscious, neurotically driven strategies of provoking dislike from one's environment. As soon as I can find my empathic stance, namely, to see a phenomenon from the patient's vantage point, I begin to sense the suffering attached to it, and the therapist in me may be evoked. A "sym-pathy" develops in me towards his suffering.

However, as has happened occasionally, when I do not succeed during the first couple of sessions to overcome my feelings of antipathy – when these feelings simply do not change spontaneously – this is a clear indication to me that I ought not to begin long-term therapy with this particular patient. As mentioned earlier, it is extraordinarily important that one's orientation to therapy be genuine and feel intuitively right. When the therapist must first overcome his antipathy in order to properly orient himself towards the patient, the whole undertaking stands on shaky ground, and something fundamental is not in harmony.

Affect attunement and transference/countertransference

As mentioned above, the organizational stage of intersubjectivity – the development of which begins between the seventh and the fifteenth month – certainly plays a decisive role in the therapeutic exchange process as well. Here we are primarily dealing with fundamental human needs for mutuality of experience and for social validation. In the exchange processes between mother and child, meanings are ascribed to things and occurrences and hints are given as to what is supposed to be attractive or unattractive in connection to self and the encounter with the world. A wide range of gestures and sounds accompanies the parent's references to the child, from stimulating sounds like "goochie, goochie, goo," "yes, yes," and "mm-hmm" to fear- or disgust-expressing vocalizations like "huh-uh," "yecchie," etc. Thus in therapy there arises the question of which aspects of such (mostly unconsciously) ascribed meanings were experienced as promoting the infant's development and which placed themselves as neuroticizing obstacles in the way of the infant's unfolding and continue to have an impeding effect. Depending on the case, there may be a necessity in therapy to question various contexts in which certain meanings are essentially taken for granted, and go unchallenged, by the patient. Sometimes such meanings, which he automatically ascribes to certain feelings or situations, have to be brought to conscious awareness; sometimes they need to be given entirely new interpretations. I will return to this matter later.

Originally, it was the infant's need for mutuality of affective experience within the organizational stage of intersubjectivity which lay at the basis of its high degree of suggestibility to the emotional climate and the quality of emotional exchange processes; and this interplay of the infant's need with the kind of responses it receives subsequently has a determining impact on continued personality development. The highly differentiated description of various forms of maternal affect attunement given by Daniel Stern (1985) is therefore highly pertinent to psychotherapists in two ways. First, it may enhance the therapist's understanding of the biographical background of an analysand's present emotional state, because there is a high likelihood that the earlier experiences, expectations, and disappointments may repeat themselves in the here-and-now. Secondly, such differentiation may contribute to the refinement of the therapist's sensitivity to the nuances of emotional exchange processes in the current therapeutic situation.

As mentioned earlier, Stern described a graduated scale of parental attunement behaviors (selective attunement, misattunement and tuning, non-authentic attunement, etc.; see Stern, 1985, pp. 138–161). He observes that, realistically speaking, complete affective "harmony" may be experienced only for brief moments, at best. As a rule, what is more at issue concerns the adequacy of selective attunements. It is these latter attunements which offer parents the stongest possibility of influencing the development of the subjective and interpersonal life of their children.

In adult clients, patterns of experiencing and ways of behaving, which originate in these early attunement experiences, engrave themselves for the most part in the unconscious psyche. From there they influence the patient's self-perception, and repeat themselves to a great extent in the expectations which the patient directs towards interactions with his therapist.

In any case, there are countless variations on how interpersonal contact is established and maintained. Since analysands cannot at first know which behaviors the therapist expects from them, they will in their uncertainty tend to fall back into habitual patterns. But after some time, in which they will have got to know one another better, it may become feasible for a skilled analyst to formulate hypotheses about the manner in which early childhood intersubjective exchanges may have been experienced by the client, and in which ways the basics of his sense of self and the world were imprinted by such exchange processes.

But here is the place to again explicitly stress that we can only talk about hypotheses – no more, no less. We do not in this respect have any definitive power of "proof." The human being is always a product of innate aptitudes and environment, and is receptive to myriad influences over the course of his development. First and foremost, how these environmental influences are processed is contingent to a great degree upon his given aptitudes. In addition, the imprinting influences of the intersubjective level of organization are also modified, overlaid, and/or warded off by a whole host of complex psychosomatic and cultural influences. As such, hypotheses can do little damage as long as they are held lightly and are not somehow reified as unchanging "truths." To the contrary, they may often become guidelines to a better understanding of emotional processes.

A clinical example

As an example, one analysand comes to mind who hardly ever took any initiative himself, and also always waited for the therapist to bring up topics for the dialogue during analytic sessions. He would often somehow lose his train of thought and then feel relieved when the therapist could take up the thread again. In such cases, some analysts tend to wait silently, and tenaciously remain so, until the patient, under a sense of pressure, finally overcomes this "resistance" and takes the initiative. I personally prefer to address this difficulty directly but cautiously, and to inquire about the inner condition that may prevent a patient from establishing or maintaining contact. A patient will often answer: "I don't know where to begin." While trying carefully to explore further, seeking to gradually enlist the cooperation of the analysand, I may come intuitively to the following hypothesis. In this particular case of my patient, it is not the *specific* topic that is the cause of his blockage. What is actually behind it has much more to do with his fear that *any subject* he might dare to bring up would meet with my disinterest. His problem thus is that he does not know if, and in which way, he can even be sure of my interest in him. And there is nothing he fears so much as a lack of resonance in response to his concerns, because in such an event, he suddenly feels invaded by a sense of being devalued, rejected, and not belonging at all. At this point, I try to put this intuition – which had just come to me in that very instance – into words; that is, into a type of verbal interpretation. For this purpose I choose the form of a question, to make sure that the analysand may clearly feel included in the exploration, and at the same time would be totally free to accept or reject the tentative hypothesis. I begin my sentence with something like: " I have the feeling that . . . " or "Might it be that . . .?" With this particular patient, in this particular interaction, I am quite "lucky" with my intervention. He feels understood, and there arise clear signs of relief in the room. In this way, it became possible for us to share some insights about his fear which has shamed him; so that it becomes more understandable and also acceptable to both of us.

Now, with regard to his difficulties that originated in the organizational stage of intersubjectivity, I arrive at a hypothesis, which corresponds to many of his autobiographical comments, that his mother was a very busy woman who could not herself relax and loosen up enough to really participate and engage with her son in play. Therefore, one of his earliest impressions was that impulses which came from him could not be "of any meaning," or worth anything much.

The fact that this sense of paralysis within my patient – in which nothing that went on inside of him was seen to have any meaning – could be discovered and understood by both of us together proved to be an important new experience for him. As essential as these experiences are, they still remain at first just isolated, individual occurrences. One can count on them being quickly covered over, even nullified, by much more deeply imprinted patterns of habit. It would be an illusion to expect that they will have much "staying power"; and soon enough, nothing may remain but the sense of a single, one-time "lucky shot," which fundamentally changes nothing in the personality. Even more so in the analysand, there may arise his fear of disappointing the therapist again, as he feels incapable of contributing anything to a sense of mutuality and connectedness with the therapist. For him, the conviction will be restored that he will be incapable of generating anything of value, or even meaning anything at all to his therapist.

Now it was important to calm down the analysand by sharing my awareness about the time-consuming nature of such transformation processes and about the patience required by both analytic partners. In this particular case, it was probably the mother's own lack of patience that had hindered her from participating more adequately in the "rhythm" of her child. Patience within analysis implies, among other things, tracking opportunities for satisfactory affect attunement, insofar as it can be tolerated by the patient. Quite often, allowing for such moments of attunement is, for certain patients, extremely difficult, especially in light of their fears of emotional intimacy. How emotionally intimate the partners in analysis may be allowed to become must often be "negotiated," very often without words, but rather by means of a subtle sense of empathy and therapeutic feel.

There are certainly countless forms of the imprint stemming from one's earliest experiences of affect attunement. It is impressive to note that, already in archaic tribes, such "knowledge" of the importance of early mothering for the development of desirable social behaviors seems to exist. For example, Margaret Mead writes about her observations of the Mundugumor tribe in New Guinea, which needed to educate their offspring to their practice of head-hunting and cannibalism:

> Very little babies are kept in a carrying-basket, a closely woven, rough-plaited basket. . . . Without looking at the child, without touching its body, the mother or other woman or girl who is caring for it begins to scratch with her finger-nails on the outside of the basket, making a harsh grating sound. Children are trained to respond to this sound; it seems as if their cries,

originally motivated by a desire for warmth, water, or food, were conditioned to accepting often this meager remote response in their stead. . . . Mundugumor women suckle their children standing up, supporting the child with one hand in a position that strains the mother's arm and pinions the arms of the child. . . . He is kept firmly to his major task of absorbing enough food so that he will stop crying and consent to be put back in his basket. The minute he stops suckling for a moment he is returned to his prison.

(Mead, 1935, pp. 194–195)

In this way violence, ambitiousness, vengefulness, jealousy, and pleasure in aggression are inculcated early on, which meshes well with the ideal type for the Mundugumor.

Translated into Western standards, such maternal behavior would be fertile soil for the development of a conduct and an inner experience marked by intense, destructive "narcissistic rage" (see Kohut, 1972).

Questions about the regulation of affect attunement

Sooner or later a patient brings his own particular inner world of emotional sensitivities into the therapeutic field. What ensues are to a great extent unconscious expectations regarding the help he hopes to receive from the therapist. The analyst will probably attempt as far as possible to place himself inside the emotional world of the analysand. By this attitude, he may achieve a certain degree of affect attunement, which generates two distinct advantages. First of all, he obtains a certain "insider's view" of the analysand's emotional condition. At the same time – as experience shows – an actively participatory form of listening in itself often has an amazingly therapeutic effect.

Certainly it is important first and foremost to tune into the "melody" of the analysand, because only in this way is it possible to truly listen for and detect noticeable dissonances. The therapist undoubtedly brings his own "melody" and "rhythm" into the field as well; and soon enough, discrepancies between the two individuals may develop. Yet when two people "make music" together, a consistent and mutual listening to one another, along with mutual adjustments, is essential. Of course, it is primarily the therapist who must consciously adjust himself to the emotional state of the patient, without at the same time losing himself in the emotional world of the person sitting across from him.

Daniel Stern, based on his infant observations, rightfully speaks about two distinct motives being at the base of affect attunement on the part of parents. First, there may be the intention or wish to *share* in the infantile emotions; but secondly, there may also be a wish to *alter* them. The boundaries between these two motives are not always clear, and sometimes they are not consciously perceived at all. For example, well-meaning parents may be far too ready to console their child immediately when he suffers from emotional or physical pain, with the attendant message that everything was not so bad after all and will soon go away, etc. But, in the face of such a response, the infant's emotion finds no resonance; it is not taken seriously enough on its own terms. In such instances, it is often the parents who need a contented child for their own comfort and would prefer not to be bothered.

In this context, a female client of mine comes to mind. Whenever she wants to seriously share her distress with me, she always prefaces with: "Surely you will think that I'm exaggerating terribly once again." In reality however, such thoughts as she attributed to me were quite remote from any of my reactions – particularly in light of the profound degree of her psychological woundedness. This all seemed to be much more a projection on to me of her mother's voice, who had always tried to quickly console her, implying that she was not so bad off after all, and that she actually exaggerated a great deal by her complaining. The patient interpreted this response as an accusation, and learned later that her mother simply could not tolerate certain expressions of affect. In addition, over the course of her development, she internalized this accusation coming from without into a kind of self-accusation. Hence one of her enduring problems consisted of a deep uncertainty about the extent to which she was even permitted to take her own feelings, thoughts, impulses, or hurts seriously.

In psychotherapy at any rate, there is very often a focus on modifying painful or destructive affects. At this point, I would like to remind the reader of Stern's observations about affective "misattunement" and "tuning" (Stern, 1985, p. 211f.). Here the mother engages consciously or unconsciously in the following strategy: she creates an "illusion" of mutual experience, but abandons this mutuality for a small movement in the direction she desires. The child, in order to re-create the previous sense of harmony, moves back closer towards the mother. In this manner, the mother succeeds in changing the behavior and experience of the child in the direction which she intended.

By this means, Stern described the "method" in which socialization and "child-rearing" typically occur. In extreme cases, however, the danger will arise that the caregiver spends so much time and energy trying to change the child's experience in the direction of his own wishes that the child is simultaneously robbed of his own feelings.

To what extent do analysts themselves act in a similar fashion, even with the best of therapeutic intention, often without noticing it? When interpreting dreams or transference issues, for example, it is easy enough to let small emphases or accents head the patient in the desired direction. While it is likely that such influence on the analyst's part can hardly be avoided, it can also be, under certain circumstances at least, an important therapeutic agent. This is true, however, only on condition that the therapist is consciously aware of his or her "strategy." Otherwise, it is possible that an analysand may, for example, automatically ferret out the apparent discrepancies and as a matter of course seek to adjust to the real or anticipated affective state of the therapist. Perhaps this behavior comes so naturally or compellingly to him that he remains quite unaware of it; worse even, when the analyst in turn is pleased to have such a "motivated" and receptive analysand, and does not notice how the latter, by means of such behavior, slips right into a transference repetition, whereby he loses any connection to himself. Throughout the course of this process, it is chiefly the therapist who has to consciously adjust or adapt to the affective state of the patient, at the same time still remaining in touch with himself.

The demand placed upon the therapist may become unrealistically high or overbearing: namely, that he must at all times be aware whether his interventions stem from an accurate resonance in response to the emotional state of the patient, or if instead they may end up by putting a subtle pressure for alterations. Such differentiating may be quite difficult at times, considering that interventions necessitate a certain degree of spontaneity. However, a continual self-check by the therapist is vital. He needs to be in touch with his empathic sensitivity in order for him to ascertain the influence of his interventions and overall clinical style.

Patients are often highly motivated to change something about their desolate emotional or psychosomatic condition. Transformation is most often the goal of an analysis. And here it seems that, obviously, two principles of any depth-oriented psychotherapy are in contradiction to one another. On the one hand, it is always about the patient learning to *accept* himself or herself as he or she is. On the other hand, there is striving for *change* and transformation. Yet one has to consider that a change in one's emotional attitude is often necessary in order to even reach an acceptance and affirmation of oneself. But one may also find a state of complete self-satisfaction, a condition that cannot be beneficial to living a genuinely human life. Thus the twin conditions of self-acceptance, on the one hand, and striving for change, on the other, may end up always in a relationship of tension to one another.

But whenever it is a matter of self-acceptance, there is always, first of all, the question of discerning which of the inner manifestations are authentic expressions of the self. It is precisely because of socialization – which begins as early as the phase of intersubjectivity, necessitating the first steps towards social adaptation – that humans are in danger of moving into a state of self-estrangement or developing disturbances in authentic self-experience. Yet we are social beings, and the maturation and development of the self is dependent on a facilitating-enough environment. Where psychotherapy is concerned, what a therapist wants is to facilitate – by means of affect attunement, empathy, and a good-enough dream understanding – the patient's approaching the authentic being that is often hidden deep down inside him. This is in the hope of helping the patient to find his own authentic path.

21

THE VERBAL SENSE OF SELF WITHIN THE THERAPEUTIC FIELD

Affect attunement and empathy

Up to now in Part III of this book, I have followed Stern's ideas about organizational forms of the sense of self while trying to reflect how they may apply to the psychotherapy of adults. I tried to bring all this, whenever possible, into an experience-near understanding. Yet it became more and more difficult and restrictive to do so without also including some description of verbal forms of communication. This was especially difficult when trying to describe the different modes of emotional attunement between the caretaker and the child because I felt obliged to allude, by verbal means, to possible feelings, experiences, and forms of exchange for the infant which are in actuality not yet open to the infant's experience by means of language. This difficulty became most pronounced as soon as I turned my attention to issues pertaining to intersubjectivity. For instance, the question of to what extent affect attunement will be operative within the child, as confirmation or as pressure to change, is quite difficult to answer as long as the accompanying dialogue, expressed through language, has to be excluded. Even more so, when the step from affect attunement to the much more complex phenomenon of empathy is activated, verbal communication is found to play an indispensable role. In this connection, it is significant when Heinz Kohut defines empathy as "the mode by which one gathers psychological data about other people; and when they *say* what they think or feel, imagines their inner experience even though it is not open to direct observation" (Kohut, 1966, p. 450). Affect attunement means, in other words, the emotional connection to the particular affective state of another person, while empathy is aimed at "discerning, in one single act of certain recognition, complex psychological configurations" (ibid., p. 51). Put differently, one could also define empathy as the capacity to gain, by vicarious introspection, insight into the experiences of other people; and to understand them from both emotional and cognitive points of view. In other words, empathy is a temporary identification with the emotional state as well as with cognitive processes going on in another person.*

In any case, as we now include the organizational forms of the verbal self, this opens a whole world of significant connections and enables the description of a far richer palette of possible life issues. This is also the experience of the infant, for whom this developmental "burst" revolving around the emerging world of language may feel like a major "revolution." Alongside the step-by-step development of language, something new on the horizon is born; namely, the capacity to render oneself as an object of one's own reflection. Therefore one can now speak of an "objective self," which is developing *vis-à-vis* the "subjective self" of earlier phases. The fact that infants now recognize themselves in the mirror is a striking sign of this emerging capacity. In addition, the discovery that one's own person or self can now be viewed and evaluated from "outside," by other people, belongs in this developmental epoch.

About the dissociability of the psyche (Jung)

As mentioned earlier (see p. 53–54), in this phase there arises, for the child, a crisis in self-comprehension. For the first time in its life, the infant experiences itself as divided, and rightly senses that nobody can heal this split. It is language which drives a wedge between two modes of experience: one that can only be lived spontaneously and directly; another that can be verbally represented. The child becomes a mystery to itself. It is aware that there are levels of its self-experience that are, at least to some extent, estranged from those "official experiences" which are ratified by language (Stern, 1985, p. 378). In other words, the child gains entry into its culture, but at the cost of losing the robustness and wholeness of its original experience.

Jung spoke early on, and rightfully so, of the dissociability of our psyche (Jung, 1947, par. 365–370). Goethe, the German poet, grieved at having not one, but alas, two souls in his breast. In addition, Jung tells us in his memoirs about his personality #1 and personality #2 which posed a continuing problem for him, causing him so many perplexities during his childhood and adolescence. Contemporary brain researchers believe

---

* For the problem of empathy, see also Kohut, 1957, *The search for the self*, p. 205; and Jacoby, 1990.

that they have discovered the locations of different, often opposing functions or states of consciousness in the right and left hemispheres of the brain. However, as experience reveals to us, there are not just two, but rather a multiplicity of "souls" in and around us. Archaic peoples lived more closely to this understanding insofar as they experienced their surroundings animistically. Polytheistic religions – with their pantheons of gods and goddesses who are so often in conflict with each other – also reflect this fact.

This dissociability of our psyche is in itself not necessarily pathological. It is an inherent part of our human condition, as both blessing and curse. We are not simply actors with a script written by nature, as can be stated with some accuracy about the animal kingdom. It is within the design of our species-specific condition that we reach a point in development where we experience ourselves as "free to decide" – at least in certain realms of our existence. In other words, in particular areas of life we are free to choose, "liberated by nature," as Herder expressed it (1968, p. 119). This realm of apparent freedom, which we call "egoconsciousness" (rightly or wrongly), is only possible under the condition of a loss of unity with our so-called instinctual nature, that is, our original wholeness. Ironically this very freedom, in turn, makes for a dependence on general guidelines for behavior and orientation. Collective taboos and social rules, and later, ethical norms and laws are now required. In other words, we are now in need of some kind of cultural canon with its inherent world-view and hierarchy of values. Hence we are as much creatures of culture as of nature; and as such, experience endless conflicts coping with the various complexities and contradictions related to our needs. Thus it is that we experience such great difficulty in being at peace with ourselves.

But without the dissociability of our psyche, the specifically human capacity for developing self-reflective consciousness would not be possible. We must all gain a working perspective about ourselves and our fundamental way of being. The crisis in early childhood which goes hand-in-hand with the maturation of the verbal self is at the same time the beginning of this specifically human development. Thus, as mentioned earlier, the entrance into our culture, which we gain, is at the cost of our experience of wholeness.

Although this dissociability is the basis of our psychic flexibility and of the richness of our psychic experience, it has also to be compensated by energies which serve the maintenance of our psychic equilibrium. The fragmentation of the self (Kohut, 1977) is a constant menace; hence we may be quite prone to anxieties. Our psychic equilibrium – which is based on the interplay of various, often opposing motivations, affects, autonomous complexes, unconscious energies, along with conscious decisions – is very precarious. And here is where the concerns of psychotherapy have their place.

It was originally Jung who discovered a counter-movement to the dissociability of the psyche, a psychic process that – often quite subtly – aims at integration and centering. It is therefore a central concern of analysts to locate such processes of integration, to provide them space to develop, and, if possible, to remove the various disturbances that hinder them. This is in any case the aim of not just Jungian analysis, but of practically any contemporary, analytically oriented psychotherapy. If these processes, which are aimed at integration and centering, were not programmed into us by nature, then any holistic psychotherapy would never be effective. In the Jungian view, these are the processes which are directed and triggered by the self, that center of ordering and integration which is active and alive in the unconscious.

The verbal sense of self and the Jungian ego complex

The emergence of human consciousness, as Jung sees it – and the way in which he connects it to the ego complex – corresponds more or less to the organizational form of the verbal sense of self, along with its attendant, growing capacity to make oneself the object of one's own observation and judgment. Here we find the beginning of a consciousness that is capable of self-reflection based on the opposites of subject and object, inner and outer, good and evil, etc. We also find the origins of the so-called "objective" image of self, which can now be seen as a content of consciousness, linked to the ego. As is well known, children at the beginning of verbal development initially speak of themselves in the third person. They most often talk about themselves in exactly the way they have been spoken to by their caregivers. Thus they repeat – indeed, are identified with – evaluations or judgments they have heard from their environment; for instance, "Little Hans is very nice . . . or naughty . . . or tired . . . etc." It is as if they would see themselves through the eyes of their caregivers and hence evaluate themselves accordingly. Sometimes it may be observed that "little Hans," because he has been judged as being naughty, will take a doll, with which he identifies, and throw it away, scold it, or reject it. In such a case, we can see the specific beginnings of the more general phenomenon in which adults treat themselves as they have been treated by their caregivers in early childhood. This latter example represents the beginning of a process by which one comes to reject oneself.

In any case, the capacity to reflect upon oneself, and thus to observe and see oneself as if from the outside, has its roots already in preverbal experiences of the "self with others." One can see it in the imprint of earlier RIGs, which are now at least partially verbalizable. Such internal representations belong to the complex of ideas or images which center around what Jung called the "ego." But it still takes time before this verbalizable representation fuses with a sense of self and at last becomes fully integrated in terms of one's sense of personal identity.

Jung was of the opinion that the ego, "ostensibly the thing we know most about," is in fact a highly complex affair, "full of unfathomable obscurities" (Jung, 1954, par. 129). The basis of ego-centered conscious-ness – the root of human consciousness, as it were – reaches deep down into the unconscious. Its core is an active energy that arranges and organizes the entire process of self-development. It can be seen as a hypothetical center which Jung, as was mentioned earlier, calls the self.*
It is essential that the relation between the ego and self – although it undergoes many changes – not be split off or lost, because the self is the very source of our creative energies. One might even say that it creates the human being and directs the development of consciousness. It is also the source behind the emergence of the various domains of the sense of self as well as the various motivational systems, and may lead finally to a mature self-awareness.

Thus here we are on familar ground for Jungian analysts, insofar as the main activity in analysis is designed to heal the split between these two modes of experiencing that are connected to the verbal sense of self and can also be called the ego and the unconscious. As analysts, we try to find a bridge to those realms which have been left "to lead a name-less but nonetheless very real existence," including creative and/or destructive resources in the psyche (which are part of the manifestation of the "Jungian" self, operating in the unconscious). Among adults they may express themselves in dreams, fantasies, symptoms, affects, etc. For the purposes of building such a bridge, it is crucial that the analyst has acquired an adequate understanding of such phenomena. Analysis is also called the "talking cure"; and here may lie an explanation of why language may have a curative effect. Through interpretations we try to apply language to those unnamed realms of experience, hence inviting

---

* In this connection it is surely of interest that modern psychoanalysis has also proposed the notion of a "superordinate ego," a construct partially congruent with the Jungian idea of the self. The superordinate ego "always strives for the preservation of the organism by the resolution of conflict and favoring ongoing developmental processes" (Blanck and Blanck, 1986, pp. 34–35).

them to become a part of our conscious world. Via language in the analytic dialogue we attempt to ratify experiences which have been otherwise fended off – by means of such barriers as shame or fear – due to their perceived incompatibility with ego values, etc. It is true that Jung was skeptical about words, and aware of how often they may be used to serve purely defensive or rationalistic purposes. Yet in his early years he himself developed the word association experiment, which showed how certain words can be triggers for feeling-toned complexes. The choice of a particular word may determine how, and whether or not, we can cross the bridge to the preverbal realm of experience, a realm which cannot yet be verbalized, yet may be symbolically depicted. Sometimes the analyst has to be the first to give a name to whatever may have been 'unspeakable' until now.

An example from analytic practice

In providing an example here, I want to refer back to the analysand who was mentioned previously (see p. 105–107). This analysand had at various times become speechless, because anything she intended to share simply disappeared into seemingly inaccessible recesses in her psyche. As a result, she would withdraw altogether. Nothing seemed to be left other than a complete sense of emptiness. Not even such emotions as fear or shame were available to her.

It is obvious that her withdrawal into speechlessness had something to do with the domain of relationship, and specifically with her transference feelings. In one of the sessions where she had once again lost her ability to speak, I sat next to her, trying during her silence to be alert to the various thoughts and feelings which would come up inside of me. Afterwards, I made detailed notes, and I now want to share in some detail what they were. I thought: "What is this woman really doing with me? She withdraws into herself as if I do not even exist. Does she perhaps withdraw into her shell because my presence is too threatening for her? Here I remembered that she had a very critical father, who had devalued her quite cruelly. But is it also possible that she might have somehow pushed him into taking this devaluing and destructive attitude towards her? Had she reacted to this criticism with her own silence and stubbornness, in a way perhaps that is similar to how she now behaves in the transference? Has she developed a masochistic pattern, which repeats itself in our interactive field, in order to provoke me to become angry with her and reject her? Would it be therapeutically helpful if I were to interpret this repetition? In doing so I would be applying a method used by some psychoanalytic theorists of 'object relations.' That is, through my own feelings of countertransference I may become aware of what the client is unconsciously doing to, or with, me. Thus armed, I may be able to give an interpretation of her unconscious patterns of relating. I would not, of course, present it with a rejecting, angry tone in my voice. I would resist acting in any way like her father. Instead I would express, in a calm voice, that something seems to be forcing her into making me into the rejecting father. Perhaps this would be a pathway towards beginning to address her unconscious masochistic pattern. But then I remember that some weeks ago I made a very careful attempt to this effect. I had told her that she seemed to be quite afraid of me, just as she had been afraid of her father. Her reaction was: 'Maybe. I don't know.' This defensive answer – 'I don't know' – really evoked frustration and some anger in me, which of course I did not express."

Consequently I sensed that this particular train of thought, along with my accompanying attitude, would no longer serve us in any therapeutic way. I also realized that, in my countertransference fantasies, I had been too intensely focused on the question of what she was unconsciously *doing* to me by her withdrawal. So I decided to take a different approach. Now I began trying to put myself in her shoes; to immerse myself as much as possible in her emotional situation. I tried to find, and operate out of, an attitude of empathy. One could also say that I tried to immerse myself even more deeply in the atmosphere of the therapeutic space between us. When I actually accomplished this, I realized that I no longer experienced anger towards her at all. What I experienced instead was a kind of emotional paralysis, together with a very heavy sense of fatigue.

Now I viewed it as my task not to succumb to this leaden tiredness, but rather to mobilize enough energy to name my perceptions, to verbalize them. But I needed to be sure that my words would have no hint of reproach in them, nor suggest that it was in any way her fault or responsibility that this heavy atmosphere existed. At the same time, I was fairly sure that the phrase "leaden paralysis" could be relevant here, not only to my state, but also to hers. A more precise description of this emotional state would be "paralyzing isolation." She felt isolated from me, and I from her. In addition, it seemed to me that all her feelings and thoughts, her entire inner life, had somehow been lost or stolen from her; that she was lying there just completely empty on the couch. All of this reminded me of phases in early infancy in which experiences of abandonment – especially if they are too lengthy and/or too frequent – bring about a profound sense of resignation. The infant loses any expectation of ever experiencing satisfying interactions with significant others.

Thus it became increasingly clear to me that I should try to verbalize, as well as I could, exactly what I was feeling. I decided to risk articulating the following: "I have a sense that it must be a torturous and paralyzing feeling for you, right here in this moment, because at home you were so full of things you wanted to tell me. But now, here in my presence, all of the electricity simply gets extinguished; everything comes to a halt." It seemed that these words were not entirely off the mark. Obviously something had reached her, for she answered: "Yes, I really feel just blank, completely empty. It is exactly as you say."

The question remains: What did my intervention actually trigger in her? First of all, she heard my voice. Having myself experienced similar isolating paralysis at times, the tone of my voice surely came from a corresponding place; and was probably affectively attuned, at least sufficiently so, to her own. At the same time, I had apparently been successful in finding some apt words for expressing her current emotional state. Perhaps this had the effect of helping her to feel much less isolated. It is evident that her awful feeling, of having lost any sense of human contact, found adequate expression in my words. Yet words are not just words, but rather language as an expression of profound communication, of what we human beings share, of what is collectively "ratified," according to Stern. Through my intervention she must have experienced that there are verbal expressions even for her own isolated state. Even this state belongs within the general range of human experience. Thus she was able to "rejoin humanity," even when at times she felt like an outcast in her state of empty isolation.

It would seem that this client has no inner figures to protect her from falling into the abyss of desperate isolation. It is my fantasy that this state reflects multiple experiences of total abandonment and a lack of empathic mirroring in early childhood, as well as painfully traumatizing experiences with an insensitive father and a helpless mother. Of course, this fantasy – even based as it is on her concrete memories – must remain a hypothesis. In any case, after a few more incidences of mutism, one example of which I have described above, the patient at last found her voice and her will to cooperate in the treatment.

She thus found again her own voice, her words, her feelings, her thoughts, and could now enter into the therapeutic space where mutual exchange and common exploration became possible. She had previously been overwhelmed by her inferiority complex, which had at times dominated her entire personality, yet at other times receded into the background. Fortunately, the openness towards corrective emotional experiences had not been completely sealed off in her.

The healing potential of language

The ancient Greeks already knew that language can possess a healing potential. In the dialogue "Charmides," Socrates expressed (Plato, 1961, p. 132) that everything stems from the soul – both the good and the bad – as well as the body; indeed, the whole human being. Therefore one must first of all treat the soul with utmost care, if one wishes for the head and the rest of one's body to be healthy. "But the soul, my best friend, should be treated by means of dialogue in order for equanimity to come about. Then it will be easy to bring health to the head and the whole body, as well." In addition to whatever else he may have meant here, at the very least it seems clear that Socrates recommended a method of treatment which was holistic, which included the whole human being, including states which we would today call "psychosomatic."

In any case, to express oneself in language, to talk about oneself, is a specifically human need which is linked to various motivations. First of all it serves purposes of interpersonal communication, which is why people who talk out loud to themselves are rare and quite conspicuous amidst their surroundings. Thus language is a medium for making oneself understandable to others, whether directly or indirectly. Many motivations express themselves in a verbal way, as well. One immediately thinks of the needs for attachment or belonging. One may also think of aversive motivations like anger, hatred, sadness, etc. In addition, the motivation to explore things and to assert oneself may use an aggressive, witty, or ironic form of language. In connection to needs of a sensual/sexual nature, language may move into the background as one seeks satisfaction of those needs. Here language may serve instead an auxiliary function to enhance understanding between partners; and when it comes to satisfying needs for physiological regulation, it is quite similar.

Within language, alongside concrete communication, the whole universe of possible needs may be contained, whether or not it expresses itself in a manifest way. But language can also serve to cover up inner states and may be used for defensive purposes, for example, through so-called rationalization. Language comes right up to its limits wherever there is an issue involving hunches, unfathomable experiences, or whenever one feels things which simply cannot be adequately expressed in a verbal way. Language can also fail us, such as when emotions are so strong that they can only be expressed in direct actions, or whenever the entire person is so overwhelmed by an experience as to be rendered speechless.

Socrates was right when he said that certain types of dialogue could help the soul to increase in equanimity and self-awareness. Such states of equanimity might be best understood as consciousness of oneself, along with a flexible kind of self-control, one which is adequate to each respective situation. At its best, this would point to a form of the verbal sense of self, which has integrated, to a satisfactory degree, preverbal experiences. Equanimity is also related to contemplating the meaning of life, in general, and the purpose of one's own existence. The possibility of becoming conscious of oneself extends all the way down into an inner world which has already been formed in a preverbal manner; and, by becoming conscious, one connects up to this world.

Verbal interpretations in analysis

I do not want to deal with the philosophy of language at this point. Much more important here is the question of why and when language may be seen as having a healing effect; and in what ways verbal interpretation – which is in fact the main instrument of psychoanalysis – can be either effective or not.

Stern has stressed, rightly so, that by means of language, the child gains access to its culture, taking into consideration that all real-life issues are tremendously complex and any identification with one-sided simple answers is harmful to the truth. Those people who do not belong, by virtue of their language differences, will be most easily rejected or expelled from a culture or other social group. "We speak a common language," therefore, has the metaphorical significance of: "We understand each other, and belong to each other. Whoever does not speak our language is a stranger." One has only to remember all those many conflicts – even wars – around language, which too often have a most aggressive, even deadly, outcome.

In analytical psychotherapy therefore, where mutual understanding is so important, any verbal intervention or interpretation must by necessity be expressed in a language that the analysand can really understand. Here the intersubjective realm has its "say" and is always a very essential part also in every form of psychotherapy which is based on dialogue. Yet it is sometimes questionable whether even the very same words or sentences signify for the analyst the same meaning as for the analysand. Here lies the crucial issue of empathic sensitivity, primarily where the analyst is concerned. To increase mutual understanding, I personally have made good use of repeating, in my own words, the content of certain, important sentences by the analysand, beginning with: "If I understand you correctly, you now want to tell me. . . ." The analysand's response may be: "Yes," or "No" or, perhaps most promisingly, he may correct me, leading to further, helpful differentiation of our mutual understanding. For many people, particularly those who have an inner sense of "not really belonging to humanity" or of being marginalized, it may be very helpful and healing to experience being mirrored by the responses of the therapist. Once they feel mirrored, they are often quite amazed to find that anyone else could form a mutually shareable connection with their own experience.

An example from analytic practice

Regarding this issue, I would like to provide at this point a brief example from my analytic practice. A 40-year-old woman, who tended towards depression and suicidal thoughts, brought a dream to our session, in which she had felt devalued and ridiculed by her father, brother, and husband.

This dream reiterates, in my opinion, those internal attacks which are so typical of emotional states of self-devaluation and depression. In Jungian terminology, one would speak of "negative animus attacks" (Jung, 1928a). But in my reaction to such a dream I usually avoid using the term "animus"; although in this case my client would have "understood" it, as she was well-versed enough in Jungian terminology. Yet it is a technical Jungian term which seemed too abstract for this specific moment, insofar as it is "drawn out" (the literal meaning of "abstracted") from a much larger palette of possible emotional and cognitive meanings. Even more importantly, so often technical abstractions – in this case, the word "animus" – only serve to offer the patient more potential ammunition for launching attacks against her own self-esteem. Clothed in words, these "attacks" may say: "I'm hopelessly 'animus-possessed.' I'm just a pest to everyone in my surroundings: hopeless, out-of-place, and destructive. I should just kill myself. That would be the best for me and for everyone else. *In addition, the analyst confirms this because he, too, thinks I am 'animus-possessed.'*"

In this particular moment I am convinced that my patient has shared this dream with me for some reason other than just getting a straight interpretation of its contents, because she tells me her dream in a vulnerable, painful, and hesitating voice. She seems to be expressing just how badly she feels. I sense that I should focus on her depressive feelings as best as I can. Thus, trying to immerse myself in her emotional state, I risk articulating the following: "I sense somehow that you are experiencing a heavy burden which is pressing you down right now. It also seems as if the rug underneath your feet has been pulled away. And so it seems as if there is no stability or support to be found anywhere. Everything that was previously important in your life suddenly, in this present moment, seems to reveal itself as a complete illusion. It is so very painful for you that you even long right now for some very literal accident or whatever else might take you from this world altogether. You feel like your life is in shambles; and, more than anything, just want to get rid of this feeling. All this is understandable, even though it probably feels to you like no one in the world seems to understand you." She listens more and more attentively and finally says, with obvious relief: "Yes, it is just like that. You seem to understand this."

Thus a moment of true concordance, a "coniunctio" in the Jungian sense, had transpired. In this situation, the use of language left in its wake a helpful, healing effect. It felt as if my formulations were flowing to me out of deep, inner resources in response to the mood pervading the interactive field. In other words, I really seemed to be in touch with the deep, inner self (in Jung's sense), and let it take part in the process. In any case, I sensed now a definite shift in mood within the patient. Such an experience is like a "little brick" which is needed in the overall process of building increased personal stability.

Of course, I had also kept her dream and its content in the back of my mind. In dreams like this there is always the question as to what extent I must include myself with those masculine dream figures who devalue and despise her. Normally it would be important to bring up for discussion negative and ambivalent feelings towards the analyst, and, sooner or later, it is indeed crucial that mistrust and reservations towards the analyst be openly explored. But, as her depressed mood was pervasive in the therapeutic field, it would surely have been counter-productive to talk about possible ambivalences in the transference relationship. This would have been out of context with the need for affect attunement. It was obviously more important for me to engage directly in mutual intimacy by means of an empathic-enough feeling-language.

In general I believe it to be therapeutically essential to develop very fine antennae for the elements pertaining to transference/countertransference – which so often resonate in the background of the various explicit themes. Whenever verbalized interpretations of transference phenomena are necessary, a therapist is in need of a refined sense of tact and a well-developed empathic sensitivity. It is often therapeutically counter-productive to focus the patient directly upon his or her transference feelings, because there is always the risk that such feelings might only get "talked about," intellectualized, and finally, simply rationalized away. This is especially the case whenever a patient's feelings are just beginning to open up and germinate in the therapy. Nor is it necessarily recommended for verbal interpretation to assume the foreground during phases in which there is a mildly positive transference, with sufficient confidence or trust, accompanying in a helpful – but more background – way the explicit therapeutic dialogue revolving more around life problems and/or dreams. However, it is an urgent necessity to bring into the open, and to interpret, elements within the transference whenever aversive emotions present themselves, especially when they prove to be disturbing to the relationship or provoke resistance. It must be acknowledged here that negative-toned feelings, sometimes in a disguised form, will crop up in every in-depth analysis. For many clients it represents a novel experience to be able to express their anger, rage, or criticism – in this case, towards the analyst – without the expected consequence of being punished by withholding love.

In all verbal expressions within the therapeutic situation, one must always pay attention to the intersubjective or interaffective dimensions of communication as well. This is necessary insofar as every verbal interpretation has not only a cognitive aspect, but also an emotional significance. It is therefore an essential component of the "art" of being an analyst to have some "feel" for what emotional significance our way of interpreting may have in the experience of the analysand. I feel this to be vitally important for any therapeutic process to become meaningful.

It is a general anthropological given that we always have to interpret our experiences and perceptions in order for them to take on personal meaning or significance. Our mind is somehow filled by interpretations which we have assumed unconsciously, very early on, from whatever was deemed significant by our parents and surrounding environment. Those interpretations seem to be taken for granted, and play a most decisive role in the formation of our deepest seated convictions. They form our unconscious hierarchy of values, which influence our various, broadly sweeping prejudices towards ourselves and the world. They also provide us with the evaluative criteria by which we ascertain what to idealize or disdain. Of course, those unconsciously held value judgments often have a neuroticizing effect and do damage to our social relations. It is therefore crucial to find, with the help of the therapist, words for such unreflected ideas in order to bring them to conscious awareness. And here we have to differentiate to what extent our verbal interpretations may be clarifying and explanatory, or when it is more a matter of re-interpreting or providing an alternative to the patient's view. The latter possibility is usually coupled with calling into question various convictions which serve to maintain the patient's neurotic balance. Precisely because they are so essential to the patient's neurotic equilibrium, it is a delicate matter of just how to call these core beliefs into question – as necessary as it may be – insofar as it brings forth such deep fears. Thus, resistance against analysis becomes more clearly understandable.

One should expect an analyst to be able to deal effectively with interpretations of unconscious contents in dreams and imagination. But he or she must also have very sensitive "antennae" in order to perceive the nuances of the "affective climate" in an analytic session and be able to verbalize these perceptions and give them their proper place in the overall life of the psyche. And here, to my mind, the findings of infant research are a very significant aid towards this goal of greater integration and understanding.

22

ON INTERPRETING
DREAMS

Introductory remarks

In many people's mind, analysis consists in the task of the analyst interpreting the dreams of his or her clients. It is assumed that he, as a highly trained dream interpreter, can somehow decipher these coded contents of the patient's unconscious, telling him what they mean. But dealing fruitfully with dreams is an act of the greatest complexity. What transpires in dreams definitely affects waking consciousness; and in most cases, profound reflection in the form of dialogue is required in order for the dream content to come alive. The dialogue takes place, on the one hand, between the ego and the unconscious; and on the other hand, intersubjectively, between analysand and analyst. In the course of interacting with the patient, it is basically the analyst's task to encourage linkages between the ego and the unconscious, to aid in deepening them, and to function as a mediator or partner in the ensuing dialogue.

Thus one has to consider two levels, both of which play a role in addressing dreams within psychotherapy. First there is the matter of obtaining some kind of meaning out of the actual dream *content*. To that end, the associations of the dreamer are necessary, as well as a certain degree of information about the life circumstances of the dreamer – of his or her conscious attitude, as Jung used to call it. Simultaneously, various associations will also emerge within the analyst, and the question is what to do about them. Here in particular, the analyst's capacity to differentiate is most needed, because it certainly cannot be simply a matter of him expressing his free, unchecked associations. Rather, the analyst has to discriminate between those associations occurring in the frame of his or her empathic relation into the patient's world, and those which stem more properly from his personal, lived experiences. As to the latter, precautions are obviously quite important, as they may have the effect of disrupting mutual efforts to discover the meaning of a dream, and can thus derail the entire therapeutic process.

Alongside dealing explicitly with dream *contents*, one must also keep close tabs on how the *communication* between the analytic partners is taking place. For instance, there are any number of ways to tell dreams, to accentuate certain parts of them, to forget other parts, to indicate that they are being taken seriously, etc. There are also countless ways in which the transference relationship may impact the dream interpretation. In any case, sensitive attention is necessary, not just with regards to the dream content, but also to the accompanying exchange processes. These are two perspectives which both belong under the general rubric of dealing with dreams, together with the therapist's awareness of his own feelings and thoughts which might emerge spontaneously while working with the patient's dreams, even when they apparently have nothing to do with the manifest dream content.

Difficulties related to the symbolic dimension – a case example

One has to realize that emotional openness to the *symbolic* dimensions of understanding dreams cannot be taken for granted. Thus many people – mainly those who suffer from early damage – often only have access to the concrete level of the dream content. I want to demonstrate this particular difficulty by means of a clinical example, referring again to the previously mentioned Mr E, an unwanted child, whose most conspicuous symptom was agoraphobia, namely, his fear that he would fall apart outside the four walls of his home (see p. 140–41.). In his dreams there were two main themes which emerged again and again in different variations. The first theme had to do with an urgent need to defecate. Yet he could never find an opportunity for relief; no appropriate location. Often, in the case of dire emergency, he was forced to defecate in a place in which he was exposed to the disapproving looks of passers-by. Needless to say, he felt horribly ashamed as a result. The second, frequently repeated theme in his dreams focused on the director and brothers within his religious order. There he was forever being sadistically scolded, tortured, and humiliated by this director. At the same time, the brothers simply laughed at him gloatingly.

Whenever he told me dreams which took place in the house of the religious brotherhood, he began to whine afterwards: "It shows again just how terrible those religious people really are." Regarding his dreams of defecation, he had no interest whatsoever in exploring them, as they evoked in him unbearable shame. He just gave a hint, indicating that he had once again dreamt one of those "dirty" dreams, and demonstrated his disgust.

Of course, it was my intention to bring the content of those dreams – which, to my mind, expressed so appropriately his inner state – more into his conscious awareness. But as soon as I even tried to open my mouth, he immediately began to lament about something or other. I simply could not get a word in. He constantly made defensive gestures, and it appeared as if I had suddenly become, for him, the very director in person, from whom he expected brutal devaluation and scorn. It was therefore not possible to deal with his dreams collaboratively, and even less so to get at their symbolic or psychological content.

Thus I was left alone with these dreams, to meditate on their signficance, if only for my own understanding. In order to approach a possible meaning of a dream, I usually try to immerse myself in the actual experience which a dreamer encounters within his or her dream. Thus, concerning my patient's defecation dreams, there arose the question: How does it feel to experience an emergency in getting rid of one's "business," but then not to find an opportunity to do so? When one must at last simply give in to this urgent need, one either becomes "he who shits in his pants" (*Hosenscheisser*) or ends up in some un-protected place having to expose oneself in a most embarrassing fashion – rather than in what the Europeans call a water closet (from the Latin *clausus*, closed). This could by itself be a sufficient reason never to leave one's own private room and its adjoining toilet, which is available at all times. Moreover, this may be a possible explanation for my patient's fears of going out into public places; and the symptoms related to agoraphobia.

With this, a hypothesis had come to my mind about what could be in the psychological background of his agoraphobia, his fear of leaving the privacy of his room. However, when I attempted to explore such a connection with my client, two obstacles would immediately present themselves. First of all, his feelings of shame almost completely hindered him from dealing with this theme. Secondly, he would argue with conviction that his fears of being in an open space had nothing to do with those "dirty" experiences in the dream. He stuck adamantly to a purely literal, concretistic understanding, and apparently had no access to possible, symbolic dimensions.

He also showed very little openness to another hypothesis; namely, that those dreams might in some way be related to very impactful experi-ences in his infancy. He could, of course, no longer remember such experiences. But insofar as this particular dream content repeated itself so often, it was supposedly a matter of an important life theme – in his case, of a traumatic nature – which had much broader significance than just the concrete narrative in his dream.

Surely, in the first place, one would think about his early toilet training. It is easy to imagine that his mother wanted to train him – probably much too early – to sit on his potty chair, if for no other reason than to avoid such unappetizing work for this child she already experienced as such a great burden. At the same time, one might conjecture that she was very often unavailable at those times in which the child needed urgently to be seated on his potty chair; thus he had no choice but to again soil his diapers, of course to her major displeasure. In any case, from early on he was probably never able to "do it right" in his mother's eyes, as in the dream, where there is not even a place for him to relieve himself without feeling ashamed. (This same difficulty continued later on for him with regard to his sexual needs.) My hypothesis, that experiences around his toilet training may have left special wounds, is quite plausible in light of the many relevant indicators. His dreams – dreamt at the time of his psychotherapy, thus depicting his state in the here-and-now – consistently expressed his feelings that, no matter what he did, he could never be all right. There was the persisting expectation that his needs would again be met only with rejection, disdain, mockery, or blame.

It is a quite general experience that dreams, dealing with getting rid of one's shit, may be a metaphor for the therapeutic situation, especially in light of the fact that the therapeutic situation is legitimately a kind of "closet" (again, in the European sense), a closed-off place where things which are burdensome may be disposed of. This is another reason why the analyst's readiness to provide an accepting space is so crucial.

Obviously, Mr E could at that time not yet trust that he had found such a space in our encounter. The sadistic director of his dreams tended to interfere, so to speak, between us. Thus his transference feelings were quite ambivalent. My patient's anxious anticipation, of being scolded and tormented by me, had many similarities to the fears he experienced when faced with his director. And again, his fears of the director had similarities to anxious feelings he had experienced in connection with his highly unpredictable and tyrannical father. But such connections had not become evident to him at that time, and this was not necessarily due to a lack of intelligence, but much more to his incapacity to combine ideas or experiences in a symbolic way, which had simply not been developed. Feces were feces and the director was the director, and that was that. Thus it was not feasible for him to see that this director might also be viewed intrapsychically, for example, as a "superego" figure operating most sadistically within him. The patient was simply not able to "play" with the images which emerged in his dreams. Hence he was not capable of imagining. The world of the "as if" was still quite closed to him. Here also belongs the observation that he had virtually no ability to reflect upon himself more objectively; and as a result, he completely lacked any sense of humor.

In such cases it is particularly important that it is at least the analyst who understands as fully as possible the symbolic dimensions of the dream contents. This may help him to gain some degreee of empathy into the inner state of the dreamer. The therapy in such cases has less to do with interpretations than with direct empathic reactions to the patient's emotional state. In the case of Mr E, that meant making available to him a kind of "lavatory," or "closet"; that is, a place where he could get rid of his burdensome "ballast." Practically speaking, it was a matter of having the patience to listen to every bit of his lamenting and complaining, and to take it all seriously on its own terms. In other words, I needed, by means of a good-enough affect attunement and empathic attitude, to help build and support his own sense of self-esteem. It was also very necessary to undercut the destructiveness of the figure of the director operating within him, a figure which he also projected on to me. Here it was crucial that all his expectations of being scorned and sadistically devalued were never actually to come true. On the contrary, I found it quite genuinely possible to embody a "good-enough," attentive father figure and to honestly accept my patient, even amidst his rather severe limitations. As mentioned earlier, this case was referred to me early on in my developing practice, when it was time-wise still possible to visit him and see him therapeutically in the home in which he has been placed – although this is against every analytic rule. Nonetheless, considering his severe agoraphobia, this was the only way for him to get some help, although in a thoroughly literal, concretistic way. In any case, it was possible for us, over the next two years, to witness a transformation in the sadistic figure of the director, which was followed by a reduction in his overall fears and a gradual increase in his sense of self-sufficiency.

The difficulties of this patient in dealing with his dreams were due in large part to his problems in forming or maintaining clearly differentiated boundaries between "real" versus "dreamed-of" experiences. These problems made it difficult for him to talk with me *about* his "shameful" dreams of defecation or dreams *about* the sadistic director. In fact, I often simply *became* for him this sadistic director, even when, from a purely cognitive level, he could still see me as, "maybe," a well-meaning therapist. This "maybe" expressed his mistrust, his doubts as to whether in some corner within me there might still lurk some traits of the director, with which I could in fact condemn him all the same. If he would have been able to find a genuinely symbolic attitude, he might have experienced me "as if" I was bound to have similar reaction patterns as this director. Yet, *at the same time*, he would have known that this was probably a transference fantasy stemming from his anxious expectations and that he would have the option to discuss this fantasy and its meaning with me, his therapist. But for him, in his current developmental state, the fact that his defecation dreams had a variety of possible interpretations was also totally obscured by his overwhelming sense of shame.

Today, there is the plausible assumption from infant research that the development of the capacity to symbolize in a meaningful way is based to a large extent on caring attentiveness and well-balanced stimulation from the infant's immediate environment. But the early experience of Mr E was greatly determined by repeated experiences of rejection, with the result that, whatever wishes or expectations he might harbor, they were overshadowed by a plethora of aversive affects. Such aversive affects had the unfortunate, though understandable, effect of dramatically limiting his capacity to be receptive to symbols in their wealth of possible meanings. His sense of self remained without any anchor insofar as he had never experienced reliable mirroring of his own way of being-in-the-world. In Jungian language, one might speak of a very weak ego, which must hold on to an exclusively concretistic understanding out of a fear of fragmentation.

An "archetypal" dream and the experience of the "emergent self"

In the following I would like to give an example of a so-called "big" or "archetypal" dream, which to my mind also shows the "emergent self," in the sense of Stern's, in operation. It is a depiction of the *emergent* self, being operative in an adult, which has the potential of a "new beginning," to use Balint's term (Balint, 1968). The dreamer was a 34-year-old academic, quite artistically gifted, whom I will call *Mr A*. For him, the symbolic dimension of the occurrences in the dream held deep and genuine significance, and opened up for him a new horizon of experience. He told me this dream in the 120th session; it runs as follows:

> *I am in a gigantic, castle-like home. There is a woman owner, with lots of servants and a chambermaid. The woman has nothing to do all day and spends her time idly playing cards. She owns a gigantic dog, which she has trained strictly and which does everything she says. The chambermaid is, more or less, forcing herself on a young man in the house, in hopes that*

he will return her affections. The mistress of the house, however, also seems to like this man. The two of them play lots of games together. Due to this apparent conflict of interests, the mistress of the house resolves to bring about the chamber- maid's downfall. The mistress calls her dog and jams her finger into its mouth, all the way to the back of the fangs. She then sets the dog on the maid. I [the dreamer] am terribly afraid of the dog myself, thinking it might mistakenly attack me, too. So I ask the mistress of the house to stay right beside me, since her presence would seem to provide protection from the dog. But she assures me that the dog does only exactly what she orders it to do. Now I hear the dog yelping. The light goes out and I am now in a huge, dark room. I believe I am already being pursued by this dog, but in the midst of this immense fear, I have the feeling that I must simply yield to my fate.

This scene is now over. The mistress of the house calls me and tells me, cold-bloodedly, that the maid is now dead, having been torn apart by the dog. She also informs me that the young man no longer means anything to her. Over a meal, she recounts in vivid detail how the dog tore the maid to pieces. I cannot listen any more and ask her to change the subject. I think about how much I would like to get out of this house, where so many evil things transpire. At the same time, I am afraid that she will then set the dog on me, as well.

At that very moment, there is a knock on the door downstairs. A man's voice calls up, saying that he wants to speak to the mistress of the house concerning the death of the maid. Relieved, I think that the mistress is perhaps not so all-powerful after all. It seems as if she still has to answer for what she does.

So much for the dream; I want to start by offering a few observations in connection to the anamnesis of the dreamer. The young man came into analysis because he suffered from very intense problems in self-esteem, as well as depressions with suicidal tendencies. From feeling "high," in the sense of grandiosity – that within him there must be something truly extraordinary – he could plummet, for even the most minimal of apparent reasons, into an emotional "low," where he felt like a complete and abject failure. In other words, one could diagnose him as a "classic" narcissistic personality disorder, as described by Kohut (Kohut, 1971).

Mr A described his mother as a jealous, envious, extremely moody "house tyrant" with a strong need to always be the admired center of attention. Depending on her mood, she could either be "spoiling" of her son or dismissive of his needs. She would shift from being proud of his gifts and talents to becoming envious and devaluing of him, insofar as she was of the opinion that he was far too conceited about himself. His father was, according to Mr A, quite ignorant of the world; he identified completely with his profession and could be easily manipulated by the patient's mother. In any case, it was impossible to rely on him.

Both dreamer and analyst were deeply impressed by the dream in its significant, mythical character. According to analytic experience, this is often a sign that impulses towards transformation and development – which are a species-specific potential in all humans – have an urge to be realized in the personal experience of the dreamer. In the described case, one may think of his vital urge to become more autonomous, to free himself from maternal dependence, and to strengthen masculine gender identity through experiences with the father.

In interpreting this dream, one might see the powerful mistress as obviously representing the dreamer's personal mother, but this interpretation would be far too short-sighted. Rather, this mistress represents an archetypal figure. That is, she is one of innumerable manifestations symbolizing that realm of experience which is generally associated with the maternal, feminine world. She may be associated with the mythological figure of the "mistress of animals," as she is embodied, for example, in the goddess Artemis. Yet, though archetypal, this figure contains at the same time the image of the dreamer's personal mother. She may largely be a symbol of those feelings and behavioral patterns which have imprinted themselves upon Mr A through the many interactions – which have scarcely been facilitating – with his mother. In the dream, he is a prisoner in her realm; he cannot escape. On the contrary, his fear of being torn to pieces by her dog compels him to stay with her; even to seek her protection and remain nearby. (To be "torn to pieces" may mean, psychologically, to fragment or disintegrate as a result of his mother's perpetually "sniffing" at his weak points with her "dog's nose," and uttering undermining criticism.)

Mr A is thus a prisoner in his negative mother complex. Practically, the result of this is a profound weakness in his ego standpoint. He has great difficulty finding a sense of groundedness in himself, and easily lets himself be knocked down by the slightest aversive "breeze." He believes he is much too easily influenced by others and is too emotionally labile; hence he is always victimized by his own moods and fears.

But this archetypal feminine figure which emerges in the dream could also symbolize – though in a negative way – the feeling aspects of the realm connected to intersubjectivity. This can be shown by the following.

The analysand was full of fears about really sticking to his own standpoint, because having his own view could be disappointing to the expectations of others. Thus he tried to attune himself as much as possible, and to share the same opinion with people in his surroundings. In his memories of childhood, he recalls that his having an opinion which diverged from his mother's always meant to her that he must not love her anymore, or that he intends to be offensive by putting her in the wrong. Thus he always tried to be in accordance with her, and over-adapted, for example, by never being able to say "No." He only managed to criticize his mother behind her back, but subsequently despised himself for being such a cowardly hypocrite. This is expressed in the dream, where he had to remain very close at all times to the mistress out of his fear of being attacked by her vicious dog.

But who is the male figure in the dream who knocks at the door and compels this cruel, tyrannical feminine figure to account for her deeds? It was quite obvious to the dreamer to associate this figure with myself, his analyst. This association has to be relativized, however, in view of the mythical character of the dream. Surely in his idealizing trans-ference, he expected to find in me the "redeemer" who would free him from the prison of his various complexes, which always threatened him with fragmentation. But *I*, of course, am no such savior; and it would be a sheer act of inflation if ever I became identified with such an expectation of myself.

In reality, it was first of all probably the patient's own strong urge to free himself which motivated his analysis in such a fertile and productive manner. As his analyst, I was spontaneously interested in his way of experiencing and thinking, and a very good rapport had developed. This served a key role in satisfying his needs for mirroring and inter-subjectivity, and validated his own way of being. Otherwise, it was mainly the exploratory–assertive motivational system which operated in our therapeutic field. He experienced for himself just exactly what is meant by the saying: "Knowledge is power." Due to our mutual explora-tion of the dynamics and history of his deeply wounding mother complex, he found more and more inner peace, along with a definite sense of assuredness *vis-à-vis* his previously undermining self-doubts.

The scene in the dream, where the just and powerful male figure appears, can thus be interpreted as the dreamer's emerging sense of having the *right* to claim for himself his own point of view, which he had won through courageous self-exploration. Thus the right to his own point of view is confirmed as the mistress loses her position of irresponsible omnipotence and now has to account for her misdeeds. Consequently, his inner assuredness, his own sense of self, and his overall ego strength have the freedom to grow. I suppose that I, as an analyst, may have been helpful by empathizing with his own subjective point of view and by facilitating our common exploration. I may also have been instrumental in helping his personal sense of firmness and self-delineation to materialize.

This dream is very impressive insofar as it depicts a kind of "model scene" within the process of inner transformation. After that "big dream," there were many dreams which obviously continued on the same line. Interestingly enough, the mother-figures in his subsequent dreams merged with qualities associated more directly with his personal mother. It was also interesting to note that in the dreams the mother-figure's behavior, as well as the interaction between her and the dreamer, gradually transformed over time. She became understanding, supportive, even needful of help for herself. This meant that, within his dreams, he could now relate to her in a totally new way. This was all an intrapsychic process, because in reality he had very little contact with his mother at this time. Nevertheless, he sensed in himself the benefits of newfound liberty, freedom, and the courage to stand behind his own views, all of which in short order affected his human relationships.

Thoughts on the "emergent self"

In the aforementioned dream there emerges from somewhere a new figure who is in possession of power and competence, and who organizes in a completely new way the previously imprisoning one-sidedness of the psychic state which had heretofore been so dominant. Thus a new organization comes about: a psychological world that is more just, more liberated, and filled with new possibilities for experiencing life and more connected to the sense of wholeness. The emerging of a new organization can be observed again and again in dreams which depict transformation, sometimes directly in the form of a birth. There are also many fairytales which follow this pattern in countless variations.

In the Jungian view, these patterns point to an urge which operates in the unconscious, the innate urge to realize one's specific individuality. The source of this urge is the self (in the Jungian sense), which from the unconscious stimulates the process of individuation, as well as regulating psychic equilibrium. Jung also calls the self "the personality in all its aspects, originally hidden away in its embryonic germ plasm" (Jung, 1928a, par. 186). But the self is imperceptible and can only be mediated by the effect it has on consciousness; effects which manifest themselves in their respective symbolic configurations. Is it therefore possible to see the male authority, who emerges in the dream of my

analysand, as symbolizing an aspect of the self? In any case, he symbolizes a very decisive aspect of this young man's subjective experience,
which had only been operational until now in subjugated and distorted
forms. The emergence of this aspect provides previously uncharted
grounding for the sense of identity of the dreamer. A regulating force
seems to be operating; one which creates, over the course of analysis
and under the conditions of a facilitating environment, a new psychic
balance. This process succeeds due to the fact that the previously one-
sided dominance of the mother archetype is now compensated by the
masculine, paternal principle.

At this point I would like to return to Stern's ideas of the "emergent
sense of self." According to his view, the infant forms, during the first
two months of life, the sense of an emergent self. It consists of a sense of
organization which is in the process of becoming formed. This particular
sense of self remains active for the rest of one's life (Stern, 1985, p. 35).
It is therefore the infant's experience that, rather than being exposed only
to a chaotic whirlpool of inner and outer stimuli, he instead gradually
and systematically organizes the various components of his experience,
and begins to identify those invariant aspects related to self and other. It
is by means of this process that he begins to experience the emergence
of organization.

While the infant senses these occurrences in a global way, Stern
invests enormous effort into differentiating them into their individual
components, and to analyze, even dissect them from various scientific
points of view. In my view, such refinement can hardly be formulated
any further, and Stern's latest analyses are quite difficult to understand in
any experience-near way (Stern, 1995). In any case, it is a matter of the
infant's subjectively sensing that something is moving and emerging,
and of expressing itself initially in a quite global form. Stern calls this
sense:

> the subjective world of emerging organization. This is and
> remains the fundamental domain of human subjectivity. It
> operates out of awareness as the experiential matrix from which
> thoughts and perceived forms and identifiable acts and
> verbalized feelings will later arise. It also acts as a source for
> ongoing affective appraisals of events. Finally it is the ultimate
> reservoir that can be dipped into for all creative experience.
>
> (Stern, 1985, p. 67)

In Jungian language, this realm of the sense of an emergent self has
archetypal characteristics. It belongs to the function of the self, which

operates as an unconscious factor, organizing our entire personality. The self stimulates the successive development of consciousness, which is centered in our ego-complex. The miracle associated with witnessing the gradual awakening of consciousness brings one closer to spontaneously appreciating the creative forces evident everywhere in nature. The significant caregivers in the infant's environment are those who can observe this creative and natural unfolding, and can therefore facilitate the infant's emergence into new life.

So far, the question – of how this early development is experienced by the infant itself – has been left to a great extent to the speculation of adults, because the infant remains incapable of reflecting upon, and even less so of verbalizing, its own experience. In the meantime, it has become the primary focus of modern infant researchers to gain deeper insights into the subjective experience of the infant. Such insights may even lead deeper into the struggle with the question of what is really the source and the essence of human subjectivity.

The "sense of the emergent self" is not a structure *per se*, but rather an unfolding of a process which may itself lead to new structures. It is essentially the creative and vital aspect of the psyche which manifests itself on various levels. They include internal experiences, ideas, insights, and emotions, all of which emerge, transmitting a sense of inner vitality.

I cannot evaluate whether Daniel Stern "vitalizes," so to speak, the infant with his own creativity; or whether Stern senses, in those emergent aspects, what actually transpires for the baby from within. It may be the "secret" hidden within these processes of emotional exchange which enabled the extraordinarily creative and unendingly empathic researcher, Stern, to write his *Diary of a baby* (Stern, 1990), by in essence somehow slipping inside the baby's "skin." Thus he is able to narrate to adults just what the infant may be experiencing within itself. It is very probable that – alongside those processes of maturation and becoming conscious – much is emerging inside the infant. That is to say, much is being set in motion within the infant's subjectivity. In any case, this selfsame process of the "emergent self" is not far removed at all from Jungian views about the lifelong dawning of consciousness in the process of individuation guided by the self.

CLOSING REMARKS

Something still needs to be said in conclusion. When one investigates, as a therapist, the findings of infant research, it seems to me quite necessary to immerse oneself in one's own emotional history. As this occurs, memories often come alive again, allowing one to trace back and look more deeply into how exactly it felt to be understood, isolated, shamed, or devalued, how it felt when one openly "conquered" something, what it was like when one was truly joined "heart and soul" with another person; for instance, on a trip somewhere, or perhaps later on, during sexual intercourse, or how it felt in situations when all the intimate experiences one yearned for just did not happen at all. Due to the fact that the infant's experiences are so foundational, accessing them in one's experience ought not to prove too difficult, even if there is access only to occurrences which happen in later childhood, or even later in life. It seems to me that one's own evoked memories are the ideal prerequisite for being really able to best utilize the findings of infant research for cognitive understanding, as well as to aid in enhancing one's empathic attunement. It is, however, important to remember that clinical methods based upon infant research are never effective when fixed rigidly or concretely. It would be much more desirable for them to be available to the analyst as spontaneously resonating options.

But beyond that, one might ask what more an analyst could learn from infant research, particularly as it applies to adults. It certainly would be naive to assume that the exchange processes between mother and infant could somehow be seamlessly transferred to the interactions which transpire within the analytical situation between adults. It is patently obvious that an analyst is neither mother nor father any more than analysands are babies. What is most noteworthy about the findings of infant research is precisely the realization that foundational human motivations, needs, and emotions are innate. And even though they may initially manifest themselves quite early on developmentally, they maintain themselves in the most diverse ways throughout the entire lifespan, insofar as they belong to the human being's fundamental constitution. Thus the model of infant–mother interactions is also maintained amidst the therapeutic field, and serves as a basic blueprint for any kind of therapeutic communication. The recognition of this fact is based in particular upon the following experiences.

1   There is the observation of basic, early patterns of a mutual relationship between mother and infant as being indispensable to the baby, not only for its survival, but also for the advancement of its physical and emotional maturation and development. The infant's interconnectedness with its environment – the primary representative of which is typically the mother – belongs, according to Stern, to the earliest postnatal experience. One could formulate: "In the beginning of every human existence was relationship" – for example, in the form of what Stern termed RIGs (Representations of Interactions which have been Generalized), or schemas "of-being-with." In the same context stands Balint, who as early as 1937 spoke of "primary love" (Balint, 1965), in contrast to Freud's concept of "primary narcissism" (Freud, 1914). The experience within the relational exchange between mother and child – consisting of regular feedings, changing of diapers, cuddling, but also being left alone and frustrated, etc. – is retained in the infant's memory and expected to repeat itself again and again. Over time, it imprints itself as an enduring attitude of expectancy.

Exchange processes in a species-specific form are part and parcel of the survival and maturation of any human being. In other words, they are archetypal. Jung also expressed this, for example, when he asserted that the soul "lives only within human relationship" (Jung, 1946, par. 444). Accordingly, infant research examines the main forms of emotional exchange. It attempts to establish what kinds of interactions promote the foundational needs of infantile maturation, and in what specific ways the influence of caregivers occurs and is most effective. These highly detailed examinations are, to my mind, extremely beneficial for the psychotherapist.

2   During the course of the first two years of life, the different senses of self – which are to be understood as foundational experiences of one's being in the world – mature on a relatively fixed timetable: the emergent self, the core self, the intersubjective self, and the verbal self; each one of these stages consists of the relational needs that correspond to its respective level of maturation. It must be

repeatedly emphasized that these four corresponding experiences of self remain intact throughout life, and develop and differentiate themselves further, according to one's life circumstances. They can, of course, also become stunted or defended against, rejected, etc. In any case, they play a major role in one's experience, as they do in the analysis of adults.

3　The integration of the innate motivational systems with their corresponding affects (which have been researched by Lichtenberg) are also of substantial help. These systems, too, may become stunted or ignored. They provide expression for one's particular emotional inclinations; and are, in Jung's words, key elements of the "energetics of the soul." They stimulate us to perceive and recognize our foundational needs, and motivate us to strive for their fulfillment. At what level this takes place, and to what extent conflicts may arise due to the demands and expectations of one's culture, are often topics within psychotherapy.

4　A crucial factor within Jungian analytic psychotherapy is the analysand's receptivity to working with symbolic experience and imagination. As mentioned above, for therapists it is essential to realize that this key capacity – of symbolic understanding – necessitates a certain modicum of personal maturation, and cannot be taken for granted. People suffering from early developmental damage often lack the freedom to open up to the symbolic dimension.

In summary, one could say that infant research seeks to establish hypotheses about the innate psychological constitution of humans. Furthermore, it examines in what ways the influence of caregivers occurs and is effective; and which kinds of interactions are facilitating or are, rather, obstructive to the foundational needs of infantile maturation and development. So far infant research has provided highly detailed explorations which may be of great benefit both to child therapists and psychotherapists of adults.

The findings of infant research are of significance to analytic psychotherapists in two ways. First, they offer hypotheses about how the inner world of an analysand developed; namely, in what ways its various internal representations and emotional complexes may have evolved. Secondly, they describe the subtleties of emotional exchange; how they correspond to general, human needs; and how often they operate in the here-and-now of analytic interactions. As a result, there exists the hope that disturbing emotional complexes may be modified through facilitating therapeutic exchange processes. In light of this, it is in my view extraordinarily beneficial for therapists to develop fine-tuned antennae for recognizing the fundamental mechanisms of emotional exchange processes – and here is the point that ultimately matters in any psychotherapeutic encounter.

REFERENCES

Asper, K. (1992). *The inner child in dreams*. Boston, MA: Shambhala.

Asper, K. (1993). *The abandoned child within: on losing and regaining self-worth*. New York: Fromm International.

Balint, M. (1937). Developmental states of the ego. In M. Balint, *Primary love and psychoanalytic technique*. London: Tavistock Publications.

Balint, M. (1965). *Primary love and psychoanalytic technique*. London: Tavistock Publications.

Balint, M. (1968). *The basic fault: therapeutic aspects of regression*. London: Tavistock.

Blanck, G., and Blanck, R. (1981). *Ego psychology* (2nd ed.). New York: Columbia University Press.

Blanck, R., and Blanck, G. (1986). *Beyond ego psychology*. New York: Columbia University Press.

Dieckmann, H. (1999). *Complexes: diagnosis and therapy in analytical psychology*. Wilmette, IL: Chiron Publications.

Dornes, M. (1993). *Der kompetente Säugling*. Frankfurt/Main: Fischer Taschenbuch.

Dornes, M. (1997). *Die frühe Kindheit*. Frankfurt/Main: Fischer Taschenbuch.

Eibl-Eibesfeldt, I. (1974). *Love and hate: the natural history of behavior patterns*. New York: Schocken.

Emde, R. (1980). Toward a psychoanlaytic theory of affect. In S. Greenspan (ed.), *The course of life*. Washington, DC: Mental Health Study Center.

Emde, R. (1981). Changing models of infancy and the nature of early development. *Journal of American Psychoanaltyic Association*, 29, 179–219.

Erikson, E.H. (1963). *Childhood and society*. New York: Norton.

Fordham, M. (1969). *Children as individuals*. London: Hodder & Stoughton.

Fordham, M. (1989). Some historical reflections. *Journal of Analytical Psychology*, *34*, 213–224.

Fordham, M., Gordon, R., Hubback, J., and Lambert, K. (1973). *Technique in Jungian analysis*. (Library of Analytical Psychology, vol. 2.) London: Heinemann.

Fraiberg, S. (1982). Pathological defenses in infancy. *Psychoanalytic Quarterly*, *51*, 612–635.

Freud, A. (1973). *The ego and the mechanisms of defense*. New York: International Universities Press.

Freud, S. (1909). Analysis of a phobia in a five-year-old boy. In J. Strachey (ed.), *The complete psychological works*. London: The Hogarth Press.

Freud, S. (1913). Totem and taboo. In J. Strachey (ed.), *The complete psychological works*. London: Hogarth Press.

Freud, S. (1914). *On narcissism: An introduction. CW XII*. London: Hogarth Press.

Freud, S. (1922). Group psychology and the analysis of the ego. In J. Strachey (ed.), *The complete psychological works*. London: Hogarth Press.

Freud, S. (1923). The ego and the id. In J. Strachey (ed.), *The complete psychological works*. London: Hogarth Press.

Freud, S. (1928). Brief an Ferenczi. In J. Cremerius (1990), *Vom Handwerk des Psychoanalytikers*, *2*, 389. Stuttgart-Bad Cannstadt: Fromann-Holzboog.

Gordon, R. (1993). *Bridges*. London: Karnac Books.

Greenberg, J., and Morris, N. (1974). *Engrossment: the newborn's impact upon the father*. In: Lichtenberg (1989a).

Harris, M., and Bick, E. (1987). *Collected papers*. Perthshire: Clunie Press.

Hartmann, H. (1964). *Essays on ego psychology*. New York: International Universities Press.

Herder, J.G. (1968). *Reflections on the philosophy of the history of mankind*. Chicago, IL: University of Chicago Press.

Izard, C.E. (1981). *Human emotions*. New York: Plenum Press.

Jacobi, J. (1959). *Complex/archetype/symbol in the psychology of C.G. Jung*. New York: Pantheon Books

Jacobi, J. (1976). *Masks of the soul*. Grand Rapids, MI: Eerdmans.

Jacobson, E. (1964). *The self and the object world*. New York: International Universities Press.

Jacoby, M. (1975). Autorität und Revolte – der Mythus vom Vatermord. *Ztsch. f. Analytische Psychologie*, *6*, 524–540.

Jacoby, M. (1984). *The analytic encounter: transference and human relationship*. Toronto: Inner City Books.

Jacoby, M. (1985). *The longing for paradise*. Boston, MA: Sigo Press.

Jacoby, M. (1990). *Individuation and narcissism*. London and New York: Routledge.

Jacoby, M. (1994). *Shame and the origins of self-esteem*. New York: Routledge.

Jones, E. (1957). *Sigmund Freud: life and work*, Vol. 3. New York: Basic Books.

Jung, C.G. (1973). *The collected works (CW)*, (H. Read, M. Fordham, and G. Adler, eds.). London: Routledge & Kegan Paul.

Jung, C.G. (1910). Psychic conflicts in a child. *CW 17*.

Jung, C.G. (1912). *Symbols of transformation*. CW 5.

Jung, C.G. (1915). Foreword to 2nd edition of "Psychic conflicts in a child." *CW 17*.

Jung, C.G. (1921). *Psychological types. CW 6*.

Jung, C.G. (1926). Analytical psychology and education: Three lectures. *CW 17*.

Jung, C.G. (1927). Introduction to Wickes' "Analyses der Kinderseele." *CW 17*.

Jung, C.G. (1928a). The relations between the ego and the unconscious. *CW 7*.

Jung, C.G. (1928b). The significance of the unconscious in individual education. *CW 17*.

Jung, C.G. (1929a). The aims of psychotherapy. *CW 16*.

Jung, C.G. (1929b). Problems of modern psychotherapy. *CW 16*.

Jung, C.G. (1934). A review of complex theory. *CW 8*.

Jung, C.G. (1938). Foreword to 3rd edition of "Psychic conflicts in a child." *CW 17*.

Jung, C.G. (1940). The psychology of the child archetype. *CW 9/I*.

Jung, C.G. (1943). Archetypes of the collective unconscious. *CW 9/I*.

Jung, C.G. (1946). Psychology of the transference. *CW 16*.

Jung, C.G. (1947). On the nature of the psyche. *CW 8*.

Jung, C.G. (1951). Fundamental questions of psychotherapy. *CW 16*.

Jung, C.G. (1954). Mysterium coniunctionis. *CW 14*.

Jung, C.G., and Jaffé, A. (1963). *Memories, dreams, reflections*. London: Routledge & Kegan Paul.

Kalsched, D. (1996). *The inner world of trauma*. New York: Routledge.

Kast, V. (1991). *The creative leap: psychological transformation through crisis*. Wilmette, IL: Chiron.

Kast, V. (1992). *The dynamics of symbols: fundamentals of Jungian psychotherapy*. New York: Fromm International.

Kast, V. (1997). *Father–daughter, mother–son: freeing ourselves from the complexes that bind us*. Rockport, MA: Element.

Klein, M. (1930). The importance of symbol-formation in the development of the ego. In *Contributions to psychoanalysis*. London: Hogarth. (Hanna Segal (1964) *Introduction to the work of Melanie Klein* (London: Hogarth) gives a bibliography of Klein's work.)

Köhler, L. (1988). Neuere Forschungsergebnisse auf dem Gebiet der Kleinkindforschung. Seminar in Zürich, November.

Köhler, L. (1990). Neuere Ergebnisse der Kleinkindforschung. *Forum der Psychoanalyse*, 6. Berlin: Springer.

Kohut, H. (1957) Introspection, empathy, and psychoanalysis. In Paul Ornstein (ed.), *The search for the self*, Vol. 1. New York: International Universities Press.

Kohut, H. (1966). Forms and transformations of narcissism. In Paul Ornstein (ed.), *The Search for the Self,* Vol. 1. New York: International Universities Press

Kohut, H. (1971). *The analysis of the self*. New York: International Universities Press.

Kohut, H. (1972). Thoughts on narcissism and narcissistic rage. In Paul Ornstein (ed.), *The search for the self*, Vol. 2. New York: International Universities Press.

Kohut, H. (1977). *The restoration of the self*. New York: International Universities Press.

Kohut, H. (1984). *How does analysis cure?* Chicago, IL: University of Chicago Press.

Lambert, K. (1981). *Analysis, repair and individuation*. London: Academic Press, Library of Analytical Psychology, vol. 3.

Laplanche, J. and Pontalis, J.B. (1980). *Das Vokabular der Psychoanalyse*. Frankfurt/Main: Suhrkamp. Orig. *Vocabulaire de la psychanalyse*. Paris: Presses Universitaires de France.

Leibbrandt, A., and Leibbrandt, W. (1972). *Formen des Eros*. Freiburg: Alber.

Lichtenberg, J. D. (1983). *Psychoanalysis and infant research*. Hillsdale, NJ: The Analytic Press.

Lichtenberg, J.D. (1989a). *Psychoanalysis and motivation*. Hillsdale, NJ: The Analytic Press.

Lichtenberg, J.D. (1989b). *Modellszenen, Affekte, und das Unbewusste*. In E.S. Wolf, *Selbstpsychologie*. Verlag International Psychoanalyse.

Lichtenberg, J.D. (1992). Hass im Verständnis der Selbstpsychologie: Ein motivationssystemischer Ansatz. In C. Schöttler (ed.), *Sexualität und Aggression aus der Sicht der Selbstpsychologie*. Frankfurt/Main: Suhrkamp.

Lichtenberg, J.D., Lachmann, F.M., and Fosshage, J.L. (1992). *Self and motivational systems*. Hillsdale, NJ: The Analytic Press.

Lichtenberg, J.D., Lachmann, F.M., and Fosshage, J.L. (1996). *The clinical exchange*. Hillsdale, NJ: The Analytic Press.

Lichtenstein, H. (1961). Identity and sexuality. *Journal of American Psychoanalytic Association*, *9*, 179–260.

Ludwig-Körner, C. (1993). Psychoanalyse und Kleinkindforschung, *Praxis der Psychotherapie und Psychosomatik*, *38*. Berlin: Springer.

Mahler, M. S., Pine, F., and Bergman, A. (1975). *The psychological birth of the human infant*. New York: Basic Books.

Mead, M. (1988). *Sex and temperament in three primitive societies*. New York: William Morrow.

Neumann, E. (1954). *The origins and history of consciousness*. Princeton, NJ: Princeton University Press.

Neumann, E. (1955). *The great mother*. Princeton, NJ: Princeton University Press.

Neumann, E. (1973). *The child*. Princeton, NJ: Princeton University Press; London: Karnac, 1988.

Ogden, T. (1984). Trieb, Phantasie, und psychologische Tiefenstruktur. *Forum der Psychoanalyse*, *2*, 177–196.

Papousek, H., and Papousek, M. (1975). Cognitive aspects of preverbal social interaction between human infant and adults. In *Parent–infant interaction* (Ciba Foundation Symposium). New York: Associated Scientific Publishers.

Parin, P., Morgenthaler, F., and Parin-Matthey, G. (1972). *Die Weissen denken zu viel*. Munich: Kindler.

Piaget, J. (1954). *The construction of reality in the child*. New York: Basic Books.

Plato (1961). *The collected dialogues of Plato*. Princeton, NJ: Princeton University Press.

Plaut, F. (1993). *Analysis analyzed*. New York: Routledge.

Portmann, A. (1958). *Zoologie und das neue Bild des Menschen*. Hamburg: Rowohlt.

Rank, O. (1909). *The myth of the birth of the hero*. New York: Vintage.

Samuels, A. (1985). *Jung and the post-Jungians*. London: Routledge and Kegan Paul.

Sander, A. (1983). To begin with – reflections on ontogeny. In J. D Lichtenberg (ed.), *Reflections on self psychology*. Hillsdale, NJ: The Analytic Press.

Sander, L.W. (1975). Infant and caretaking environment. In E.J. Anthony (ed.), *Explorations in child psychiatry*. New York: Plenum Press.

Schöttler, C. *et al*. (eds.) (1992). *Sexualität und Aggression aus der Sicht der Selbstpsychologie*. Frankfurt/Main: Suhrkamp.

Schwartz-Salant, N. (1989). *The borderline personality*. Wilmette, IL: Chiron.

Sedgwick, D. (1993). *Jung and Searles: a comparative study*. New York: Routledge.

Segal, H. (1964). *Introduction to the work of Melanie Klein*. London: Hogarth Press.

Slavin, M.O., and Kriegman, D. (1992). *The adaptive design of the human psyche*. New York: Guilford Press.

Spillmann, B. (1993). *Zeit der Seele*. Unpublished diploma thesis. Zürich: C.G. Jung Institute.

Spitz, R.A. (1965). *The first year of life*. New York: International Universities Press.

Stern, D.N. (1971). A microanalysis of mother–infant interaction: behaviors regulating social contact between a mother and her three-and-half-month-old twins. *Journal of American Academy of Child Psychiatry*, *10*, 501–517.

Stern, D.N. (1979). *The first relationship: infant and mother*. Cambridge, MA: Harvard University Press.

Stern, D.N. (1985). *The interpersonal world of the infant*. New York: Basic Books.

Stern, D.N. (1990). *Diary of a baby*. New York: Basic Books.

Stern, D.N. (1995). *The motherhood constellation*. New York: Basic Books.

Stern, D.N. (1996). *A model of infantile representations*. New York: Basic Books.

Stevens-Sullivan, B. (1989). *Psychotherapy grounded in the feminine principle*. Wilmette, IL: Chiron.

Tomkins, S. S. (1962/1963). *Affect, imagery, consciousness*. New York: Springer.

Trevarthan, C., and Hubley, P. (1978). Secondary intersubjectivity. In A. Lock (ed.), *Action, gesture, and symbol*. New York: Academic Press.

Wickes, F.G. (1923). *The inner world of childhood*. New York: Meredith Press.

Winnicott, D.W. (1958). *Through paediatrics to psychoanalysis*. London: Tavistock.

Winnicott, D.W. (1965). *The maturational processes and the facilitating environment*. London: Hogarth Press.

Wolf, E.S. (1988). *Treating the self*. New York: Guilford Press.

Wolf, E.S. *et al*. (1989). *Selbstpsychologie: Weiterentwicklungen nach Heinz Kohut*. Munich: Internationale Psychoanalyse Verlag.

Zinkin, L. (1991). The Klein connection in the London school: the search for origins. *Journal of Analytical Psychology*, *36*, 37–62.

AUTHOR INDEX

SUBJECT INDEX

DATE DUE

GAYLORD   PRINTED IN U.S.A.